ALSO BY TED CONOVER

Immersion: A Writer's Guide to Going Deep

The Routes of Man: Travels in the Paved World

Newjack: Guarding Sing Sing

Whiteout: Lost in Aspen

Coyotes: A Journey Across Borders with America's Mexican Migrants

Rolling Nowhere: Riding the Rails with America's Hoboes

CHEAP LAND
COLORADO

CHEAP LAND COLORADO

Off-Gridders at America's Edge

Ted Conover

ALFRED A. KNOPF | NEW YORK | 2022

Library of Congress Cataloging-in-Publication Data

Names: Conover, Ted, author.
Title: Cheap land Colorado : off-gridders at America's edge / Ted Conover.
Description: First edition. | New York : Alfred A. Knopf, 2022. |
Includes bibliographical references and index.
Identifiers: LCCN 2021055124 (print) | LCCN 2021055125 (ebook) |
ISBN 9780525521488 (hardcover) | ISBN 9780525521495 (ebook)
Subjects: LCSH: Self-reliant living—Colorado.
Classification: LCC GF78 .C665 2022 (print) | LCC GF78 (ebook) | DDC 304.209788—dc23
LC record available at https://lccn.loc.gov/2021055124
LC ebook record available at https://lccn.loc.gov/2021055125

A portion of the proceeds from sales of this book
will benefit La Puente Home, in Alamosa, Colorado.

Jacket photograph by Jon Cohrs
Jacket design by Jennifer Carrow

To my parents and to my sisters, for all the help,

and

To Margot, again

This is the country I love the most. The look of this country is what I would want to see every day, though I live in the mountains now. I think of the high plains, the great plains, the short grass prairie, as the way country should look: this stark clear flat land, so open and wide, with its sandhills, and overhead the tremendous clouds, and the wind blowing, and nothing to stop it from Canada to Texas except barbed wire fence.

It's dry, but it's not an empty place, never mind what so many people think. It may not be pretty, but it's beautiful if you know how to look at it. You have to quit thinking of trees. You have to quit thinking of green. You need to slow down, be quiet. You have to get out of your car and be still.

—KENT HARUF

Contents

CHEAP LAND
COLORADO

Prologue

IT BEGINS WITH a moment of contact—of driving up to a homestead and trying to introduce yourself.

The prospect is daunting: a lot of people live out here because *they do not want* to run into other people. They like the solitude. And it is daunting because many of them indicate this preference by closing their driveway with a gate, or by chaining a dog next to their front door, or by posting a sign with a rifle-scope motif that says, "IF YOU CAN READ THIS YOU'RE WITHIN RANGE!"

The local expert on cold-calling is Matt Little, charged by the social service group La Puente with "rural outreach." Matt has let me ride around in his pickup with him so that I can see him in action. Distances between households on the open Colorado prairie are great, which gives him time to explain his approach, which he has thought about a lot, as he does this every day and in three months has not gotten shot.

If you're thinking the checklist is short, you're mistaken. Before you ever see the homestead, you need to consider the visual impression you'll make. Matt drives a 2009 Ford Ranger with a magnetic "LA PUENTE" sign on the door. It is not fancy. Nor is Matt fancy: he is a forty-nine-year-old veteran of two tours in Iraq, a slightly built man from rural West Virginia with an easy smile. He smokes cigarettes and often he is whiskery. He tells me not to wear a blue shirt, because that's the color worn by Costilla County code enforcement, and you don't want to be mistaken for *them.* La Puente ordered him a hoodie and a polo shirt in maroon with their insignia, and he usually wears one or the other, along with jeans and boots.

He'll drive by a place, often more than once, before actually stopping, so that he can reconnoiter. Is there an American flag flying? That often suggests a firearm inside. Are there children's toys? Is there a small greenhouse or area hidden behind a fence that suggests that marijuana is being grown? (Initially I thought that might be a good sign, since cannabis can make people mellow. But Matt emphatically said no. "A full-grown plant could be worth a thousand dollars, and people steal 'em!") More to the point, is anyone even living there? Are there fresh tire tracks? Smoke coming from the chimney? Many prairie settlements have been abandoned or are lived in only during the summer.

Matt had noticed one property with berms constructed inside its perimeter of barbed-wire fence. He saw bullet casings and suspected the owner was a vet with some psychological issues: "I thought he was probably playing war games, reenacting things he'd been through." He drove by to show me—the place was at the end of a dead-end road, which made it kind of hard to pretend you were just passing by. Matt said that the first few times, he paused at the road's end, waved at whoever inside might be watching him, and turned around. He continued in that vein over the next month, waving or honking but not lingering, until one day he saw a man outside the house dressed in camo gear. Matt parked his truck and stepped outside.

"I'm Matt from La Puente," he said. "I've got a little wood." He gestured at the firewood stacked in the bed of his truck, something useful conceived of by his employer as a calling card, an icebreaker.

The man picked up an AK-47. "You're a persistent son of a bitch," he said. Then: "How much is it?"

"It's free," said Matt.

The guy walked toward the gate. He opened it. He waved Matt in.

Normally, Matt had shown me, you didn't see somebody outside, so the procedure was to stop at the end of their drive and tap the horn. At the first sign of life, he'd often step from his truck so they could see him, a (hopefully) unthreatening presence. He might leave them with some firewood, a business card with his cell number, an offer to come back should they find themselves in need of food, help with filling out an application, a ride to town for a doctor's appointment, or a pickup of a prescription.

I paid close attention because I was starting to volunteer with La Puente. It seemed like a good way to meet isolated prairie dwellers, and Matt said he could use the help.

I set myself a goal of three new contacts per day. La Puente loaned me a "RURAL OUTREACH" sign for the door of my own pickup truck. I chose an area and drove around, as slowly as I could without look-ing suspicious; I guessed that many of the places I was sizing up were abandoned.

I finally settled on a place with a short driveway, figuring that would make me harder to ignore and easier to evaluate. It was a modest house with various pieces of junk around it, including non-working vehicles, but I could see by tracks in the dusty dirt that someone had been driv-ing in and out. I stopped and beeped the horn. That's when I realized that the Jeep Wagoneer in front had somebody in it. I rolled down my window. A moment later, he cracked his own window. I climbed out of my truck and, in a show of my confidence and good intentions, walked over to him.

"Hi, I'm Ted, from La Puente," I said.

"Hey," he said. His green Corona beer baseball cap matched the color of his eyes.

I told him about the firewood.

"I don't usually accept charity and stuff," he said.

"I get that," I said. He was just back from rehab, he said. I asked for what, and he said opioids.

"And how are you doing?" I asked.

"Okay so far. You want a soda?" He offered me a Sprite, which I accepted.

It was November and cold and windy, and I had left my jacket in the car. I should have gone to get it, but I kept hoping that any minute he'd invite me into his truck, which was warm enough inside for him to be in a T-shirt; its front said, "SINGLE AND READY TO JINGLE."

He didn't invite me in, but he liked to talk, and it wasn't long before he told me how he had once let a guy live in his place for a spell while he was gone. Then, when he came back, he and the guy got into an argument and the guy shot him. "Right here." He held out his arm to show a big, complicated scar.

Instead of needing to pry information out of a hermit, as I had expected, I found myself with a chatty, self-revealing guy who really wanted someone to talk to . . . even if he didn't want to invite them into his car.

I tried honking outside three places where either nobody was home or nobody lived, and I left each feeling kind of foolish. But then I saw a humble place close to the road, with a horse in a small corral and a couple of chickens in a pen. I parked at the gate and honked. I was immediately swarmed by several heeler dogs, some of them growling, but I made soothing noises and crossed my fingers. It took a couple of minutes for a Hispanic guy about sixty years old to appear and start walking toward the gate, from about fifty yards away. While he ambled over I read an official notice from the county that had been stapled to a fence post. "CEASE AND DESIST," it said. I pointed to it after the man reached me and I had introduced myself.

"Are they after you about no septic system?" I asked. It was a common problem.

"No, it's over taxes," said the man. "They didn't send the bill. I'm working with them." I offered him wood, which he accepted, as well as some new bedsheets I happened to have, which he declined ("I sleep in my clothes"). He said he owed ten hours of community service to a court and asked if he could work it off with La Puente. I gave him the office phone number and encouraged him to call. We said goodbye and I climbed back into my truck. I turned the key and . . . nothing. Embarrassed, I tapped the horn again. The dogs swarmed me again. The man came out again and immediately offered to give me a jump—it was in his interest, as well, as I was blocking his gate.

"Circling the wagons" was the expression that came to mind at the next place I decided to hit. An array of old vehicles—a Lincoln, an RV, a pickup truck, a Volkswagen bus, an SUV, and more—were arranged in roughly three-quarters of a circle, like a wagon train hunkered down on the prairie in anticipation of attack, or a doughnut with a big bite missing. I saw goats outside, a sign of life, but paused: the settlement was about a football field away from the road. Honking would bring nobody to my window. *What the hell,* I thought, and decided to drive in.

I tapped the horn as I approached, and tapped it again for good measure once I had entered the little circle inside the perimeter and placed my truck in park. The apparent dwelling was on the far side of my truck, so I rolled down the passenger window to make it easier to see me.

A middle-aged white man wearing wraparound dark glasses with reflective lenses and a baseball cap came out a door, descended a few steps, and walked around to my side of the truck. He kept his distance and also kept his right hand inside the pocket of his hoodie; I suspected there might be a pistol there.

"How ya doin'?" he asked in a tone that said, *Declare yourself.* I told him I was Ted from La Puente, new to the area, just wanted to introduce myself, got a little wood—

He interrupted me: "That's dangerous, just rolling up on people. You must be either brave or a little dumb." He smiled in a way that was hard to interpret.

"Probably a little dumb," I acknowledged.

He was just visiting from California, he eventually told me. "Tony will probably be back a little later."

I put that name and all the vehicles together. "Wait—does this place belong to *Tie Rod Tony*?" He was a person I had already met. The man nodded. Suddenly I was no longer afraid. But I was wistful, feeling like a cat who had wasted one of her nine lives.

1

Cheap Land Colorado

We come for the scale of it.

—LINDA GREGERSON, "Sleeping Bear"

These times are too progressive. Everything has changed too fast. Railroads and telegraph and kerosene and coal stoves—they're good to have but the trouble is, folks get to depend on 'em.

—LAURA INGALLS WILDER, *The Long Winter*

MY FIRST EXPERIENCE of the San Luis Valley came on a family car trip when I was eleven. We stayed on the paved roads, but even that was impressive. The Great Sand Dunes National Monument, now Great Sand Dunes National Park and Preserve, looked like fake scenery from a movie until we were in it. I was amazed by its origin story: grains of sand blown from one side of this huge expanse, about the size of New Jersey, had formed gigantic dunes on the other. The San Juan Mountains to the west hold the remains of an enormous ancient supervolcano whose eruption was one of the largest explosions in Earth's geologic history.

When you grow up in a beautiful place that seems to lose some beauty to settlement (i.e., development) every year, you treasure the unchanged. The San Luis Valley still looks much as it did one hundred, or even two hundred, years ago. Blanca Peak, at 14,345 feet the

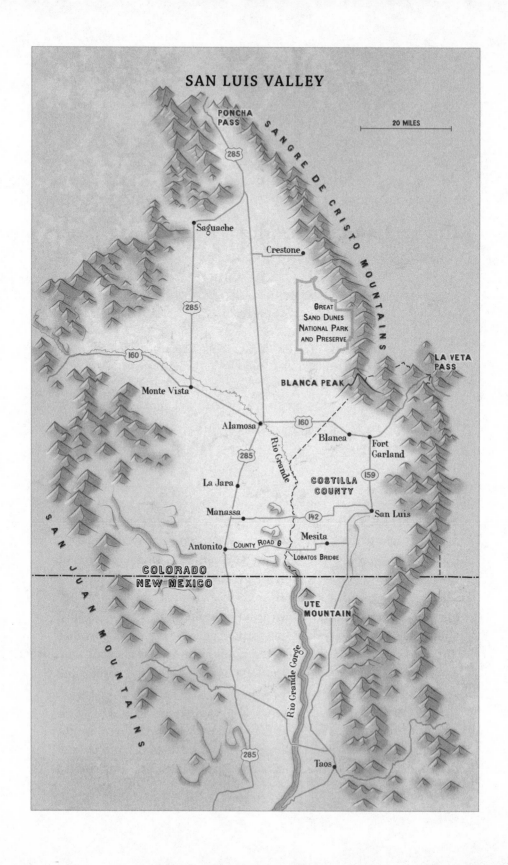

fourth-highest summit in the Rockies, overlooks a vast openness. Blanca, named for the snow that covers its summit most of the year, is visible from almost everywhere in the valley and is considered sacred by the Navajo. The range Blanca presides over, the Sangre de Cristos, forms the valley's eastern side. Nestled up against the range just north of Blanca are the amazing sand dunes. The valley tapers to a close down in New Mexico, a little north of Taos. It is not hard to picture the Indigenous people who carved images into rocks near the rivers, or the Hispanic people who established Colorado's oldest town, San Luis, and a still-working system of communal irrigation in the southeastern corner, or a pioneer wagon train. Pronghorn antelope still roam, as do feral horses and the occasional mountain lion.

It's also not hard to see a through line between the homesteaders of the nineteenth century and the people who move out there today. The land is no longer free, but it is some of the cheapest in the United States. In many respects, a person could live in this vast, empty space like the pioneers did on the Great Plains, except you'd have a truck instead of a wagon and mule, and some solar panels, possibly even a weak cell-phone signal. And legal weed. By selling or bartering weed and picking up seasonal labor, you might even get by without having a job, though if you have no income, things can get tricky, especially when winter comes around. It would be extremely difficult to live completely off the land, especially out on the open prairie.

I left Colorado for college, and again for grad school, and finally for New York and my city-loving wife. But on my office wall hangs my last Colorado license plate, from 1990. Family kept me coming back on visits, and often I would meet up with old friends. One of these was Jay, whose family had a cozy A-frame cabin in Fairplay, Colorado, about an hour and a half from Denver in another high basin, this one called South Park. Mocked as a backwater by the animated TV series, South Park is a great foil to the busy, popular Interstate 70 corridor that leads to ski areas like Copper Mountain and Vail. It is windy, mostly treeless, and sparsely populated. Jay's family A-frame was in trees at the valley's edge, but it got famously cold there in the winter (and often even in the summer). We did a lot of cross-country skiing in the backcountry and joined up with friends for parties there, starting in high school and continuing for many New Year's Eves after.

In 2016 a Denver magazine called *5280* asked me to write about South Park. Jay and I reconvened there for a few days. The "park" is very wide, and we wanted to visit areas we'd never seen before. A local offered directions to one particularly remote area, musing that "once you're on 53, you will swear you'll never find your way back." We headed there the next afternoon and found a place nearly devoid of people that was overlaid with dirt roads from a moribund 1970s subdivision that had never taken off, just as in the San Luis Valley. This area, a few months before, had made the news as the home of a disturbed man named Robert Dear who had attacked a Planned Parenthood clinic in Colorado Springs, killing three people and injuring eight. *The New York Times* ran a photo of the little trailer he lived in on five acres. The trailer was surrounded by snow and miles of empty space, the very picture of isolation and desolation. I thought, *What would it be like to live out there? What would drive you to it? Who would you get to know? How would you manage?*

We saw some isolated trailers and shacks and assumed a handful of people were living off-grid. We heard from a teacher in Fairplay that some of the kids from that area had parents with pretty extreme religious views, which had created friction with the school district. We knew that the local sheriff's department had recently had shoot-ups with white supremacists in remote parts of South Park. We had to pause, as we drove around, to wait for a herd of bison to finish crossing the dirt road we were on, leap over a fallen gate on the far side, and move into an empty field. We kept looking for a cowboy who might have sent them on their way, but they seemed to be on their own.

Denver and New York are complex urban areas. Out here, by contrast, it seemed that life must be simple, but how could I really know? That feeling of ignorance grew stronger a month later, in November, when Donald Trump was elected president of the United States. The day before, in New York, I had told a French radio station that Trump could never win the election. (Of course, I had plenty of company in this delusion.) The American firmament was shifting in ways I needed to understand, and these empty, forgotten places seemed an important part of that.

I told my sister about the place. In her work for a Denver-based foundation, she said, she had recently visited Alamosa, the San Luis

Valley's biggest town, and heard about off-grid settlement on a much larger scale. Staffers from a social service group called La Puente had shown her slides of how people were living out on "the flats" and told her about their Rural Outreach initiative; later she sent me some photos in a pdf file. I got in touch with La Puente, which had begun as a homeless shelter—one of the first rural homeless shelters in the country—founded by a nun. And then I visited.

Lance Cheslock, the executive director, showed me around, starting with lunch at the shelter. It's a big old house on the humbler side of Alamosa, converted to allow for separate facilities for men, women (who get buzzed into their part of the upstairs), and families, for whom there are separate bedrooms. There are forty-five beds in all, but on this day in June, only twenty-six guests were registered. Most of the downstairs is a dining room and kitchen. The shelter was serving three meals a day, with lunch and dinner open to walk-ins from the community—but only after enough diners had signed up to clean the kitchen afterward. The AmeriCorps volunteer assigned to this task wasn't having luck. Lance took the clipboard from her and began walking down the queue, cajoling and appealing to diners' better natures, engaging with them one by one until he had his volunteers. A few minutes later we sat down at a table for six, along with shelter clients and a staff person, the shelter's director, Teotenantzin Ruybal.

Tona, as she was known, had grown up in the valley and had run the shelter for more than nine years. She was from one of the extended families that have been in the area for generations and identify as Hispanic. (The terms "Latino" and "Latinx" are less often used in the valley.) Her demeanor was on the gruff side—you can't run a shelter if you're a pushover—but it was clear from our conversation that she had a big heart and was deeply committed to helping the poor.

She explained the direct link between the shelter and the off-gridders I was interested in: "You're living in a slum, and you see an ad about owning five acres for five thousand dollars, and you have a view of Blanca Peak—to them it's an opportunity, it's the savage wild, their piece of the rock." People would come to the valley just to own their own place, free from landlords and utility bills. And free also from being judged: "Sometimes the attitude is, I'd rather live a rough life out there than live in town and be looked down on," Tona explained.

"Regardless of if it's a stupid choice, it's their choice," she continued. But it wasn't always sustainable, because though they might be
living on their own land they still were poor, with slender margins for
surviving if things went wrong. Often, said Tona, they turned up at
the shelter once it got cold and they saw how unforgiving the winter
could be. The most durable off-gridders often had a fixed income of
some sort—veterans' benefits, for example, or Social Security disabil-
ity payments—because otherwise it was hard to make a living. The flats
were far from jobs, and getting to jobs required reliable transportation,
which many lacked.

Tona's partner, Robert, was a former corrections officer and sheriff's deputy who had spent a year and a half as La Puente's first Rural
Outreach worker. That weekend Tona and Robert drove me out to the
flats for a tour. We met in the little town of Antonito—the last town
before the New Mexico border—on a day that was unusual because it
was overcast. Tona and Robert lived outside town, in the countryside
but not off-grid, with three Chihuahuas; one of them, Diego, came
along for the ride. We rendezvoused at the Family Dollar store, where
I parked my truck and transferred into their SUV.

Antonito was once a center for sheepherding and the wool trade
and a stop on the Denver & Rio Grande Western railroad. It still had
a bronze statue of Don Celedonio Mondragón, a labor organizer, next
door to the empty onetime lodge of the Sociedad Protección Mutua de
Trabajadores Unidos (SPMDTU), the union he founded for shepherds
and farmworkers circa 1900. Amid some empty storefronts, Antonito
had two marijuana stores, two liquor stores, a grocery store, and two
good Mexican restaurants. It had the seasonal Cumbres & Toltec
narrow-gauge railroad, a tourist draw, as well as a baroque outsider
art structure known as Cano's Castle. It had a small hotel with a tame
pig that lived outside and wore a purple collar. But to me, the coolest
thing about Antonito was what Tona and Robert were about to show
me: its unsung status as a gateway to the flats.

From the Family Dollar, we crossed the tracks and headed east.
Town quickly yielded to irrigated farmland. A huge center-pivot sprin-
kler shot water onto the road, forcing Tona to turn on the windshield
wipers. Interspersed among humble houses were some very old mobile
homes and, even older, some decaying one- and two-room adobe

houses, their mud bricks slowly eroding away. The pavement ended at a small church, the Sagrada Familia Mission, past which a small bridge lifted the dirt road over an irrigation ditch, and then in a mile or two the irrigation ditch ran out, too: no more trees, no more agriculture, and not many fences. We entered a large tract administered by the Bureau of Land Management, and the horizon dropped lower and lower. Tona's SUV shot over one cattle guard,* then another, and another, now in a terrain of low sagebrush and chico bushes, a cloud of dust shooting up behind us. We were in a very pretty, gentle saddle between two sets of rounded hills, and the view kept getting wider and longer.

Finally, as we topped a rise, the whole of the giant San Luis Valley seemed to spread out in front of us. On the far eastern side were the still-snowcapped Sangre de Cristo Mountains, many of them higher than thirteen or fourteen thousand feet. The most prominent was Blanca Peak. Way to the south was rounded Ute Mountain, in New Mexico, which the valley extended into. Between them they cradled a huge volume of space that rested on a vast tawny plain that Tona and Robert called "the flats" and most locals, as I would learn, called "the prairie."

The road ahead of us continued gently downhill toward a dark, narrow notch in the landscape that was the Rio Grande River. As we got closer, a pattern became visible on the flats—the same sort of giant grid I had seen in South Park. These roads had been cut across the land as part of a real estate scheme in the 1970s. Closer yet and a few dwellings and former dwellings came into view, most of them trailers, some of them trailers augmented with small additions. Tona braked as the road narrowed to a one-lane iron bridge, the Lobatos Bridge, built in 1892. Its deck was two long courses of thick wooden planks that thumped and creaked as we drove slowly over them, with the Rio Grande River below, mostly shallow, its canyon not deep.

The area had been Robert's Rural Outreach beat for over a year, until January 2017, when, he said, he hurt his back lifting heavy boxes of

---

* A grid of bars installed on roads where they cross a fence line. Cattle guards let vehicles pass over easily, without needing to stop for a gate, but prevent the crossing of cattle, which are reluctant to walk on the spaced bars.

The Lobatos Bridge, eastbound, over the frozen Rio Grande River

food. (Matt Little was just getting started at this point.) Robert hadn't been back in five months, and as we drove up from the river and onto a road he used to visit, he marveled at the several dwellings that had appeared since the winter, and at what had been abandoned. Several times he referred to what I heard as "groves" behind wooden fences or in temporary greenhouses; I pictured fruit trees. But when I asked for more details, Robert explained that he was referring to people's "grows"—shorthand for marijuana gardens. The option of being able to grow marijuana legally had attracted many residents to the area, he explained. Those with medical marijuana permits could grow up to ninety-nine plants. The limit for others was six, which was often exceeded without legal consequence.

Tona steered us to the edge of the river canyon, where we got out and stretched our legs. She warned me to be careful of rattlesnakes and told me about the fall migration of tarantulas, which would begin in a couple of months. Peering over the canyon's edge at the river, she related how her father had brought her and her siblings out here to catch crayfish when she was a girl. She and Robert liked fishing and hunting. Tona pointed to a bald eagle soaring over the river and made a hawk-like screech.

Robert told me about the job, which he remembered fondly in part because it "let me walk away from being a cop." He was naturally funny and outgoing and enjoyed being able to show it. But the biggest challenge was getting to know people. "It took about three months before I knew a core group," he said. Many were extra suspicious because Costilla County, which we were in and which probably had the greatest number of flats dwellers, had begun a crackdown on code violators, with the goal of reducing nonconforming uses (if you asked the county) or of reducing the number of poor people out on the flats (if you asked them). The absence of a septic system was the violation that got most people in trouble. The requirement for one had been on the books for years but was seldom enforced until recently; now code inspectors were giving people who might have lived there for years a mere ten days to "correct the deficiency" before they would incur fines of $50 to $100 *per day.* Septic systems cost in the neighborhood of $7,000 to $12,000, contractors were few, and getting one to do the job within thirty days—to say nothing of ten days—was all but impossible, even if you could afford it. So paranoid were some locals that Robert said they would seed their driveway with nails in order to disable visiting inspectors and deter inspections, and build a second entrance that was safe. He said he had gotten several flat tires this way.

Knowing Tona gave him a head start on meeting locals, as she had already met many of them at the shelter. Often they had a substance-abuse problem. Occasionally they would grouse angrily about government overreach and threaten revenge (she mentioned three names). Other times it just seemed as though the shelter was their cold-weather base and the flats their warm-weather home. One such person was Armando, the resident we'd visit first.

Armando's property had four main features. The first was a sort of gate consisting of two posts adorned with "KEEP OUT" signs. There was barbed wire strewn between them and a board with nails but, oddly, there was no fence on either side. On Robert's instruction, Tona tapped on the horn and simply drove around it, as it appeared

Armando must usually do, as well. We approached a small wooden corral with a horse, a small camper trailer with a Great Pyrenees dog tied outside, and a low stone structure with Armando outside it.

Armando was tanned, hairless except for a beard, barefoot, and wearing only shorts. Tona and Robert rolled down their windows; Armando recognized them and waved us in. He seemed happy to see them and immediately offered us a tour. He was working on the crude stone structure, which had one mostly enclosed room with an earthen floor, ill-fitting windows, and a fireplace for cooking (a very large knife was lodged in the stones above it). Adjacent to the room was a garden for marijuana, and next to this, at the end, what Armando called a swimming pool. It was actually a hole just big enough for the inflatable raft that was floating in it, an integral part of his vision of summer living. To him it was beautiful; he called it el Templo del Cielo (the Temple of Heaven). He told me he was originally from Puerto Rico. We visited for a while, niceties were exchanged, and Armando complained to Robert about "the fag" over the hill who he had some gripe with.

Paul was the neighbor Armando had been referring to. He was charming and funny, seemed unsuspicious, and lived in two trailers joined into an L shape. He had a tasteful wooden fence along the road, painted white, and, amazingly, three trees, a rarity in these parts. The dogs who swarmed our car seemed friendly. We parked near his three vehicles, not all of which appeared to be running: a 1991 Mercedes wagon, a Chevy Blazer 4x4, and a Dodge Dakota pickup truck.

Robert introduced us and Paul said, "Pleasure to meet you, and yes, I'm gay!"

Paul invited us in and brought out chairs and sodas. He passed around a letter thanking donors to La Puente, signed personally with a note by Lance Cheslock. "See? I'm a client but also a donor." He had donated something like fifty dollars. Paul said he'd been here since 1994, when he'd paid $2,300 for five acres. "I came because I wanted to own my own land, and I couldn't in California." Monthly disability checks for social anxiety disorder were his main income. "When I'm around too many people, it's not good. Like after a few minutes in Walmart, I get a little crazy." He admitted that he tended to focus too much on his closest neighbors, who lived in a trailer down the hill. Their trash blew onto his property. A young man and woman lived

Paul with his "girls"

there, "left behind by the old man, without a car." The old man, from Alabama, had recently been arrested on child-abuse charges. Paul said he had initially gotten along with them, until he didn't, at which point the woman called him a fag and cursed him as "devil spawn."

He was also sometimes bothered by cattle. Oddly, though the land had been subdivided, it was still treated by Costilla County as open range, which meant that residents were responsible for fencing cattle *out*. Paul's property was fenced except for the entrance, and sometimes cattle would come in that way, despite the dogs.

Paul said he tried to get away twice a year, taking a bus from Alamosa to the Denver airport after choosing a destination by the lowest price—"always less than three hundred dollars." He had been to North Carolina, Texas, and California this way but always returned to his trailers.

Our last stop was a fenced-in property that had an actual swinging gate, which was closed. Tona honked, and after a couple of minutes honked again. When there was no response, Robert opened the gate and we started slowly driving in.

That's when a small SUV parked in front of the house headed straight toward us, blocking our progress. Tona and Robert got out, the two women in the car recognized them, and we all headed to the house. There we convened over the snarling of dogs chained to various objects out front.

Kea and Rhonda were talkative and animated but did not invite us inside. Rhonda, Kea's mom, had wild hair that stuck straight up and out. She told me she was from Chicago and California and had known from the moment she'd met him that Robert had been a cop, "because he has the aura of a cop. He was standing like *this*." I recognized *this* as the "bladed stance," a diagonal stance law enforcement officers use to reduce their vulnerability to attack when speaking to somebody they don't know. I told her I had worked as a corrections officer and had been taught that position as well.

Kea said that she had been suicidal a year ago over a failed relationship. She was recently back from California, where she had sought medical treatment—she didn't say for what—and referred to her ballooning weight. She now weighed 410 pounds and looked uncomfortable perched on the back deck of the SUV, which had its rear door up. She said that she and her mother were of Creole descent, and that she loved dogs and writing. I said I did, too, that I was working on an article and maybe a book about the valley, and that we should talk. They were among the few Black people I had seen out there, and I was curious about what forces had attracted them to this place—or pushed them from somewhere else.

Our return drive to Antonito was delayed by a flock of hundreds of sheep that occupied the dirt road in front of us and the land on either side as far as we could see. They changed the horizon to white and fluffy. The mass of them parted when Tona got near, although not quickly. We couldn't see the shepherds, but Robert said they were typically Mexicans or Central Americans who stayed seasonally in small camper trailers.

Tona turned on some music, and Diego, the long-haired Chihuahua, who was with Robert in the back seat, came alive. Tona turned it up: AC/DC, heavy metal from the 1980s. Diego caught the spirit, putting his paws on the back of the front seat and sort of howling, sort of singing.

YOU . . . shook me all night long

YOU . . . shook me all night long
"AC/DC is his jam!" said Tona. "But he likes Hispanic music, too."

I had not known that this kind of place existed. I had a long experience of the mountain towns and the national parks and forests that support Colorado's tourist economy, and I knew a bit about ranching, but this off-grid world, like the one in South Park, was completely foreign— and, to me, fascinating. It combined the soaring beauty of the Mountain West and resonances of the pioneers with the hard-bitten realities of life on a shoestring.

To be clear, life on the prairie was not typical of life for most in the San Luis Valley. Tona said longtime Hispanic residents tended to have a low opinion of people like the ones we had just visited. They would use the word *roñoso*—roughly, squalid—to describe them or would refer to them as squatters, even though most owned the land they were on. Nobody reputable would live out there, went the thinking, when it was so much nicer around the valley's edges, where there were trees and creeks and some civilization.

But La Puente's project of building bridges to these outsiders struck me as virtuous, a demonstration of what we needed on a national level to heal the American divide. I wanted to learn more, I wanted to stick around, I wanted to get involved.

Back at the shelter the next day, Lance Cheslock and Tona introduced me to Geneva Duarte, a lifelong valley resident and longtime La Puente volunteer. She lived in a double-wide trailer with extra space, which she enjoyed offering to those in need, be it AmeriCorps volunteers or a visiting writer. I moved in for a few days. Geneva's *chante*, to use the local lingo for "house," had a TV room bursting with Denver Broncos regalia, as well as several posters of a handsome, athletic-looking young man in what I thought was boxing attire. Geneva corrected me: her son, Angelo, had been a mixed martial arts fighter of some renown before he'd died, eleven months before, by coming too close to power lines while trimming a tree. She pointed through a window to a homemade monument to Angelo she had constructed out back; it was next to one for her husband, who, grieving and with dementia, had passed away only six months after Angelo. Geneva had had a tough year.

Geneva lived in Alamosa but knew I was interested in life out on the flats; she asked if I wanted to see Angelo's place.

"Angelo lived out there?"

"Yes, after I threw him out!" Her son, she said, his girlfriend, and the girlfriend's son had lived for a time at her house but then overstayed their welcome. Seeking a new start, Angelo had bought five acres on the flats and built his own place.

As we drove to see it, Geneva told me what a great guy her son had been, and how everyone had loved him. It's what you'd expect a mother to say, and yet I'd find that in Angelo's case, it was true. A La Puente worker had gotten to know Angelo when he'd hawked Geneva's fresh breakfast burritos around town. "One of the best people ever!" he raved. Alamosa's mayor knew Angelo through games of poker at Geneva's house and liked him, too—even after stories like the one about Angelo getting pursued by police in Fort Garland and deciding he would try to outrun them, and succeeding for twenty-five miles, ending the chase by parking his car in front of the Alamosa jail. The three years he had done in state prison over domestic-abuse charges suggested a dark side. But he seemed to have come out of the experience a better person.

"I've had a lot of problems with shame over my past but Uncle Ang never made me feel judged or badly," Geneva's granddaughter wrote to me. "Actually it was exactly the opposite—he made me feel as if I wasn't alone. We all screw up, we just have to strive for better. I owe a lot of my success in life to being able to forgive . . . myself. And that's what my uncle was all about was second chances and being true to wanting a change." And Geneva's daughter Wendy confirmed this: "He learned from all his mistakes. And he was never a repeat offender."

Angelo's shack—small, wooden, and ramshackle—had been slapped together using oddments of wood, aluminum siding, and plexiglass. Everything was uneven and drafty; though it had been only a few months, it looked long abandoned. The door was closed with a padlock, which Geneva set to work opening. She said she did not really share my interest in life on the flats. "The house where we grew

Angelo Duarte's shack, with Blanca Peak in the background

up didn't have a bathroom, didn't have plumbing," she said. "So living out here? I don't think so."

A neighbor appeared while we were poking around. Jimmy lived in a straw-bale house* about a hundred yards away (it looked a lot more comfy than Angelo's place) and said that he and Angelo had worked on a lot of projects together—including digging ditches for a shared well that was nixed by the county. He spoke with Geneva about the unpleasant girlfriend who had lived here with Angelo and her addiction to "black" (black heroin—Jimmy made a motion of injecting into his arm). And how she had stopped by with her current boyfriend to, basically, harass him. When the conversation next turned to a custody issue she was having, it carried me away from feelings of prairie freedom to a sadder, more universal world of poor people's pain.

Besides Jimmy's house, only one other settlement was visible from Angelo's shack. It was a down-at-the-heels assortment of trail-

---

* Straw-bale houses use bales of straw as building materials. Such bales are seen as a renewable resource and also supply insulation.

ers, sheds, and junk that appeared to be the active home of several people—we could hear dogs barking. I asked Jimmy and Geneva who lived there. They waved off the question with looks of distaste, and Jimmy said something like "Aaaah, nobody." Which, of course, made me wonder more.

When we left, Geneva told me that Jimmy had brought up the idea of buying Angelo's place from her, and she said that at some point, she would want to sell.

"How much would you ask?"

"I don't know, maybe seven thousand? But I'd take less," she said.

I found myself wondering if I should buy it. The shack was kind of cute. It came with a backstory, including a detail Geneva was just adding: "Angelo said once he got his feet on the ground, he wanted his place to become like a sports camp for kids who got in trouble," she said. "He'd run it, and he'd call it the Last Chance Ranch." *I bet she'd take five thousand,* I thought to myself.

But that night, once I was back in settled Alamosa, the dream of owning that property lost some power. There were tons of five-acre lots out there, and many could probably be bought for less than $5,000. Better to start fresh than with somebody's broken dream?

Lance Cheslock, the director of La Puente, understood this call of raw land. "Ten thousand plots of land are ten thousand potential dreams," he said. That was the meaning of that land: a base, a claim, a new start. Ownership. Sovereignty. He himself had started from scratch when he'd relocated to Alamosa from Haiti, where he'd spent three years with Habitat for Humanity after graduating with a degree in chemistry from Colorado College. He and his first wife had converted a two-room shed into living quarters on acreage just south of Alamosa and started their family there. That wife moved on but Lance is still there, living with his second wife, Rachael, in a more substantial house next to the old one, which he now calls "the bunkhouse." (Lance and Rachael held their wedding reception at the shelter.)

Lance has been leading La Puente for more than thirty years. He has overseen its expansion from just a homeless shelter to an organization that offers a wide range of services to the poor: a valley-wide network of food banks, plus social enterprises from Milagros Coffee House, at Alamosa's main intersection, to a used-clothing store, a supportive-housing office, a program for kids from at-risk families, and more. But he told me that it wasn't until 2015, when Tona and Robert went out to the flats as part of the country's annual "point in time" count—used by the federal government to allocate monies to help the homeless—that the lives of people out on the back of beyond really reached his radar. "We heard stories of people skipping diabetes medication for want of gas to get into town, of running out of food, of being isolated in abusive relationships, and collectively thought, *We need to be out there,*" said Lance. "We should have known this long ago. But like everyone else in the community who drives on paved roads, we hadn't paid attention."

A grant was secured from a foundation called Caring for Colorado, with the premise that engaging far-flung poor people was likely to improve their health, even if that didn't happen overnight. Robert had been the first Rural Outreach worker; Matt Little was now the second. Lance suggested I go to work with Matt if I wanted to learn more.

Matt's pickup truck was his office, and I climbed into the cab the next morning near the town of Blanca. We were about an hour north

Matt Little

of where Robert had worked. Unlike Robert and Tona, Matt himself was a flats dweller. He told me he had arrived from West Virginia a few months before, following the death of his wife. With him he brought his disabled adult son, Joshua, a wolf-dog named Allie, and a horse, Roxy Dancer.

He told me that a lot of people on the flats seemed to be military veterans, like him, and "a lot of them got PTSD." But there were no easy categories that applied to everybody. Over the next few hours we checked in on two women who had arrived from Oklahoma a few months before, having both divorced their husbands. They called their little house at the bottom of Blanca Peak the Muumuu Ranch. Among their many dogs (Matt knew all their names) was a Chihuahua dressed in a leopard-skin sweater "so the hawks won't eat him." Next we visited a sixty-year-old retired plumber and his wife who had left suburban Denver "after the gang shootings got too bad"; they lived in a shed. An air force jet roared overhead, alarmingly close to the ground. She made me instant coffee while he opened a beer at eleven a.m.; on the rough-hewn table was a jar of marijuana buds. The couple had added a loft inside the shed where they sometimes slept, particularly in the days after they found a rattlesnake inside the little marijuana green-house they had built in front. (In the floor was the bullet hole from when they shot it.)

Later we passed a family from Pueblo engaged in the very first act of settlement: scraping a patch of land clear with shovels. It's where the house will go, the dad explained to Matt after we stopped. Matt told them he was about to do the same thing on land he was buying nearby. He left the man his La Puente business card and said that down the line, if they needed "a little firewood," they should let him know.

Matt was working hard to make himself known, and of use, to those living on the flats; unlike others at La Puente, who referred to them as "clients," Matt called them "my people. And I don't like to say I'm 'serving' them," he added. "That's what you do at a restaurant. I'm just lending neighbors a hand. People helping people." I liked his take.

Matt's major frustration, he said, was that the valley was so big and there was only one of him; he was never going to meet the need. In just three months on the job he had put nearly twenty thousand miles on his pickup truck, traversing the vast space to get to where people were.

(Tona's partner, Robert, had told me that he might drive 130 miles just to visit three or four clients.)

That's when a light bulb went off. As a journalist and writer, I have often researched by participating. Perhaps I could learn about this rarefied world by helping Matt, by doing what he did. I asked what he thought of the idea. It took a minute or two to sink in. I said he could always take the lead, but the need was great and I might as well be useful while I poked around. He actually looked kind of happy, said, yeah, it was cool with him. I told him I'd need to ask Lance.

I'd been able to see Lance several times during my initial week-long stay. Besides eating lunch at the shelter and comparing notes in his office next door, we'd met for coffee at Milagros Coffee House. Finally, he and his wife had invited me to join them for disc golf at the local course (where one of the best parts was the sign at the entrance that said to watch out for mountain lions), followed by spaghetti and salad at their place, and then a bit of the NBA finals on television. Lance had asked about my time spent with Matt and I'd told him about some of the people I'd met living out on the flats.

"Did you get some good stories?" he asked.

"I feel like I started some good conversations," I said. "But I'd have to go back to fill in some of the stories. They don't all come, um, fully fledged."

Lance laughed. "Sometimes I feel like the manuscript was left on the roof of the car and wind blew the pages all over. I ended up with pages 9, 182, 191, and 258, not in that order." Actually, I said, that was it exactly. I was starting to like Lance. Though he freely admitted he was not a big reader, he sometimes had a literary way of looking at things. He also had a big heart and was passionate and funny.

I didn't ask him about becoming a Rural Outreach worker myself until I was back home and speaking to him on the phone. I said I wanted to try to do what Matt did—and help Matt out when possible. I wanted to know who lived out there and why, and what it was like. I would wear two hats: when I had a conversation with someone who seemed interesting, I would explain that I was also a writer and ask if I could interview them, take notes. My teaching job meant I couldn't move to the valley from New York, but I could spend most of August there, and then visit every month or two. Also, I wanted to live out on the flats myself, somehow, though I didn't exactly know how. Could he use a volunteer outreach worker?

Lance said that he needed to check with his team but he thought it could work. When he called me back, he jumped immediately into the value of working with marginal people out on the flats. "It's the opposite of the entitlement culture," he began. "Those with the frontier mentality are trying to make it on their own. In what they're trying to accomplish, sometimes you see a reflection of yourself." Plus, he added, "the fringes of society really define who we are. They are the extreme fringe, asking questions about how we all should live." Then he was quiet. I braced for a no.

Finally, I had to ask: "So what about the idea of my volunteering for you?"

"Oh, of course!" said Lance. "Did I forget to say that?"

While La Puente was responding to the arrival of poor people on the flats by offering them a hand, local authorities were taking a different approach. County services were growing strained by demand from prairie dwellers—the new people were perceived as needier than most, and more likely to require attention from law enforcement (and occupy jail cells) and social services. And then there was the aesthetic challenge. The county provided no trash pickup out on the flats. Most people burn it, in barrels or in a pit. But trash is hard to control in a windy environment, and some of it gets away. Perhaps more of a problem is what could happen when a would-be settler's dreams fell through. In pioneer days, they would leave behind a log cabin or an adobe hut, which would weather and decay in picturesque fashion. But in the era of prefab mobile homes, what gets left behind can be a piece of junk that just looks junkier over time, as windows get broken and the shell gets stripped of wiring and any other parts that have value.

Costilla, with more than forty-five thousand five-acre lots, had been zoned for years. Yet as in many western counties with lots of space and a small tax base, there had been little enforcement of many rules, such as the one requiring dwellings to have at least six hundred square feet of living space (no "tiny houses" allowed) and restrictions on long-term camping. Many homesteaders had lived out of compliance with the code for years, undisturbed. But in 2015 the county leaders launched a crackdown. They hired a new land use administrator and transferred a couple of deputy sheriffs to enforcement detail. By all accounts these officers took to their new job with gusto, usually focusing on the septic system requirement: landowners found to be lacking one (they might be using an outhouse instead) were often given ten to thirty days to put one in or else face those heavy fines. (Six different counties make up the San Luis Valley in Colorado: Alamosa, Conejos, Saguache, Rio Grande, Mineral, and Costilla.)

Fear spread as low-income residents of the flats received summonses regarding septic systems that were tantamount to an eviction notice. People who had invested their every penny in a home got ready to just walk away, leave everything behind. I kept thinking some would challenge the order in court, but as the county had probably guessed, nobody had the money to hire a lawyer.

Even as many bid tearful good-byes to longtime homes, others found common cause in far-right ideologues who said the government had no right to force people from their property. A handful of people declared themselves "constitutional sheriffs," outside the dominion of the United States government, which they declared illegitimate. In late 2015, a self-appointed "judge" who would later visit and advise the ranchers who were occupying the Malheur National Wildlife Refuge, in Oregon, came down to the flats to counsel citizens on their "rights" and help them organize. Armed confrontations ensued, and several prairie people landed in the Costilla County jail.

Before I became identified with flats dwellers, and possibly one myself, I thought it could be enlightening to do a ride-along with Costilla County code enforcement. And so I found myself one summer day in 2017 in an old SUV with an AR-15 assault rifle in the back, heading out onto the sagebrush prairie with Trinidad Martinez, the land use administrator, and one of his officers, Cruz Soto.

Soto, who wore a bulletproof vest, drove. He was short, compact, tattooed, and armed with a pistol—very cop. Martinez, taller and with a shaved head, wearing an orange Denver Broncos T-shirt, was harder to pigeonhole. He told me he'd left the valley to study criminal justice in Denver but had moved back because this was where his people were. He had no training in land use or planning, but he felt his cause was just. "I'm tired of seeing shacks and campers—what you can see off the highway," he said. And he was tired of "people with modest ambitions doing as little as possible." He believed that their reluctance to spend money complying with the code wasn't always tied to poverty—some "spend a huge amount feeding their animals," for example. They "show up here out of the blue and disrespect our culture" by not obeying the law.

I asked if we were heading to particular addresses or were just looking around, and Martinez said the latter. "We can't cover the whole county, but we always find something." He told me they had twelve hundred square miles to patrol, and thirty thousand parcels of land. I shared with them that people I had spoken to felt certain they were using satellite imagery or aerial surveillance to spot shelters, which they then cross-referenced with a permit database to see who was a scofflaw. One resident had told me the spotter plane was blue. Another said it was yellow.

Martinez laughed. "We don't have anything remotely close to that," he said. The Ford Expedition they were driving, for example, had been purchased used from Jefferson County, in suburban Denver. "On our budget, we are barely able to afford tires."

More properties were vacant than occupied. The first place we approached was fenced, with the gates closed. But Soto drove over the adjoining lot, which was unfenced, around to the far side, and up to the trailer. This wrecked a bunch of sagebrush and chico bushes but was easily doable in the SUV. We got out and walked around.

There was a marijuana grow of about twenty plants, which looked pretty healthy. Nobody was home. "But," Martinez observed, "they must come out here or these plants would be dead." A visual inspection showed no septic system, and so Soto wrote up a summons and posted it on the door of the trailer.

Fifteen minutes later we stopped at another place, this one looking much more abandoned. Soto and Martinez had been here before and told me the owner "used to post a lot of sovereign citizen signs on his fence." To get to the house, we had to open a barbed-wire gate and drive through. Like so many others who have walked away, this person had left a small structure, now open to the elements, and a lot of junk. And he'd left one last sign, a warning to would-be intruders:

Code enforcement officers at a hidden marijuana grow

"FATAL SICKNESS," it said, next to the drawing of a skull. "Deer mice which carry *deadly* Hanta-Virus have inhabited this building. ⅓ of people that get infected *die* within 1–2 weeks. For *your* safety, Please Stay Out!" Soto and Martinez chuckled—this was a new one.

Back on the highway, Martinez pointed out an empty trailer they had stopped at the month before. They'd contacted the owner by mail, he said, only to discover that, to the owner's knowledge, the lot was completely empty: he hadn't visited in years and had no idea that somebody had put a trailer on it (and then, completing the cycle, abandoned it).

"I want you to see that gravestone I was telling you about," said Soto to Martinez, as we drove up a hill to an old RV parked with nothing around it. Underneath its front door was the marker in question. It read, "Zacarias H. Ruiz, Jan. 8, 1950 – Nov. 1, 1965." There was an iron superstructure next to the camper—pipes that look as though they had once supported plastic for a greenhouse. Soto intoned, "So you can see they had a grow and then they abandon— *Whoa, what?*" As he was sweeping his arm toward me, we both saw that a different grow, this one buried in a wide trench to keep it out of sight, was very much in operation. It had about a hundred happy, healthy marijuana plants, flourishing in big plastic sacks that held potting soil and were irrigated via tubes from cisterns that held water with fertilizer dissolved in it. Martinez appraised the plants with a connoisseur's eye—he knew several of the various strains of cannabis—and said that the people who kept this going "really know what they're doing." I asked if they were going to report it, and they shrugged—apparently not. "Not really a code thing," said Martinez.

A while later, they stopped to tell a man from Denver and his son that unless they had a camping permit, it was illegal for them to park their RV on their property *for any length of time whatsoever.* The man seemed not to believe that could be so.* Soto handed him a pamphlet, and Martinez told him to come by the office and get a permit—"or we'll be back."

We avoided a section where deputies had apparently been fired upon recently, Martinez saying, "I'm not gonna go in there if I think they're gonna shoot." I asked who did the shooting.

"Right-wing terrorists," he said. "We've got a couple of them in jail now." A while later, when we pulled into a different property, he said, "This was one of their friends, Vince."

Martinez and Soto stayed in the truck as a skinny, highly agitated man emerged from his makeshift compound, brandishing a cell phone and using it to record the encounter on video. I realized he was Vince Edwards, a member of the right-wing opposition. Edwards had been arrested about a year earlier on a warrant for failure to appear in court—and not quietly. When deputies arrived, he messaged out an SOS to his confreres, who passed it on via Facebook: "All Costilla County Colorado people in need of rapid response to country rd. 12 and 27 st. The police are trying to arrest someone unlawfully." The deputies, rightly believing Edwards to be armed, called for backup, too. It took three hours before Edwards surrendered. He had recently finished nine months in the county jail, and now he declared that the officers (who he knew by name) were harassing him: "You're trespassing and I am asking that you leave this property immediately."

---

* In fact, camping is allowed for up to fourteen days without a permit.

They responded, "We heard somebody bought this from you, so we came to tell them it was still in violation." They mentioned the lack of a septic system and other code deficits. "Show us some paperwork to prove it's still yours."

"You're the county, get your own paperwork!" Edwards responded.

They seemed to enjoy how upset Edwards was getting. But finally they retreated. "The problem with guys like him," said Martinez as we slowly drove away, "is that they tell all the other people in this area that they can do whatever they want without permits, without septic systems, and everything else. So everybody that buys property out here and comes to start developing it looks at their videos." Edwards and others used social media to post about their struggles. "And then they get the impression that they can do whatever they want. And then they get mad at us when we cite them and put them in the court system.

"My inspectors know," he continued as we returned to headquarters in San Luis, "which people are heading the snake, so to speak."

Martinez's skepticism about flats dwellers seemed of a piece with the scorn that Tona had referred to, the indigenous perspective that flats-dwellers were dirty, or squatters. "Growing up," he said, "I would look out there on the flats and think, *Why would anybody put a house out there?*" Many longtime residents of the valley, who tended to live in wooded precincts at its edge, felt you'd have to be a weirdo or a barbarian or just desperate to live on the flats. And that life had been better when fewer people did.

"What's sad to me," Martinez went on, "is, I grew up here, and when I was in high school there was almost nobody here. We used to be able to ride four-wheelers and motorcycles and go hunting, but now you'll be on trails like ones my father built, and you run up against a trailer! Since the new people came, we can't use the land that is rightfully ours, by Spanish land grant! We're fighting to maintain our culture and way of life."

While I'd known about the long-running dispute between longtime Hispanic residents around San Luis and the owner of the giant tract of mountain property to the east known as the Taylor Ranch, I had never heard anyone suggest that even these undesirable subdivisions belonged in some essential way to Hispanics.

———————

I bought my pickup truck in New Mexico. My youngest sister, who lives in Santa Fe, is mechanically astute, drives a very old Subaru (and so knows about life with old cars), and said she'd help me. The goal was something cheap but reliable, with four-wheel drive. On Craigslist she found a white 1998 Toyota Tacoma that seemed to fit the bill. The seller, she learned when she called, ran a small car lot in Española, New Mexico. She liked him over the phone and drove us there when I came back in August.

The truck, nearly twenty years old, had more than two hundred thousand miles on it when the odometer stopped working. It had a manual transmission and old-fashioned four-wheel drive: to engage the front wheels you had to get out and turn a dial on the hubs. Miraculously, the maintenance records of its five previous owners were stored in the glove compartment. It had a cap over the bed and a big blue BERNIE sticker on the back, amid smaller stickers for ski areas and craft beers. It felt like the right karma, and I bought it. (And, yes, removed the BERNIE sticker so as not to provoke strangers.)

Next, where to live? Homes on the flats were seldom advertised for rent. Matt Little told me he'd once found one via a business card on a bulletin board at the Blanca RV Park, but now there was nothing. Lance and Tona volunteered to keep their ears open for a room I might rent in somebody else's place, but the more I thought about it, the less that sounded promising: too many people out there were eccentric and used to living alone. The odds of finding a good fit were slim.

But then Tona told me about a family that had come into La Puente's outreach office, which was next door to the shelter. The Grubers were a mom, dad, and five daughters, whom they homeschooled. They lived in a mobile home on the flats, the dad had recently had cancer surgery, and they could use some extra money. "But they said there's not really room in their place," Tona advised. "Would you consider buying a little trailer you could take down there, leave it on their property?"

I said I would. Matt said he would drive me down and introduce me to the family.

We went the next day. The route happened to take us near the shack built by Geneva's son, Angelo, and so I asked Matt if he knew anything about the neighbors across the way, the ones with a dilapidated collection of trailers, sheds, and other junk who Geneva and Jimmy had declined to comment on. As it happened, he had heard that one of the residents had recently triggered an explosion when he was attempting to make shatter. (Shatter is a cannabis concentrate that takes the form of small, translucent yellow pieces that are typically breakable; thus the name. Manufacturing it requires heat and solvents, and is famously dangerous.) A couple Matt knew who lived nearby said they had heard a boom and seen "a mushroom cloud." The guy who'd triggered it apparently suffered a concussion but was spared further injury because instead of being indoors, he'd been inside a fabric-walled greenhouse (which was incinerated).

"Wow," I said, and quoted Dorothy's line from *The Wizard of Oz:* "We're not in Kansas anymore."

"Oh, it probably happens in Kansas, too," said Matt with a chuckle.

"Did it make the news?"

"The news? No, I don't think so. There isn't that much news out here." I took that to mean that most of what happens on the flats does not end up in a newspaper or other medium. Without a guide like Matt, a visitor would never learn these things.

As we continued through the flats toward where the Grubers lived, Matt entered unfamiliar territory. The flats are so huge that you would be hard-pressed to know the entire area. Our phones often had no signal, and so he was navigating by instinct. "Do you ever use a regular map?" I asked. I had pulled out a large-format DeLorme road atlas Lance had loaned me; it divided Colorado into ninety-four pages and offered a close-up of practically every area. But the flats were so huge that the atlas was not up to the task. Specifically, it did not include details about the hundreds of dirt roads. I'd been trying to follow our progress but now was having trouble figuring out where we were, because many of the roads weren't marked and some of them were marked incorrectly—both on the map and on the occasional road signs, which likely dated from the 1970s, when the roads were created.

"Yeah, those don't really work," Matt told me as I riffled through the big atlas. "You need to get one of these." He held out a tattered map of a kind I'd never seen. "It's a DIY Hunting Map," he said, explaining that the brand was well known to hunters in the Rockies. "You can get one in Monte Vista."

I took it and helped Matt navigate to Frank and Stacy Gruber's place. Its main feature was a mobile home whose newness stood in contrast to the chaos around it: jury-rigged pens and a shed for a pig, goats, and geese; an old yellow bulldozer; solar panels mounted to sticks and branches; a broken-down sedan and a working pickup truck; the ruin of an aged RV that had a sort of external wall added to its front side, like a lean-to; a trash pit near that, partially fenced in, from which a whole lot of trash had escaped (again, there is no garbage collection on most of the prairie); and, finally, a six-foot-tall chain-link fence enclosure extending from the mobile home's front door to create something like a yard for the dogs and the kids' toys.

Right now, though, several dogs had run up to our truck after Matt tapped the horn. The dogs were friendly and so was Stacy, who emerged from a back door holding her youngest daughter, Raven, just a few months old. Matt told Stacy who I was, and Stacy said to wait and she'd get Frank. He came out a few minutes later wearing a Denver Broncos T-shirt and clearly in pain. Several inches of his colon had been removed at a hospital in Colorado Springs two weeks before. Their daughters watched us through the windows as the dogs calmed down and we were able to talk. He had been a house painter and drywaller but hadn't been able to work for a while. They pointed out a spot about two hundred feet from their house, a clearing in the low bushes just off the dirt driveway, that they thought might be a place where I could live if I had my own trailer. The rent would be $150 a month.

I told them that this sounded fair but I'd need to find a trailer; rather than a security deposit or the first and last month's rent, what you needed to live on the flats was your own home to live *in*. They said to let them know.

"I bet Geneva would sell you hers," said Tona when we got back to town. I knew the one she meant—I had seen it sitting in Geneva's driveway. It was venerable but clean.

Later that day, Geneva gave me a tour: it was twenty-five feet long with a full-sized bed, a kitchen table/booth that could be converted into another bed, a tiny bathroom with a shower, and a small galley kitchen. She had used the trailer only on summer fishing trips, she said, and was looking to sell. To sweeten the deal, Geneva offered to throw in a bunch of kitchen things I lacked, bed linens, and temporary use of a little generator she owned, until I got one of my own. The price would be $4,000. I looked through some old documents she had saved. The owner's manual showed the trailer, a model no longer made called an Aerolite Seven, set up on a groomed lawn by the side of a lake, an elderly couple in lawn chairs alongside it and nearby a well-groomed mom—their daughter?—and her two young sons. It had been manufactured in 1998, the same year as my truck. Synchronicity. I told Geneva I would meet her price—she had been generous to me. The Aerolite was about to have a new experience.

2

My Prairie Life, Part I

Before enlightenment; chop wood, carry water.
After enlightenment; chop wood, carry water.

—ZEN PROVERB

We think of addictiveness as a property of certain chemicals and addiction as a disease that people, in effect, catch from those chemicals, but there is good reason to believe otherwise. Addiction may be less a disease than a symptom—of trauma, social disconnection, depression or economic distress. As the geography of the opioid and meth crises suggests, one's environment and economic prospects play a large role in the likelihood of becoming addicted.

—MICHAEL POLLAN, *The New York Times*, July 9, 2021

I RETURNED TO THE VALLEY in December 2017, eager to start living on the flats but also apprehensive, as the valley can get quite cold in wintertime. Geneva kindly picked me up at the Alamosa airport, since my future home and my pickup truck were both parked at her place in town. I went to put my suitcase in the back of her little sedan, but when she opened the trunk I saw there was some piece of a large animal already in there, partly wrapped in a garbage bag.

"Umm . . . ," I said to her, and pointed.

"Oh, sorry. It's a deer leg. I'm taking it by my sister's now." I didn't really ask more questions until after we had dropped it off at her sister's place. "It's for eating," Geneva explained. "We make jerky out of it."

"Have you been hunting?"

"Not exactly," she said, and changed the subject.

Excited to be back, I told Geneva how Matt had agreed to come by the next day, hitch the trailer to his truck, and drive it to the Grubers'. My own truck, as Matt had explained, was not ideal for the task—the hitch was the wrong size and too high. Geneva showed me around the trailer again and gave me some details about how everything worked. She also handed me the keys to my truck and said that everything had gone fine—she and her daughter had picked it up for me at the Denver airport. (I had missed my plane in Alamosa's tiny airport a few weeks before and had to drive to Denver.) I told her I was grateful and went outside to make sure it was ready for the next day's journey. Then I came back to Geneva with a question.

"Umm . . . the dried blood in the truck bed. Do you know what that's from?"

I had not connected it to the deer leg, but Geneva, looking abashed, filled me in. Her daughter and son-in-law, she said, had driven my truck home from Denver, after driving up there with her. They had been crossing La Veta Pass at night when they saw that a deer had recently been hit and killed by a vehicle—a state trooper with his flashing lights on had the deer in his headlights and was pulling the body onto the shoulder. Joe and Lenora parked in front of him and asked if they could take the deer. He said yes, as long as they reported it to the game warden the next day. They heaved the body into the back of my truck.

They had hung the deer inside a shack in Geneva's backyard and dressed it the next day. That's when Geneva had kept one leg for her sister, and another for herself. "Sorry they forgot to clean the truck," she said.

"Do you make jerky, too?" I asked. Geneva had once had a restaurant and was a very good cook. She brightened, said yes, told me how she dried and cured it, and promised to save some for me.

Matt, who had pulled a lot of trailers, wasted no time the next morning hooking mine up to his hitch. He discovered that the wiring harness (which would activate the trailer's brake lights when he touched his own brakes) was old and wouldn't work. This worried me, but he said it was fine. I'd follow him in my truck. We'd just get off the main roads as soon as possible.

I liked that aspect of the flats—not only was it off the grid, but generally it was outside the sphere of law enforcement. Within about fifteen minutes of departing Geneva's, Matt had left the main road and was proceeding away from civilization on an unmarked dirt road—at a high rate of speed, I should add, and generating a huge contrail of yellow dust behind him.

Just about every aspect of this passage intrigued me. It was going into the wild, a place with more pronghorn antelope, feral horses, and coyotes than people. But also it felt at times like a postapocalyptic landscape à la Mad Max, with ruins of old vehicles and junk and things that had burned, some of them still smoking. When the subdivisions had been created, presumably each new road had been marked by a street sign. Most of these now seemed to have disappeared, with the occasional remainders evocative of a faded dream, an enterprise that didn't work out. Instead of an American suburb circa the 1970s, I was headed, in winter, to the far margins to live among the self-sufficient, the alienated, the smokers, the wounded, the dreamers, and the hermits.

Matt continued going fast, which made me nervous because most of the intersections lacked stop signs. The chances of somebody approaching were slim, but they were not zero. I'd asked Matt about this before and he'd said he was always scanning left and right, looking mainly for dust plumes—they were often considerable and more conspicuous than other vehicles. *A good strategy unless it's raining,* I thought at the time. On this day there was not a cloud in the sky, and I hung back so as not to be enveloped in Matt's dust plume.

After about forty-five minutes Matt slowed down; we were moving away from his area of familiarity, and he wasn't exactly sure of the turns. Some zigzags and backtracking ensued, but finally, coming over a rise, I saw what Matt would always call "Frank and Stacy's place."

Again we were surrounded by dogs; there seemed to be even more this time than last. Most calmed down when Stacy emerged from the house, again holding her youngest, and introduced me to them. They ranged in size from a slobbering dusty Saint Bernard named Tank to the ferocious Chihuahua mix, Bear. Between were a smart heeler mix named Lakota (Stacy was part Lakota Sioux), who launched herself into the bed of my truck, and a couple of boxers. Girls could be seen peering out from windows, and eventually some of them shyly came outside and Stacy introduced them, too. They were, in order of descending age, Trinity, Meadoux, Kanyon, Saphire, in a diaper, and baby Raven, in Stacy's arms. Frank, still moving gingerly, also emerged. Though it was December the sun was bright, the wind was not blowing, and nobody wore more than a light jacket. We confirmed where my trailer would go and then Matt, practiced at driving trucks for the military, expertly backed it into its spot and worked with Frank to level it, putting boards under two wheels and adjusting the trailer's scissor jacks. I opened the trailer door to peek inside and saw that a cleanup job awaited: boxes and bottles had overturned on my trailer's race to the prairie, and everything was covered in a layer of dust. But I wasn't bothered—I was home.

Frank explained to me some basics of off-grid trailer life. Finding water and keeping warm were going to be my main ongoing projects. His family, like many others, had added a wood-burning stove to their mobile home, and they stayed warm with that. For water they had a 275-gallon plastic "tote," which they kept on a trailer and periodically refilled at a neighbor's well. He offered to share this with me if I needed it, and even to let me take showers in their place—they usually had propane and would use it to heat water as needed. They also had an array of solar panels (though the wind had broken some) and a bunch of batteries for their electrical needs: lights, a fan to circulate the warm air around the wood-burning stove, a television. "And sometimes we use a generator."

I showed Frank my small generator and single battery. I was upbeat: the night before, I had experimented with sleeping in the trailer in Geneva's driveway with its furnace set to about fifty degrees, I told him, and had been fine. He looked surprised but said that was great, and maybe I'd be okay. But in the long term I'd probably want more batteries and a couple of solar panels, to save myself having to buy gasoline and having to run the generator all night.

For waste, he said, we could figure out a way for me to dump my "blackwater" tank into their septic system.

I'd brought sacks of groceries and gallons of water with me from town. Frank asked two of his girls to help me carry them from my truck to the trailer, then instructed them to leave me alone while I settled in. Stacy said, "You can show him the animals later on," and the girls looked happy.

Meeting the animals turned out to be a major undertaking, because there were so many of them. In addition to the dogs there were geese (nearest to me), goats, chickens and ducks, a potbellied pig, and, inside their mobile home, two cats and a cockatoo named Sugar. "And we used to have horses," said Meadoux, "but they died." She gestured to a mound of earth about fifty feet from my trailer. Her dad had buried the four horses there last winter, using the bulldozer.

I had situated my trailer so that the door was on the opposite side of the family's home, which gave me more privacy and a beautiful view of open prairie with mountains in the distance. But that prairie was empty and, almost by definition, a lonely place. I was happy that behind my trailer was a lot of life.

When the sun went down it got cold and then, before long, very cold. It had been a long day, and so right after dinner, with the trailer's furnace running, I put on long underwear, pulled a down comforter over me, and went to sleep.

Three or four hours later, I awoke, either from the absolute, complete silence or the cold. The furnace had gone off. I sat up and flipped a light switch: nothing. The battery was dead. Shivering, I contemplated getting dressed, going outside, attaching the battery to its charger and the charger to the generator and getting the furnace back on. But that was a lot of steps, and outside would be even colder. Instead I unpacked a very heavy sleeping bag I had used in the Himalayas, wrapped the down comforter around *that,* and zipped the bag completely up so that only my mouth and nose were exposed. To some degree, I went back to sleep.

In the morning, I saw that frost had covered everything inside the trailer. I stuck out my arm and checked a thermometer on the night table: minus seven degrees Fahrenheit. Needing to relieve myself, I unzipped the sleeping bag, jumped into my boots, pulled on my parka, and grabbed my truck keys. My thought was to start up the truck, turn on its heater, and then return to the sleeping bag while it warmed up.

But the trailer door wouldn't open. Was it locked? I fiddled around and concluded no, it was frozen. Some of those frost crystals had

My truck and camper

joined the metal door to the metal frame and were holding on tight. I guessed I could kick it open if I really needed to, but I didn't want to damage it—the trailer had lasted twenty years, and this was only my first day inside! I'd need to wait until everything warmed up a bit. I could go back to bed for that, but first, I thought, I might as well brush my teeth, my theory being the more you stick to your routine, the less you'll let these challenges bend you out of shape. The jugs of water I'd brought were frozen, but I'd anticipated that and placed a filled water bottle in my sleeping bag so that it wouldn't be frozen when I awoke. I found my toothbrush, put on the toothpaste, started to brush, and ouch! The bristles were frozen and felt like a jagged rock in my mouth. They must have been damp when I went to bed. I poured a bit of water from my bottle over them to soften them up and tried again.

After waiting back in bed for the sun to rise and hit my trailer, I thought about how, over the years, the valley has had some of the coldest winter temperatures in the continental United States. But yesterday had been so balmy! When sunshine finally poured through the window of the door, I tried it again and was released.

My goal was to meet one new person on the prairie every day, and the Grubers had told me they'd help. For the first time Stacy invited me into their mobile home, with many apologies for the mess. And messy it was—though with so many kids and so many dogs, it would be surprising for a home to be otherwise. The front door opened into what had been a combination living room and kitchen. It now was also Stacy and Frank's bedroom. They had moved their queen-sized bed in, and it had become a playground for kids and dogs alike. The television was on, and when Sugar the cockatoo saw me, she began to make earsplitting shrieks from her cage at the end of the room. Girls jumped on and off the bed, preceded by dogs, followed by more dogs. Frank and Stacy smoked homemade cigarettes, and occasionally weed from a glass pipe. Despite the chaos, they seemed calm and happy.

They were worried by the news of my cold night, and sympathetic. When they'd first moved out, from a rental house in the Denver exurb of Greeley after periods in New Mexico and Wyoming, the family had no house and had lived in a tent. Then they'd moved into the now-decrepit RV I had seen when I'd arrived. Some of this had been in wintertime, so they knew about being cold. I'd probably need to keep my generator running all night when it was this cold, said Frank. I readily agreed.

A tragedy had let her pursue this dream, said Stacy. At age fifteen, in Casper, Wyoming, she was in her boyfriend's car when it was T-boned at an intersection by a fire truck driving with its lights off. The boyfriend "basically died in my arms," she said. Her skull was fractured by the knob that held the mike to a CB radio, which was forced up through her eye into her head; injuries to the frontal lobe of her brain "still give me headaches." Her face required surgery ("I looked like Frankenstein"). Money from a legal settlement had allowed her to buy forty acres, enough that "each of my girls can have her own land someday." Three years later, an inheritance from her stepfather had let her purchase the mobile home, a septic system, and a pickup truck. Some money left over as a cushion had been stolen from an online account, said Stacy, which, after Frank got sick, had placed them in a position where they'd sought help from La Puente. They had lots of good things to say about the group, and I felt that my association with it was about as positive a reference as I could have.

As we chatted, the girls' attention wandered between the television and the animals and me. Mostly they kept their distance. But they, and

The Gruber family

the dogs, loved it when I reached out a hand to pet an animal, and particularly when I decided to try to win over Bear, the Chihuahua, who had snarled at me the day before. At one point, seated on a beaten-up L-shaped sectional couch, I let the little dog onto my lap. Two of the girls happened to be looking when, completely by surprise, the little mutt reached up and licked me on the lips. I made a face and they burst into laughter.

I explained to Stacy and Frank that one of my goals was to meet more flats dwellers and see what they needed. Was there anybody they might suggest? They came up with some names, and Frank walked me outside to point out the general direction in which each one lived; he drew some maps in the dirt using a stick. They also said I should come with them late in the day, when Stacy drove the girls to feed two horses for their friend Jack.

I stopped in on a few of these new people and also renewed acquaintances with some of those I had met with Robert and Tona six months before. At first I dropped Frank and Stacy's names, but then I would mention them only when asked—people almost always already knew about La Puente, but it was impossible to predict neighbors' feelings about one another.

Though Robert had never gotten to know him, I kept hearing about a guy named Troy. He had one of the oldest houses around, he'd lost a leg in a farm accident, he'd tow you out of a ditch. He lived on a main road, he'd been around a long time, and he knew lots of stories. Everybody knew him. He'd been married, had kids, been divorced, and now had a new wife named Grace. Late in the afternoon, a few days later, I decided to introduce myself.

There was the customary gauntlet of barking dogs en route to the front door, but I waded through and knocked. Troy Zinn opened the door, dish towel in hand, and invited me to sit at the kitchen table while, drinking from a can of beer, he finished his work at the sink. The dogs stayed out. I told him that I was a writer, volunteering for La Puente; he already knew about La Puente, said he thought they did good work.

I asked him about his house, which was humble but well-built for the area. It had three bedrooms, said Troy, and dated from the 1940s or 1950s, when the Bankers Life insurance company had owned a huge tract of land and run a cattle operation and a farm. This had been the headquarters. Directly across the street were two other buildings that had been part of that compound, including a now-abandoned bunkhouse and a bungalow that had housed a kitchen for the hands. Troy now rented out the bungalow. All three structures, a bit the worse for wear, had white stucco walls and red roofs. Troy's house and the bungalow, notably, were on the grid: two electrical lines bisected the valley in the area, and they benefited. And he had an agricultural well that dated from the ranch days. Bankers Life had sold the ranch to land developers in the 1970s, and Troy's parents had become caretakers of the property. He had spent much of his childhood here. When he married and became a long-distance trucker, he moved ten miles away, to the little town of Jaroso. But when the house became available again, he moved back.

Grace, a charismatic middle-aged mom who had struggled to make ends meet after a divorce in California, arrived home with two teenagers. I'd seen her name on a list of local residents that Robert had assembled, back when she'd lived a mile or two away. She had bought land sight unseen and moved out here with her four kids, only to discover that it was not walking distance from a town, as she'd been led to believe, but "in the middle of nowhere." Eventually she and Troy connected. "Of all the alcoholics out here," she would tell me, with Troy in the room, smiling, "he was by far the nicest." She acted as though somebody new at the kitchen table was a normal thing and unpacked some groceries.

Not long after that, another mom arrived with teenagers. Grace introduced me: *Sam, meet Ted.* Again I thought I recognized the name, but this one had different associations: Samantha McDonald was connected to trouble, in the person of her husband. Zanis "Zane" McDonald, a tattoo artist from Alabama, had allegedly threatened staff members at the high school in San Luis, which his four children attended, after feeling that his son had been slighted by the music program. He had expressed solidarity with his neighbor Jeremy Costley, also from Alabama, who promoted resistance to county code enforcement and had declared himself a "common-law marshal." But worse by far, he had recently been arrested, along with Costley, on charges of sexually abusing their daughters, through a swapping arrangement. The men were in jail in San Luis, the county seat, half an hour away, awaiting trial.

Sam looked about the same age as Grace, but like she'd been through a lot more. She and her kids were on their way home from Mesita, a very small town with only three or four households, where the school bus had dropped them off. I offered her some firewood from the back of my truck, and she accepted, saying they were almost out. Might I follow them home and unload it there?

Her minivan was battered, with a side door that didn't slide completely shut. Her son, Arik, fifteen, was the driver. I followed them a mile or two to an unusual place I had seen before: a small wooden house with no windows, and a front door held fast by a padlock. Arik stayed outside to help unload the wood. Then Sam came out and we chatted for a while, though it was cold. Her last name was Hanson, she told me, adding that most people knew her by the last name of

her husband, whom she was in the process of divorcing. I acknowledged having heard the name, said I bet it was a tough time, and asked
what kind of help I might give. Besides more wood, she said, her son
needed a better coat and one of her daughters a new pair of shoes; and
food was always welcome. I said La Puente could help with all of those
things, and I would bring them. Then she mentioned other needs: new
tires and more minutes for the Tracfone (a brand of cheap cell phone).
I said I didn't know if I could help with those, but I'd look into it.

The next day I was back in Alamosa. I needed to pick up another load
of firewood and see what else I could get for my "people," as Matt called
them. But also I wanted to talk to Matt himself. He understood the
job I was trying to do better than anybody and could teach me things.
Also, he was just fun to hang out with.

We met up at eight a.m. at La Puente's Milagros Coffee House. It
was a laid-back, open space in an old room with high ceilings. It was
homeless-friendly, so you'd sometimes see people spending time there
you might not be so likely to find at Starbucks (which Alamosa also
has, on a commercial strip outside the town center). Its Wi-Fi pass-
word was "loveothers." Matt wasn't paid a large salary, so I always
tried to buy him breakfast, but normally he'd accept only a coffee and
always leave more than the cost of the coffee in the tip jar. He'd been
both a chef and a restaurant manager, he said, and knew how much
tips meant to those workers.

He shared with me his worries about some of his people, now that
it was getting cold. He revealed that a fellow he'd introduced me to
at the RV park in Blanca had resorted to burning his barn the winter
before, piece by piece, when he ran out of firewood. "I think I've got
him taken care of this year, but I need to check again." This idea of
freezing to death seemed to haunt him, perhaps because he'd come
close to it himself: he had been laid off from his previous job, as a cook
at Alamosa's Adams State University, in the middle of last winter and
had lived in his pickup truck, which had a camper top, along with his
disabled son, during several of the coldest weeks of the year.

I asked Matt to fill me in on his life before then, and he obliged. He'd
grown up in Weirton, West Virginia, one of eight kids. Weirton had a

huge steel mill, which had mostly shut down when Matt was a teenager. The area had then become one of the nation's opioid-addiction
epicenters. His wife, Sarah, had grown up there, too, and worked as
a beautician, in a supermarket, and in a bank, and finally as a registered nurse. Matt had left for stints in the air force—first in Panama, to
oust Noriega, and then in the Middle East for Desert Shield and Desert Storm—and returned home to a job market with limited choices.
College-level courses in biology helped him find an office job doing
lab work, "but to spend all day in a cubicle—nah," he said, shaking his
head. He'd worked three years driving a garbage truck, and had also
gotten a degree in restaurant management in Pittsburgh (only an hour
away); that helped him land a job as a chef at a racetrack and, later, as
manager of a Ponderosa Steakhouse.

He and Sarah had had two sons; one, Joshua, was schizophrenic and
had been a challenge to raise. Matt had actually won the West Virginia
lottery, and he and Sarah had used the money to buy a house. But in
2013 that house, uninsured, had burned to the ground. Three months
later, Sarah had died of COPD at age forty-two. (Matt was a smoker,
too.)

"My oldest had an apartment, so I was, like, living with him, and it
was just . . . everywhere I went I was reminded of her. I mean, it was
both our hometown . . . so I was just, *It's time to go, there's nothing holding me back.*

"I'd never been west of the Mississippi except to Lackland Air Force
Base, in San Antonio. So I was looking . . ." An avid hunter, Matt had
read about Colorado in *Field & Stream* in the 1980s, and that was "like
a seed. So I'm like, 'Let's try Colorado.'" He tried searching online for
"cheap land colorado" and saw there was a lot of it for sale in the San
Luis Valley. He had less luck with job listings in the valley, so he cast a
wider net and found a job as a chef in Pueblo, about a hundred miles
from Blanca. "Three months in Pueblo. If it sounds like a prison term,
that's kind of what it felt like." But once in Pueblo, he kept looking and
finally found the new job in food service at Adams State.

Matt asked how it was going with my trailer. I told him about getting frozen in on my first night, and he said he'd had the same thing
happen on the shore of Mountain Home Reservoir, where he and
Joshua had camped after he got laid off from Adams State. The space

inside his camper top was cramped, and with him and Joshua in there, the condensation could really build up if a window wasn't cracked. He said that one night it had gotten down to thirty-six degrees below zero; he woke to a layer of ice all the way around the door inside, which he had to chisel off in order to be able to get out.

From Milagros we went to La Puente's wood lot in town and filled the beds of our trucks. Then, en route back to the flats to distribute the firewood, Matt offered to show me his land, where he hoped he and Joshua would soon be able to live.

The ten acres were right at the foot of Blanca Peak. It was a spectacular landscape that, in many other parts of the state, would have commanded a premium price. But because it was in the valley, with its seemingly limitless supply of small lots, he'd been able to buy it for only $8,500. Since then he'd been planning and preparing. He had ordered a shed, which he planned to expand into a small house, and he showed me where the shed would sit, where the septic tank would go (the land was outside Costilla County, and code enforcement was less draconian), and the outline of a horse corral. He had no machinery apart from his pickup truck—but he'd made the most of it, borrowing the heavy tow hitch from a neighbor's mobile home to clear a driveway through the sagebrush. Otherwise he was using a shovel to prepare the ground for laying blocks for the shed, to set fence posts for the corral, and to dig a trash pit.

He seemed especially excited about the corral, which would finally provide a real home for his horse, Roxy Dancer, who was currently picketed at the small place he was renting out on the flats. I asked about the horse's trip from West Virginia to the valley.

"After I had a place to keep her, I made another trip—brought her from there in a U-Haul."

"You mean you rented a U-Haul horse trailer in West Virginia?"

"No, I rented a U-Haul and put her in the back." Matt chuckled. "Propped the rear door open so she'd have plenty of air. That rail that goes around the inside is a perfect hitching post." The day the county had given him an address, he told me, he'd saddled up Roxy in her new corral and ridden the hundred yards to his "front" fence post, to hammer the street numbers into the wood.

Matt also had a wolf-dog, Allie, and was looking for another. I've known others who've loved these semi-feral animals, which always strike me as a little spooky. Matt extolled Allie's differences from a regular dog: she didn't bark (she howled), she wasn't territorial, and she was more loyal than a regular dog.

Matt started every day by visiting a nearby spring to get water—I had seen this place, off the roadside, in the shadow of a big cottonwood tree. It often had a line of off-gridders with trucks and cubical "totes" they were waiting to fill. He said that Joshua, now thirty years old, would sometimes accompany him on that and other errands but spent most days at home. "I applied for him to get special housing in town [Alamosa], but it's a long wait."

Matt said he'd show me where they'd been living since the period of camping in the truck—he didn't like to call it homelessness—and en route would introduce me to Dan Schaefer.

Schaefer, a ten-year resident who had been cited by Costilla County for not having a septic system, faced mounting fines, which he was fighting not with firearms or declarations of sovereignty but through the legal system. He had found a lawyer willing to represent him and three or four other families. Matt said that Schaefer knew a lot about prospecting (something that interested him, as well) and ran a website about it, called Colorado Prospector. But he warned me that Dan tended to lecture people, and that he had seen him get mad once at a meeting.

Schaefer was a large man and seemed smart. He met us outside his trailer, which had an addition tacked on its side and a front area enclosed by chain-link fence, as the Grubers had. Schaefer walked beyond the enclosed area to speak with us. A woman he did not introduce also came out and appeared to busy herself with yard work, though, oddly, it was pretty clear she was just trying to overhear our conversation. (I was later told that the couple had divorced but she had refused to leave.)

Schaefer had a lot to say—too much, really. After Matt explained why I was there, he started off on a rambling, wide-ranging speech while I tried to take notes. My hand got sore and then my feet and I started worrying about sunburn—we were standing in full sun. Certainly he had a right to be agitated: charged with a criminal misdemeanor, he'd been assigned a public defender, who'd told him he was the first resident so charged who had stood his ground. He'd been through an administrative hearing, a first certiorari hearing, and a pre-trial hearing. "In the law it says the county has fifteen days from the hearing to provide their evidence to my public defender," he argued, but it had not yet done so. Proceedings had already lasted nearly a year—"that's a fuckin' year that's affecting my life and income." He had written a post online about his situation titled "Cease and Desist Living?"

Next came a lucid and, I must say, convincing-sounding consideration of the *need* for a septic system, in light of his family's usage. His outhouse, he said, was sufficient given the small amounts they put in it: "Dilution is the solution to pollution!" He ignored me when I asked him to explain this in more detail. Then I tried to squeeze in a question about him and his background, but he ignored that, too, until Matt repeated it.

"Stop talking and hear me out!" Schaefer bellowed at Matt, who gave me a glance (*See?*). Eventually he explained that he was a former marijuana dispensary owner, and also that he had had a high security clearance in the military but had been discharged because of "possible cocaine use."

"Possible?" I asked. Schaefer ignored this, as well, and lamented the disappearance of his neighbors. He pointed out, at various far distances, the settlements of half a dozen former neighbors who'd had to leave because of county code enforcement. "Mary was this year. That one they ran off last year. Juan and Maria are gone. They're harassing Kenny. Ron and Marlene, they ran them off the week before Christmas, with all their kids in school. See that abandoned camper? They ran them off to Conejos County."

Finally we left. "Whew," I said to Matt.

"You see? Well, at least I told you," he said.

"I guess I'm sympathetic to him," I replied, "though he's a guy who will test your sympathy."

Matt's previous residence turned out to be a simple affair—basically a camper trailer with one end cut off, that space then extended into a long room. It had lots of light and views but seemed the opposite of airtight; I could almost feel the wind blowing through.

Matt's rental place

As we continued on our way, Matt drove me past the longtime home of the Worley family, neighbors of his who had also been pressured to leave. It was homemade and impressively extensive—spread out like a giant house of cards made from a hundred different decks, addition after addition after addition, none of it quite square and materials sourced from a thousand junk piles. "Are they still there?" I asked. There were no vehicles, and the homestead looked possibly abandoned. That was a good question, answered Matt. They were hoping their case would be joined with Dan Schaefer's and, in the meantime, were trying hard to keep off the county's radar. Matt had seen their empty truck parked near the highway recently—something people did when they lacked a driver's license or had an expired registration—and had more than once picked them up when they were hitchhiking into Alamosa. I had heard that the Worleys were against documentation, didn't want to be in any government computer. Thinking he might catch them at home, Matt had recently come by with a load of wood, honked his horn, shouted, and, hearing nothing, begun to unload. At that point, James and Roxanne Worley appeared from out of their root cellar, where they had hidden upon the approach of Matt's truck. "The Worleys are the Anne Franks of this situation," he told me.

I didn't know how, but I resolved to meet the Worleys.

The next morning I dropped more firewood off at Sam Hanson's place. A defeated-looking pit bull stopped barking the minute Arik came out to help me unload.

"What happened to her?" I asked him.

"Well, last year somebody shot her," he said. "That's why she limps. And then, you can see, she found a porcupine." I didn't need to ask why they didn't take her to a veterinarian. There was no money.

One of Arik's sisters, Ziza, poked her head out the door and said, "Hi, Ted." I showed her a pair of shoes I'd brought from La Puente, and a pair of jeans. The shoes were too big, but the jeans were good.

"Isn't this a school day?" I asked her.

Sam, who appeared at the door, pointed at the rear tire of the minivan, which was flat—they discovered it partway to the school bus stop that morning, she said, and just turned around and drove home. None of the four kids was going to school today. I asked if I could help— "Maybe I could drive them to school for you?"

What would be most helpful, said Sam, would be if I could drive Arik into Antonito with a tire and a rim that the tire shop there would put together. I told her sure, and in a few minutes, we were en route.

I liked Arik, and we chatted the whole way. He was sad to miss school but said it had been worse the year before, when his dad pulled him and his sisters out midway. Apparently the music teacher had told Arik he wasn't responsible enough to look after one of the school's saxophones and would have to play something else. But both his father and grandfather had played sax, Arik explained, and his dad, in a rage, complained—and in addition to his other threats had threatened to burn down the school. Now that Zane was in jail, the kids were back in school, trying to catch up. Arik was carrying a paperback with him, a fantasy about dragons and elves that he needed to write a report on for "Sped." Huh? His special ed class, he explained. He offered up an exceptionally detailed account of the book.

I dropped Arik at the tire place, which I knew well because of my own issues with flats. It turned out that Arik had other errands to do, so we agreed to meet back there in about three hours.

The timing was perfect for me to drive up to Alamosa and attend a talk at Adams State University by a *Denver Post* reporter who had recently written a story, accompanied by a video, about a family who lived off-grid in the northern part of the San Luis Valley.

The reporter had brought along slides from reporting about other off-gridders in the valley that he had done two and a half years before. I recognized a couple of people in the photos but then was shocked to see a series of pictures of the McDonalds, who at the time had recently finished building their house. One of the photos was of Arik, then thirteen, standing next to a wooden wall. "All of this was hand-cut by me," he was quoted as saying; the reporter added that he'd "used a hand saw to size the boards." The somewhat ghastly part of the presentation was that the journalist was unaware of what had befallen the family since he'd reported his story.

The McDonalds' windowless house

The family built a tiny cabin near the Rio Grande River, along with an attached greenhouse to grow pot plants and vegetables. "I grow what the state allows for two adults," [Zane McDonald] said.

"We did a lot of research, we asked a lot of questions. We all knew this was going to be a sacrifice, but it was also our last adventure with the kids before they get too cool to hang out with us."

Residents of the valley can be polite to a fault, and perhaps that's why nobody in the audience of three hundred brought up Zane's horrific record—though an organizer told me that at least a couple of people complained to her afterward. In the report Zane sounds like a law-abiding, hip dad. (The criticism I did hear, from the man seated next to me in the balcony, was that the reporter's focus on the *poor* gave a bad name to off-gridders who did not live in poverty and grow weed, and who took care to build nice places. There were many such folks, in Colorado and elsewhere, but in the valley, they tended not to build out on the flats.)

As Arik and I headed back out to the prairie, I asked if he remembered speaking to a reporter for a story in the Denver newspaper. He said yes and added, "The kids in school gave me such a hard time about that."

"Do you mean for having your picture in the paper?"

"For being a story about poverty," he said. He'd been at a tough junior high; I could imagine they were merciless. "But now they don't, since everything that happened." Even bullies would shut up when your dad was arrested for abusing your sisters.

The Grubers had me over that evening for some stew. Stacy was still embarrassed about the mess, but I assured her again that it didn't matter, that it reminded me of growing up with three little sisters. In the trailer, though, it was all compressed into a smaller space and the animals were part of the mix. So much was happening at any one time, it was hard to know what to pay attention to. Opal, a baby goat, was temporarily living inside, and Trinity (Trin) was feeding her with a bottle on the couch. Stacy moved the baby Raven from her high chair to her playpen, at which point a cat jumped into the playpen with her, and Tank, the lumbering Saint Bernard, stood up to the high chair and began slurping up uneaten Cheerios from the tray. Meadoux, the second oldest, placed her dog, Lakota, on a different part of the couch, wrapped her in a sheet, and told her she was on a time-out. Frank showed me a photo sent by their friend Josh in Oregon of a very large marijuana plant he was growing, and Stacy quipped that maybe I should raise a marijuana plant of my own "for the full experience."

Meanwhile, of course, the television was on (you could pick up more than twenty channels simply by having an antenna). Our attention drifted to a news report about a UFO sighting that cut to an interview with a witness, an older woman who was missing teeth. Stacy surprised me by exclaiming that when a believer in aliens goes on TV, "they always put someone who doesn't look good—they don't have somebody like you, who has their teeth."

I was surprised that she brought that up, but in retrospect I think she wanted to clear the air about her own lack of teeth. In a lot of rural America, people associate missing teeth in the non-elderly with abuse of methamphetamines, but Stacy wanted me to know that this wasn't the case with her. "For me it was an easy choice," she said, since she'd gotten a big infection, an abscess in her jaw that required some teeth to come out. "It was either lose the teeth or die." Frank still had a few teeth but offered that he'd lost his first as a teenager, when the two top front ones got knocked out in a fight. By age seventeen he had a partial denture. "Sometimes I wish I didn't still have the ones I do," he said, since they caused problems now and then. He had done some crystal meth in his teens, he said, but had never tried heroin, had never shot anything into his veins. Stacy had been an alcoholic with a fondness for beer. But since finding each other and starting a family, they said (and I observed), they used nothing but weed and tobacco; neither of them ever drank.

Illegal drugs, however, were all around the valley—particularly opioids and heroin. The very month I had this visit with the Grubers, *60 Minutes* ran a report on how the country's largest drug distributor, the McKesson Corporation, had fueled the opioid epidemic by turning a blind eye to massive orders from small pharmacies in the San Luis

A sign outside an Alamosa garden store in 2018

Valley. "DEA investigators discovered that McKesson was shipping the same quantities of opioid pills to small-town pharmacies in Colorado's San Luis Valley as it would typically ship to large drugstores next to big city medical centers." A twenty-nine-year veteran of the DEA put it this way: "McKesson [was] supplying enough pills to that community to give every man, woman, and child a monthly dose of thirty to sixty tablets. . . . I found it shocking."

One result was massive addictions—at the Alamosa jail, the sheriff would tell me that 90 percent of all prisoners had an opiate addiction or were in on drug-related charges. I had asked Stacy and Frank about an abandoned RV one road away from them. It belonged to former friends of theirs, said Stacy, who had moved it onto her property the year before. But the couple started using drugs and turned into bad neighbors—they failed to look after the Gruber house one weekend when the family was away, with the result that the pets left inside pooped all over the carpet and wreaked other havoc. As their relationship disintegrated, the couple abandoned the RV and disappeared.

Stacy said the woman had recently gotten back in touch. Her new boyfriend was looking for a safe place to park his car for a few days—could they leave it with them? Warily, Stacy and Frank said yes. But once the vehicle, a shiny red Mitsubishi sports car on a trailer, was parked, Frank checked on social media "seller" sites to see if anybody was missing it. Sure enough, the car was stolen. The Grubers called the sheriff's office, so as not to get sucked further into their former friend's dysfunctional world.

My least favorite part of time spent inside the Grubers' mobile home, I was pretty sure, involved Sugar, the cockatoo. Sugar had a big, pretty white cage, positioned near a window because, Stacy said, she loved to see what was going on outside. Like most of their pets, Sugar was a rescue. She seemed very smart—she knew words and sentences. But her frequent earsplitting shrieks drowned out all the other noise, which is saying something.

One day when the TV went quiet, I heard a woman's voice say, "Big Dog wants out." Stacy looked at me. "Did you hear it?" she asked.

"Yeah—Tank needs to go out?"

"No, I mean did you hear who said it?"

"Um, I'm not sure," I confessed. Stacy told me to listen some more.

"Come here, Big Dog," said a voice, and this time, following Stacy's eyes, I realized it was Sugar.

"She likes Tank," Stacy explained. "When Tank gets close, sometimes she'll pull on his fur."

In response to my fascination, Stacy took Sugar out of the cage. Sugar sat on her shoulder, then perched on her arms, then happily moved over to Trin and Meadoux.

"Watch this," said Trin, sitting down on the bed with Sugar. She folded down the sheet. Before my disbelieving eyes, Sugar slid in and lay down.

"I don't always know it's her talking, either," said Frank. He recounted how one day, as he was about to leave the house and join Stacy, who was already in the car, a voice asked, "Are you leaving?" Frank paused and said yes. "When will you be back? Sugar wants to come." Stacy said Frank was shaken.

In future days, I would also learn that Sugar had a foul mouth. "Fuck fuck fuck fuck fuck," I heard her say more than once. And to Chaps, the kitten, "Here, kitty kitty, I'll bite your fuckin' ear off!"

"Who taught her that?" I asked. Stacy said that Sugar had belonged to a couple in their eighties who had to move to a retirement home and couldn't bring her. Stacy thought the husband's name was George, because Sugar would say, in a reassuring woman's voice, "It's okay, George." But other times Sugar's voice would be that of an angry man, saying, "Shut the fuck up" or "Shut the fucking door." The girls giggled hearing Stacy tell it. "We think George was abusive" to his wife, Stacy added.

Frank said that sometimes Sugar's screeching got on his nerves, as well. Once, when he pretended he was going to toss a plastic water bottle at her cage, Sugar said, "Go on, throw it!" And another time: "Throw it, motherfucker!"

Meadoux said, "Sometimes we say 'Shut up' and she says, 'No, you shut up!'"

It seemed that Sugar was still learning new phrases. Frank and Kanyon, the middle daughter, were big fans of the Denver Broncos football team and never missed a game on television. It was after one of those that Sugar started saying, "Don't fuck it up, Broncos!"

A few weeks after I arrived, Stacy would report that the bird had started saying something else new, in the voice of one of her daughters, when she saw my pickup truck pull in: "Ted's home."

It was time for the smallest girls to go to bed. I said good night to the Grubers and moved toward the door. Stacy told Trin to show me the way with a flashlight since I hadn't brought one. I told Trin there was no need, though once past the chain-link fence, I was glad she was there. When the moon was large you could see lots at night, but on that night there was no moon to be seen—just about a trillion stars. The flashlight helped me avoid obstacles like boards and rocks and wind-blown trash. We walked to the far side of my trailer, and Trin trained the light away from us and out into the prairie. "Sometimes I see eyes looking back," she said, panning slowly across the horizon.

"What do you think it is?"

"Probably coyotes," she said. "Sometimes maybe a dog. But also it could be a mountain lion." She had only seen the big cat's tracks in her two years on the prairie, she added, never the real thing. That made me feel a little better.

When it comes to personal security, a trailer is definitely better than a tent—with the door closed, no wild animal could enter my space. But as the wind picked up one night later that week and my bed shook, I wondered, *Should I let this rock me to sleep, or should I be worried?* The wind moaned through a couple of ceiling vents that wouldn't quite close, providing a spooky soundtrack. The next day, I started asking flats dwellers if they'd ever heard of trailers blowing over. Most said no, noting that big mobile homes, like the Grubers', were generally tethered to the ground with straps. But what about little ones like mine? I asked. One person allowed that he had seen a smaller trailer than mine, used by Mexican shepherds, flipped over after a particularly violent windstorm.

On the next really windy night, I went over the scenarios in my head. The wind could blow from any direction, but mostly it came from the west or southwest. Given how my trailer was positioned, that meant that if the wind were to blow my trailer over while I was asleep and tip my bed vertical, I would land on my head. The least I could do, by way of prevention, was to start sleeping with my head at the other end of the bed. That way, should the wind upend my trailer, I'd land on my feet.

One route from Alamosa to the Grubers' passed through the small town of Manassa, where the largest building in town, occupying a whole block with its lawn, was the Mormon church. Manassa's claim to fame was that it was the birthplace of boxer Jack Dempsey (dubbed the Manassa Mauler by Colorado-raised writer Damon Runyon). Dempsey, the ninth of thirteen children, grew up poor in a Mormon family. A small log cabin in the town park houses the Jack Dempsey Museum.

A highway sign at the Manassa turn-off depicts the legendary boxer in his boxing gear, and a bronze statue in front of the museum shows him in a fighting pose. For a time, Geneva Duarte looked into getting a sign commemorating her fighting son, Angelo, erected outside Ala-mosa. She had more success arranging an annual mixed martial arts (MMA) evening at Adams State, where the proceeds went to a scholar-ship given in her son's name.

She also hoped that I would write about Angelo, and to that end invited me to join some of Angelo's cousins and friends at her house for an evening of remembrances. Present were Santino Trujillo, Gilbert Estrada (who happened to be living in Geneva's mobile home at the time), and Salina Pacheco—all of them children of Geneva's sisters. Any thoughts that this might be a Hallmark-card kind of sentimental evening were quickly put to rest as everyone present seemed to agree that Angelo had been hard-living, outgoing, macho, brave, likable, and capable of inflicting grave damage on his fighting opponents. And many of these opponents seemed not to have been on a wrestling mat or in a boxing ring or MMA cage.

Part of this love of fighting seemed to be the culture of the val-ley, and part seemed to be Angelo's aggressive nature. An essay on Jack Dempsey in the Alamosa Public Library's western history room states, "Fighting was the entertainment for all the boys in Manassa." It suggests that Dempsey began fighting before the family moved to the town of Creede when he was ten or eleven, and then to Montrose around 1905. Physical combat remains a strong part of valley culture, though Angelo started with wrestling, as many boys still do.

"He used to rough me up and put me in wrassling moves and make me cry," began Santino. But in social settings, such as bars, Angelo was always on his side and a fine wingman.

"Back in the day," Santino went on, "before I got married and me and Angelo used to run amok, we used to try and pick up girls from the bar. I picked up this one girl one time, and she was going out with this tough guy who'd been in prison, and him and his buddies wanted to beat me up. They caught me at the hot dog machine. I was by myself; Angelo was over at the soft drink area. They were like, '*Let's go out-side.*' . . . My cousin Angelo saw that I was being harassed and he goes, '*Well, what's the problem over here.*' And they say, '*We wanna take him outside.*'

"And Angelo says, '*Well, so fight me.*' Guy said he wanted to but his friends said, *No, don't do it, you don't want to fight him.* And so he didn't just then. But one day this guy's waiting for me outside an office. And Angelo comes up and said, '*Okay, it's gonna end here, and just be me and you.*' And Angelo took him out back and left him in a heap, they had to call Flight for Life for him."

Another night at a different bar, a guy named Adolph came up from behind and put Angelo in a headlock. Big mistake: Angelo spun around, picked him up, threw him to the ground, and proceeded to pound him. Afterward, Salina recalled, Angelo came up to her looking worried, afraid he might have killed the guy and would need to flee. But Adolph recovered.

"Angelo beat the crap out of the Villagomezes, both the father and the son," Santino reminisced.

Gilbert recalled how once when he was living in Denver with his three sons, Angelo came to stay. "I'd have a few beers, and he'd wait to the point where I was a little tipsy and he'd say, 'Come on, Chuck!'— like Chuck Norris, I guess. It'd only take forty-five seconds before I'd tap out—wrassling on a hardwood floor is something I didn't always want to do. But that's just who he was, that was his nature, he just loved to get physical."

Sometimes a friendly match would not end up that way. Santino recalled coming home to cousin Mikey "knocked out on the damn kitchen floor in a puddle of blood, blood splashed on walls, and Angelo in the living room, his shirt opened up, breathing real heavy. I said, 'What are you doing, you can't be killing Mikey!'"

The hell-raising wasn't always violent. Once Angelo stole a riding lawn mower and drove it home—he wanted his sister Lenora to ride it with him. Then at two in the morning he drove it over the bridge into town and by the college, over people's lawns.

I watched to see how Geneva would react to these tales. She was riveted—many of them she hadn't known in detail. She jumped in to add that Angelo got more religious as his MMA career continued and cast himself as a "warrior for Christ." But that did not prevent him from going all out to annihilate an opponent. Geneva was not far behind. "I watched every match. I'd yell, 'Get him, Angelo! Fuck him up!'" she said.

Angelo did prison time for assaulting his girlfriend and got involved with drugs. Hearing that made me think I wouldn't have liked him.

But his family said those were the dark years. Once he got out, he stopped fighting. After that, Salina recalled, Angelo "was serious about becoming a mountain man. He said, 'Fighting just doesn't do it anymore—I want to be with the lions and the bears, the wild things.' I said it made me kind of scared and he said it made him excited: 'That animal's either gonna hunt me or I'm gonna hunt it. My life or his.'" On that theme, Santino recalled the time he and Angelo were way up in the woods on Blanca Peak when they heard a bloodcurdling cry.

"It wasn't a bear or a deer, just a loud scream. You could tell it wasn't human, the way it echoed off the mountain. I was like, 'Did you hear that?' A couple seconds went by, and we heard it again. Then one more time. We looked at each other. I said, 'We gotta go, bro, I gotta see my family'—we'd left 'em at the campsite. And Angelo said, 'No, we gotta go chase him down the mountain!' All he wanted to do was track him down, go face-to-face. But I was really scared. He called me a pussy and was mad at me the whole time. He didn't wanna leave—I pretty much forced him to."

The group wondered out loud whether it was that determination to confront his fears that led Angelo to get too close to the high-tension line that electrocuted him. A crew of four, all family, were assisting him with a tree removal near Monte Vista that morning. Angelo had rented a bucket lift. Despite warnings from Santino, he positioned it closer to the power lines than it needed to be. With all of them watching, said Gilbert, he entered the bucket and directed Lenora to raise it into the air.

"He turns toward the power line, kinda like this. And it's like he reached his hand, to me it looked like he was gonna test the power line. I was like, 'What are you doing, what are you trying to do?' And from the bottom of the bucket I seen a spark, like a ball of fire, and Lenora did, too."

Gilbert paused—he was having trouble with the end of the story. Angelo was grievously burned and unconscious. He died at the hospital shortly after. "Telling you how it went down, I can feel my cousin's presence, and he's telling me, 'Tell him what happened, don't be a pussy, tell him what happened!' And that's probably giving me strength," he said.

Alamosa mayor Ty Coleman, who had played poker at Geneva's

with Angelo and been dragged out to go ice fishing with him, arrived toward the end of the evening and remembered a man who was both humble and supremely confident, who was endlessly resourceful ("I saw him making a lot out of having not much at all"), and whose memorial service was attended by more than five hundred people, from "some of the wealthiest people down to the poorest of the poor, from all ethnicities." (Coleman is African American.) "And he touched them just by being himself."

Not long afterward, Geneva threw a Christmas party at which the sister we had delivered the deer leg to brought me a gift of the venison jerky she had made with it. It was more gamy than beef jerky but not bad. Then Geneva gave me some she had made, which was better. A highlight was Geneva singing "Las Mañanitas" in Spanish with her *jita* (daughter) Wendy.

But the really big deal was La Puente's blockbuster community Christmas party.

Every year La Puente went all out on the party. The shelter was bedecked with lights, tinsel, boughs, stockings, wrapped presents—all kinds of Yule decor. A big dinner was served, and Lance was committed to the idea that any kid who turned up should also leave with a present. The line for all of this stretched out the front door and around the block. Inside, there was a giant sleigh in which Santa (a costumed resident of the shelter) and Mrs. Santa (a longtime volunteer and donor) sat surrounded by a retinue of elves (AmeriCorps workers); each kid spent a few minutes among them. There was live music played outside; there was Lance dressed as a giant elf, having the time of his life (and handing me an elf shirt to wear). There was the manager of the Rainbow's End thrift store on the electric bass, his partner on keyboard, and an employee who had been brought up Amish playing the saw. That year the theme was Harry Potter, most visible in the way the tree in front of the shelter had been transformed into the Whomping Willow, complete with a miniature Weasley's car ensnared in its branches. The party was a local institution and also, for everyone involved at La Puente, a ton of work.

During a pause in the action, I asked Lance why he felt it was so important to do *so much* by way of celebrating the holiday. (Outreach staff had prepared for days and days.) The question totally perplexed him; it was the first time I had seen Lance speechless. "Why would you want to do less?" he finally asked me.

This effusion of celebration and high spirits was, I came to see, a conscious push-back against the forces of sadness and trouble. Partway through, a policeman arrived with a warrant for a woman who had been staying there. Fortunately for the festivities, she had recently moved out. But then Judy, Lance's No. 2, told me in a low voice that she'd just received news that Sidney Arellano had been found dead in his car the night before. Was it drugs, the cold? I asked. Judy didn't know. Sidney was a familiar, singular face around the shelter: a haunted-looking man who wore his black hair long and favored overcoats, even in the summer. He was into mysticism and had once held a "birthing ceremony" for some precious stones in his room at the shelter. Lance had agreed with Judy not to share the news of Sidney's death just yet, as it was such a dissonant note on this particular day, but it was sure to be acknowledged later, as twice a year La Puente commemorated with candlelight vigils members of their community who had died.

Deep inside the shelter, seated in his plywood sleigh, Santa himself looked very real—he was an authentically big man with his own bushy beard. The only detail of his appearance that was not storybook was the oxygen cannula under his nose—like a lot of the people I was getting to know, Santa had COPD. The party lasted until every single kid had talked to Santa, received a present, and been offered the feast. I felt somewhat exhausted and went to sit outside at a picnic table—and Santa did, too. Clifford Kidder II took off his oxygen tube, lit a cigarette, and we started to talk.

He'd had the oxygen tank since the start of November, he said. But he had smoked since he was a teenager and had suffered from COPD for years. ("I know it looks bad, but I'm down to six cigarettes a day.") He'd been driving a truck until seven or eight years ago. "I'd start coughing, things'd disappear, and I'd end up fifty miles down the road not knowing how I got there. Loss of memory was part of it."

He ended up moving in with his ex-wife and her mother in Michigan. But it wasn't any easier to breathe there, next to a toxic waste incineration plant, and he landed in the ICU for ten days. When he got out, he faced up to the fact that it was a bad living situation and he hit the road. "Either I get mad at you or I just get up and leave," he said, somewhat cryptically. He hitchhiked out, headed for Yuma, Arizona, but a driver dropped him in Alamosa after Clifford realized he'd been through this town before. He'd stayed for a while at a halfway house operated by the Church of Christ, and he'd driven for Colorado Gators Reptile Park, just north of Alamosa—"I took a load of the tilapia they raise down to Texas.

"I had twenty-eight jobs before I drove a truck," Clifford told me. He was from the Ohio River Valley, forty-three miles north of where Matt grew up. Jimmy Stewart was from there, too, he said, and he had watched *It's a Wonderful Life* many times. "So maybe it's appropriate for me to play Santa."

The suit got hot, said Clifford, but he enjoyed the role. He liked working with Mrs. Santa, the La Puente benefactor—he said that she had spotted one girl who was wearing only socks and made sure she got some boots from the shelter before she left. And he liked being treated as a benevolent soul himself. "The look in a child's eye. . . . I remember the first time I went to see Santa. It's the girl who climbs into your arm and doesn't want to leave or the little boy who brings a book and wants you to read it. A boy did that today." Being treated this way, I could see, flipped his life upside down. For a few hours he was not a deadbeat, a loser, and a leaver. Instead he was like the grandpa who had everything, a guy who, rather than disappoint, granted wishes.

3

So Many Different Kinds of People, or My Prairie Life, Part II

Its virtue is that it lacks everything.

—Travel agent touting Antarctica in Tony Kushner's
Angels in America

It's our patriotic duty to see the humanity in people with whom we
disagree.   —DAVE ISAY

I STAYED ON THE PRAIRIE for the first half of January 2018, and then I was there for some of every month except November. The living was a little rough—just one reason it felt like a perfect complement to my life in New York City. Fewer people meant more space for me. I liked the slower pace, how affordable things were, the strains of Hispanic and Mexican culture (including the food). I liked the weather, which was never dull; the sky changed all day long, sometimes dramatically so, always grabbing your attention. I liked the varieties of people, many of whom you probably wouldn't find in a big city. And I appreciated the less-pressurized feel of life among those less set on leaving their mark than my circle in New York. It was a beautiful, wild, and mysterious world, home to the semi-destitute.

Most simply, of course, off-grid meant not connected to public utilities. Many people associate "off-grid" with "green," and credit off-gridders with trying to live lightly off the earth by reducing their needs, unplugging from utilities and rejecting conspicuous consumption. The model for upscale green living was headquartered just about an hour away, outside Taos: Earthship Biotecture was renowned for the creative ways their houses, known as Earthships, incorporated cast-off materials such as bottles and tires, and for their efforts to conserve and recycle water inside the house. I took one of the company's tours and saw some inventive houses it would feel good to live in: they made smart use of the area's abundant sunlight, and some had gardens inside. Teams of young people were helping with construction, all of them paying for the privilege. Their interest in such things as "tiny houses," renewable energy, leaving the grid, and reducing humankind's carbon footprint was inspiring to me, and hopeful: they saw that urgent action was needed if we were to save the planet and wanted to respond to my generation's failure to act. The company had been a pioneer in green construction and green thinking since the early 1970s. But I also noticed how expensive Earthships were—far too costly for most people I'd met in the valley. The paradigm had another flaw: most of the Earthships seemed to have propane tanks out back, painted tan for camouflage, which seemed like cheating.

Earthships were just one kind of upscale off-grid living. I experienced another on a weekend expedition to the Sangre de Cristos, where a young couple I'd met had built their own off-grid place on land in the mountains, with trees. It was more expensive than living down on the flats but also felt more protected. My hosts invited me along to a weekly potluck meal farther up their unelectrified valley, and there I saw something I hadn't imagined: a full-sized suburban-style ranch house with an expansive lawn and *enormous* solar panels on racks that swiveled to follow the sun and massive batteries that stored all that energy. The husband of the couple who owned it was a former military intelligence guy, at home with electronics. He told me that normally his system was adequate to power everything you'd want in a city, including a clothes dryer and air-conditioning. Only if a string of cloudy days left them a bit short, he said, would he power up his generators. He was proud to live independent of the grid and saw no need for all of the "hippie" trappings of the Earthships set.

(In some ways, the green tech of Earthships had had unanticipated ill effects. Their embrace of used car tires, for example, had probably resulted in the collections of them you'd see on some of the prairie lots of Costilla County. Yes, packed with pounded earth they could be used in walls to both insulate and support, but many people never got around to that part of things. Instead, they'd leave a couple dozen, or even a couple hundred, old tires strewn about their land, where they never decomposed and always looked bad.)

Certainly down the economic ladder a few rungs were the people with environmental consciousness who were drawn to the virtue of not needing much, and who appreciated the creative reuse of discarded materials, communalism, "tiny houses," and outsider art. Among these was the occasional college grad. Some college-educated people were down on the prairie, but more seemed to be up in the woods.

Prairie people overall just seemed poor and wanting a different life—one with more self-reliance, fewer bills from utility companies, and, in many cases, lots of distance from neighbors. Most seemed to be escaping more typical American lives that had become unsustainable, whether because of too many bills or too many disappointments. They arrived pulling trailers or with old RVs and set up camp. Sometimes they would build something, but often the trailer became the building block, added on to with shacks or Tuff Sheds. They drove Fords more often than Toyotas. Their political consciousness tended toward the Trumpian: anti-government, pro-gun, America first, self-reliance. Among them were preppers, homeschoolers (Christian and otherwise), sovereign citizens, weed lovers, and Hillary haters. Some had lived near a coast, but more seemed to come from the heartland, many from the South. And most were very poor. The San Luis Valley, with its extra-cheap land, was a sort of mecca for these off-gridders. There were probably more than a thousand people living off-grid here, though nobody seemed to know for sure. (Nationwide, the number is probably in the tens of thousands, though again no authoritative numbers exist. Off-grid life seems to be growing in the United States, often in regions with cheap land, like Appalachia; or sunshine, like Hawaii, Utah, Arizona, New Mexico, Texas, and Florida; or frontier appeal, like Alaska, Idaho, Wyoming, and Colorado; or environmental consciousness, like northern California, Oregon, Vermont, and even New York.)

A flip side of having all that space to yourself can be loneliness. A friend of mine who grew up in rural Vermont and Maine had spent time in Wyoming and Colorado living alone in a trailer while working on a ranch and as a hunting guide. So when he heard I was alone in a trailer in the wide-open spaces, his first reaction was concern: *Are you all right out there?* He had not always been all right. He offered to talk to me about it anytime, which I appreciated.

But I was coming to the conclusion that my life out there was, emotionally speaking, usually good and often much better than that. Some of this was my collaboration with La Puente, a group of people I admired and connected with. And some of it was having the Grubers for neighbors. A good bit of this was learning what they were thinking and talking about on the many occasions when the kids stopped by, usually Trin and Meadoux but sometimes Kanyon or all three of them, or occasionally four (including Saphire). They would knock at my trailer door, then enter and stand just inside while I sat at my breakfast table. They would bring me drawings and news of the animals. Stacy told me to tell them to go away if I was busy, and sometimes I did. But mostly I welcomed them.

They told me how Lakota had badly cut her foot (sharp things abounded at the Grubers' place) but that they had cleaned the gash and applied antibiotic ointment. They told me how one of the Nigerian dwarf goats was certainly pregnant and overdue. (They had a kids' ultrasound device powered by a radio battery.) They also told me how Meadoux had recently crashed into a pronghorn antelope on her bike.

She and Trin were on their way to Jack's RV, a mile or two away. Jack had told the girls that if they proved they could look after his two horses for a few months, watering and feeding them, they could have them. Often Stacy drove them over, as she did on my first day there, but on this day, they had decided to ride their bikes.

There were some hills between Jack's place and theirs, but the girls were strong. The bikes were nothing fancy, and Meadoux's lacked brakes, but out here that didn't really matter . . . until it did. Riding into a stiff headwind, they crested a hill and saw a small herd of pronghorn antelope resting just below. The wind was so strong the herd didn't hear them, and some didn't see them until it was too late. It was a fairly soft collision, from the sound of it: Meadoux said she "almost hit a baby" but that the pronghorn she did strike bounded away as if

Walking dogs and goats with Trin and Meadoux

nothing happened. Trin said, "I crashed my bike, but I wasn't hurt because I was wearing my parka and I rolled."

I told them that one thing I missed from New York was walking everywhere. They said they sometimes walked the goats and I should join them. Some dogs came, too. Trin, the oldest girl, helped me put names on some of the plants I'd come to recognize: those were yuccas, these were chico bushes, that was a sage. And the girls identified things that were mysterious to me, such as the hoofprints feral horses left on dirt roads or holes where a ground-dwelling owl might live. They were experts in the natural world around them.

Their book learning was less advanced. Like some other kids in the area, they were homeschooled—but this could mean different things. Some of the kids whose families had internet service were enrolled in an online curriculum called Branson. They had regular class meetings and homework assignments, and they passed through grades like kids in ordinary schools—the state of Colorado even supplied them with laptops.

The Grubers, though, didn't have internet, apart from the data on their phones. Stacy told me she relied on a series of textbooks and workbooks that the kids' old school, in Wyoming, had let them have when the teachers upgraded to a new edition. She made the kids spend time on their studies every day. Though she was smart, however, Stacy wasn't highly educated—neither she nor Frank had finished high school. And she was a truly terrible speller. So the odds of her kids getting a good education were low.

I knew that Trin and Meadoux were proud to live on the prairie but also that life for their family was hard, with few creature comforts and a constant shortage of money. The girls appreciated trips to Denver to stay with their aunt, or even to nearby Antonito, where they could get a good signal on Trin's smartphone. (Most places on the prairie had poor cell service.) They watched TV and knew what was happening in pop culture. When I shared a story on Facebook about New York City teens who had their own fashion sense, Trin was the first to like it.

One day the girls mentioned that their cousin, Ashley, was coming to stay for a few days. Stacy initially told me that Ashley just needed some time away from her mom up in Oregon. But then it became clear that Ashley's needs were a bit more specific, and urgent: she was there to withdraw from opiates, and the Grubers had offered to look after her while she did.

Frank and Stacy drove into town to pick up Ashley at the bus station. But after that, the news was spotty. The girls complained that after initially being given Kanyon's room, Ashley had taken over the couch in the living room. She seldom moved or pitched in. Around day four, Stacy asked me if I had any Benadryl, because Ashley's skin was crawling, extremely itchy. Luckily I did. Around day six, Ashley came outside to sit on the front steps in the sun for a while. I stopped over and said hi. Ashley was friendly and said she was feeling better. She'd be going back before too long.

"Back to Oregon?" I asked.

No, she said, probably to California, to stay with her dad. She'd recently learned that there was a warrant out for her arrest in Oregon— she'd crashed her car not long before she came down to Colorado. Ashley was guessing that the cops might have found her drugs. "I'm just happy they didn't find the gun," she said.

"You had a gun in the car?" I asked.

"Well, sure. If you're going to deal, you've got to be able to defend yourself." I had heard that was true.

Others came by, too. Josh had been friends with Stacy since her Casper days, before she met Frank. Then he had married Meg, and the couples had been neighbors in Farmington, New Mexico, where Josh worked as a technician examining pipelines. But Meg had never gotten along with Stacy—she insinuated that Stacy was a drug user. When Frank and Stacy moved to Colorado, Josh and Meg moved to the Northwest, where they had a daughter and Josh found a new job. They bought a house and a new truck and life was good.

But then Josh got fired and it all fell apart. They lost the house, moved into their small "fifth wheel" camper trailer, and took refuge at Frank and Stacy's, where they parked not far from my trailer. The arrangement didn't last long. Given her history with Meg, it seemed generous for Stacy to let her stay. But Meg wouldn't go in their mobile home, and before long she had taken their daughter and moved to her parents' house in New Mexico. Josh became a long-term guest.

A little later in the spring, the Grubers introduced me to Sam and Cindy, who lived a few miles to the south. It was a gruff sort of meeting; the middle-aged couple were sitting on the Grubers' couch with their coats on, smoking weed, when I arrived. Sam responded reluctantly when I offered my hand in greeting. I later learned that Sam and Frank had met in an online chat room about living off-grid in the San Luis Valley before the Grubers bought their property here. When somebody else cautioned against bringing a family with small children to live on the prairie, Sam countered, saying, effectively, *Don't listen to these people, it's great. Message me.* Frank had done so and had been persuaded. Once they were situated, Frank told me, Sam had brought them a goat and some marijuana plants.

Now Sam and Cindy were considering selling their place to the Grubers. Negotiations were well along. The price, Stacy told me, would be $30,000, with $2,000 down and monthly payments—and, presumably, a lump-sum payment when they sold the mobile home and had some cash. *But why would you move when you have a nearly new place?* I asked.

Stacy said she'd show me, and so one day we went over in her truck.

I recognized the place from my reconnaissance—I had once honked outside the front gate but gotten no response. It was one of the few properties with a wooden fence along the road, which made it look substantial. Stacy pointed out the other thing she really liked: a modest built house. It was smaller than the space they were in now, she acknowledged, but she thought they'd fit. "And it would be so nice not to have to live in a trailer"—a bit because of the stigma, I think.

There were nice touches, like a small faux railroad water tower that enclosed an aboveground water tank, and an outbuilding where she said the older girls could live. But best of all, she noted, was that it had a well. "So you could almost live like a normal person," with a washing machine (included) and shower and no need to buy water from neighbors, and constantly rationing your use and refill.

"And there's room for your trailer," she said, indicating two possible spots.

"Hmm," I said. One of the spots had a great view of untrammeled prairie. "When would this be?"

Stacy said within a month or two. Josh, she added, would stay behind, to keep an eye on the mobile home.

And so it transpired that, six months after I first joined them, as spring gave way to summer, I moved with the Grubers to their next place.

Most of the moving happened when I was in New York. My trailer was one of the last things to go. Sam did me the favor of towing it behind his powerful GMC Yukon, a task accomplished in under an hour. But that still left one more big thing: Frank's little bulldozer.

No trailer was large enough to load up the dozer, so it would need to be driven the nine or so miles. At five miles an hour, this could theoretically take under two hours. But there were problems with the hydraulics. There were problems with the tracks. There were problems with the diesel fuel: when it ran out, it needed to be resupplied from a tank in the abandoned RV where the Grubers had lived before their mobile home arrived. Frank, Stacy, and Josh got started in midafternoon, but as of nine p.m. the bulldozer had come only a fraction of the way. Sam, a skilled mechanic, got involved as well. A bit before midnight I drove out to check on their progress. I looked for the lights of the pickup truck. It was following the bulldozer, its headlights showing

Frank's bulldozer doubled as a jungle gym.

the way over the dirt roads. The tracks left by the dozer were zigzaggy, and days later would still be visible.

"Why not just leave it till morning?" I asked. "Somebody could steal it," said Frank. And so the dozer crept, and stalled, and crept, and stalled, and finally, I was told, arrived shortly before dawn, its journey reminding me of the mule-drawn wagon carrying the casket in William Faulkner's *As I Lay Dying*.

Unlike the Grubers' old place, this new five-acre property had some history. In keeping with much of the settlement in the valley, it was short and violent.

Lisa Foster had bought the land from an ad on eBay, sight unseen, for $3,027 in 2007. She and her husband, Bob, childhood sweethearts from rural New Mexico, were living in Las Vegas, their children grown. Lisa had worked as a contractor, specializing in home renovations for disabled people. "It was always a dream of mine to build a place from the ground up," she told me. "I got to live that dream out there."

Lisa shared with me a slideshow of the summer after she, her husband, and a friend first broke ground, in March 2008. No other settlements were visible in the area at the time, she said. First they put up a tent to stay in. Next, with a touch of humor, came a tall post with a house-shaped birdhouse atop it. Then they built a one-room cabin, an outhouse, and a good-sized shop building, with fences around the whole property. In the photos the three of them, none younger than fifty, look industrious, happy, and, at the end of the day, tired.

Lisa continued to build in the five years she spent there. Bob was often away (he was a manager for Verizon in Las Vegas), so in most ways it was her show. Tired of driving into Antonito for water, she soon spent $19,000 on a well. Enamored of horses, she made friends with a notorious local character known as AJ, who kept a lot of them "and had foals that needed help"—so she built some corrals. She acquired a dog and soon had five. "But the first one was just a pain in the butt," always barking, biting, and starting fights. "One day I just had it with him, and I shot him!" News of that got around the neighborhood and people started saying, *Stay the fuck away from her,* which she regarded as a positive. "The only people who found me were Jehovah's Witnesses."

For her first three years, she said, "It was just heaven." But then it wasn't.

In reality, Lisa had a soft heart, which would be her undoing. One winter day she noticed a family of six apparently living out of their car, basically in the road, not far from her home. "They had four babies out there in twenty-nine degrees below zero, and they were living in this little bitty car, nowhere to stay." They had set up a playpen next to the car. One of the children was a newborn. Lisa stopped and talked to them and later brought them food. Then "one night they just showed up at the door—it had been raining, and I just let 'em come in. I thought they'd be helpful."

Instead, they slowly took over. They helped with very little and "never paid any rent." The husband insisted that he wanted to buy the place, even though she didn't want to sell. He could get hostile and weird; she later learned that he had been a security guard and had had to flee Dallas one night after he angered members of a local gang. The couple promised to take care of her place and her animals during times she was away, but instead they neglected them, and ultimately, "they killed all my dogs. I was very naïve, I just didn't see it. I brought them in because of the kids," but the arrangement was her undoing. After the wife "got into my phone" and read texts, including one where she admitted to preferring her own grandchildren over the couple's four kids, things got worse. The husband threatened her with a gun. She moved out, perhaps temporarily—she wasn't sure. Eventually, with the help of the county sheriff, she evicted them, but not before they had burned or otherwise destroyed much of what she had built, including furniture and corrals. It was, Lisa said, an "ugly ending."

That ending was redeemed somewhat when Cindy and Sam contacted her out of the blue, saying they hoped to buy the place. "I sold it to them for the cost of the well," or $20,000—a net loss of about $30,000 on the $50,000 she'd put into it.

Sam and Cindy, both of them army veterans who had come to the valley around 2008, a few years after medical marijuana became legal, had lived only a couple hundred yards away. Sam said that the man who took over Lisa's place told people he owned it and was threatening and unhinged. "One day this crazy dude came crawling up on us with a roofing hammer! My buddy Geno comes out of the RV with a shotgun and says, *Watch out, dude, I'm gonna blast you!* He left us alone after that."

Lisa's place, even with the damage done to it, represented an upgrade—according to Sam, there were only eight places on this part of the prairie with wells. He and Cindy moved in and for a couple of summers grew a lot of weed. It was physically demanding as well as stressful from a security point of view. Sam described how one year, near harvesttime, members of a motorcycle gang had turned up and said, *We're gonna take thirty pounds and here's what we're gonna pay you, or else you're getting a couple of bullets in the back of your head.* His response: *Well, hey, fucker, I'm armed, let's get started right now because you're not taking my weed.* The gang backed off, but Sam lost his taste for the enterprise. He and Cindy also had health issues. Sam said he had stage 4 cancer, with tumors on his liver, spleen, lungs, and more, which he blamed on the years he had spent as an industrial welder in a packinghouse, breathing in harmful fumes. Cindy, for her part, had non-Hodgkin's lymphoma as well as breathing issues, likely COPD. They made a deal to sell the place to a guy in the neighborhood, who made a down payment and moved in.

Meanwhile they pursued a lifelong dream of sailing. After driving to Marathon, Florida, they bought a diesel-powered boat and chugged off toward the Gulf Coast of Texas. Unfortunately, Sam said, the guy failed to make his promised payments but remained on the property. Weeks passed, the sailing adventure ended, Sam told the man to get out, but he wouldn't—it sounded like Lisa Foster's squatter scenario all over again. Finally, the guy left. Sam, still in Texas and nervous about what shape he'd find the place in, asked Stacy if she'd go over and look around. Stacy discovered that items were missing, including a gasoline generator and a wind turbine, and that there was a lot of new, unwelcome junk on the land, including a large portable toilet.

This kind of story was common on the prairie, I would find, and a reason that renting wasn't often done and property deals often fell through. Stacy had rallied to Sam and Cindy's cause, reporting the theft to the sheriff's department, posting about it on Facebook, and, she said, trying to calm down Sam, who had worked himself up into a rage she feared might turn murderous.

And in this dramatic fashion began the summer of 2018.

Life with the Grubers was eventful already. But adding Sam and Cindy to the mix, especially Sam, upped the ante considerably. They remained the owners of record, even if they had let the Grubers move into the main house. Next to that house was a semi-enclosed area for the marijuana grow, and next to that was Sam and Cindy's little trailer. And next to them—a little closer than I might have wished—was my trailer. In front of their trailer on a couple of chains, or sometimes in cages, were their pit bulls, Fatty Wolf and Speckles, who would bark savagely and lunge at me when I walked past, even after they knew me. This was always unnerving, something I never got over.

Another source of noise and peril were Sam's firearms. He loved shooting, "modding," and collecting firearms. His Facebook profile picture featured the custom AK-47 he took with him whenever he drove anywhere. I never saw him handle guns recklessly, but just having them nearby, and subject to frequent use, put me a little on edge—particularly since he enjoyed his beer and weed and could get a little lit at night, and because he was often upset about things.

The last member of the cast at the Grubers' was Nick. He was typical of what Sam would affectionately call a "prairie rat"—young, aimless, willing to work occasionally but largely destitute, a drug user with a couple of screws loose. (Sam sometimes used that phrase to describe flats dwellers generally.) Nick was buddies with Junior, whose RV had occupied the space my trailer had moved into at the Grubers' old place. Junior had grown up locally and had once lived at a different location with Nick. The story went that they'd had a fight after Nick had failed to water his marijuana seedlings and they'd all died.

Nick had strong eyeglasses and was physically unimposing. Like Sam, he enjoyed discussing guns and the uses to which they might be put. He would say, with some frequency, things like "I'd just take a thirty-aught-six and cap him" or "a derringer would fix that problem," and then mime shooting the weapon cited.

His most prominent tattoo, on his upper arm, was of a wild-haired running figure, shaded red, brandishing a hatchet dripping red drops; it was the logo of Psychopathic Records, the label of Insane Clown Posse. Nick explained to me that when his family had lived in Aurora, Colorado, and a process server had tried to serve his dad, Nick had gone after the guy with a hatchet. That earned him a felony menacing charge, he said, which he beat in court by producing evidence that he is disabled by fetal alcohol syndrome. "My mom is an alcoholic." He had been in schools for troubled kids. But despite his challenges, he was usually mild-mannered and friendly, a follower type. The Grubers let him sleep on their couch for several weeks in exchange for helping around the house. Later he moved into a small room next to the shed (Lisa Foster's old workshop) and, still later, into a small trailer the Grubers helped him buy.

As the prairie warmed into summer, I continued to work with La Puente for part of the week. But most of my life was on the prairie, and a lot of it revolved around the Grubers. Trin caught cool lizards with blue bellies and showed me. Kanyon explained that the tiny burrs that stuck to my socks were called "goatheads." Meadoux announced that

Lakota had given birth to a brood of the cutest puppies—the family's dog population was now over twenty. Stacy filled out applications for Trin and Meadoux to spend some of the summer at a free sleepaway camp. Jack's horses were now in residence and beautiful to watch as they grazed over the five acres; early one morning I saw them move into light reflected off the window of an old truck in order to warm themselves. Occasionally, Trin or Meadoux would climb on their backs and move lazily around the property.

One of the family's pleasures was to take an outing to "the Beach"—a sandy stretch of the Rio Grande just a couple of miles away. For much of its way through the prairie, the Rio Grande was hard to access—and near the Grubers, it was sunken into a narrow canyon. But the Beach was a lovely exception. Several times I helped transport members of the crew there. One day in June, Stacy packed a picnic. While the little girls played with pebbles by the water's edge, Trin and Meadoux waded out and caught crayfish. Stacy encouraged them to catch more—"We can make a stew with them!" Frank, meanwhile, pointed out a camper trailer parked a couple hundred yards away. The occupants were squatting there, he said, which was not good—though the area was not officially a park, the Grubers and others treated it that way. The idea of somebody taking over a piece of it for the summer struck them as wrong.

Stacy said that Sam had nicknamed them "the Shims," for she-hims. That didn't sound particularly helpful. I mentioned them to Matt, who said he had first noticed them in line at the spring where he got water. The man was big and wearing purple heels, he remembered: "Unusual for around here." His partner, on the other hand, seemed to be a female who embraced a very masculine style. Since then, he'd seen them around, in Fort Garland and in Blanca and once walking between the two towns, which he guessed might have been because they had been pulled over by the police and didn't want to get busted again before correcting something they'd been cited for. And then he saw them with their trailer, parked in a hard-to-see area near where he lived. A friend of his had driven by and, noticing a distinctive, "metallic acidy smell, almost like battery acid," believed they were cooking meth. A rumor, which initially struck me as far-fetched, held that they were perhaps saving up for gender transitions in Trinidad, Colorado, a nationally known center for that located about an hour and a half away, over La Veta Pass.

I went by the camper on the Beach a couple of times after that day, to see if they needed anything. But they weren't at home. On a visit to a neighbor who lived a bit closer to the Beach than the Grubers, I asked if he'd had any contact. He answered that on a walk down there he'd seen them working on the transmission of their truck, which they had taken out and placed on the ground. In short, he'd said: "Trannies working on a tranny. You can't make this stuff up."

Somebody else told me they'd confronted the couple after seeing them pump water out of the Rio Grande, which is against the law.

Then late that summer, after I'd been away a few days, I saw that Sam's big GMC Yukon was dented up and missing its entire hood. Sam said there had been an altercation. He, Frank, Nick, and Josh had driven down to the Beach on a recent evening, around ten. As Sam told it, the larger of the "Shims" drove up to them in his truck and they exchanged words. Shortly afterward, the guy turned off his headlights and surprised them by ramming Sam's SUV with his pickup. Sam's airbags deployed. Shots were fired; a dog might have been hit. Sam drove onto a rock he couldn't see in the dark.

Sam reported that the next day, the guy had driven by and shouted at them from the gate. And that a day or two after that, he said, "lightning must have struck because his trailer burned down." I went to see for myself. Ashes were the main remnant of the trailer—that and its steel chassis. I hadn't known that trailers could burn so completely. A short distance away from it I came across a single, very large men's sneaker . . . and remembered Matt saying that the man had big feet. I took the sneaker with me.

I imagined there was more to this story and tried to learn it. But it appeared that no police reports had been filed, and nothing of it made the news. I kept asking flats people if anyone had seen the couple. Finally came a report that they were squatting at the foot of Blanca Peak, in a different trailer. I went to the place and again found nobody home. I left behind a La Puente card and a note saying that they could call me if they needed assistance. They never called. A few days later, I passed by the site again and they were gone.

Were they criminals cooking meth? It seemed possible. Were they also victims? That, too, seemed possible. Was prairie justice tainted by anti-gay or anti-trans bias? That seemed possible as well.

The Grubers had neighbors whose property was on the edge of the Rio Grande canyon and offered a way down into it. One day I joined Frank, Trin, and Meadoux for an excursion down the canyon wall (it was steep, but in this spot it was doable if you were careful). At the bottom we were suddenly in a different climate. The canyon was narrow here, the river confined to a channel with modest banks on each side. Willows and other shrubs flourished close to the water, and there were birds and butterflies. The only signs of human presence were some shallow caves in the canyon wall where people had taken shelter and built small fires to keep warm. It was easy to imagine that they'd been Native Americans, hundreds of years before.

Later, the neighbors invited us all for dinner. The place had belonged to the wife's father, she said. She and her husband had lived there for years. He was a strong, tough guy whom I had approached cold when first canvassing for La Puente. He hadn't been happy to see me but at least had come out of the house and told me in person that he didn't need any help. I now knew that he worked at a local ranch, had had brushes with the law (like almost everyone around here), and was successful at growing weed. He also liked guns.

Sam and Nick joined the party, arriving with firearms, which they added to a table already full of them. There were pistols, including an old six-shooter; an AR-15 that fired .22 rounds and another that had been "modded" into a pistol; a .50-caliber rifle; and a shotgun. I had nothing to contribute, but they invited me to join in the shooting anyway. Our target was a post maybe a hundred feet away onto which were attached or balanced various bottles and pieces of wood and metal.

I enjoy target shooting. But earlier that year, a beloved member of my extended family had been killed in an alcohol-involved gun accident at a hunting camp in Alabama. And so the fact that this was shooting while drinking made me less enthusiastic. I also don't like shooting without ear protection. I was pleased that evening when we

A little after-dinner shooting

put down the real guns and our host brought out the potato gun. This makeshift cannon of PVC tubing, a mainstay of rural America, used hairspray as a propellant, a barbecue clicker as an igniter, and a potato as projectile. Frank especially seemed to enjoy launching the potato into the atmosphere; I liked it as well, since I had never heard of anyone killed by a potato.

La Puente held monthly all-staff meetings in the community room of a church in Alamosa. Different units of the organization gave reports, and Matt was usually tapped to talk about Rural Outreach. The reports were supposed to feature a quick story about some way in which people had been served by the unit. Matt, whose rough and dirty hands, dusty boots, and worn jacket make him stand out in the group at La Puente, was initially loath to speak but got more comfortable with it as the months went by. People seemed to appreciate his stories for the glimpse they gave of the unknown world of the flats. Matt also saw that everyone loved a story about snakes. For example: One of his "people," Matt had said recently, had a problem with mice in his walls and ceiling. Many locals solved this problem with a cat, but Matt said the guy didn't like cats and wished out loud that he had a bull snake under his house like one of his neighbors did. "Are you sure?" Matt asked, and the man said yes. The next day, a three-foot-long bull snake at the side of the road caught Matt's eye. "I grabbed it, and it wrapped up my arm," he explained, demonstrating. "I didn't have a bucket or anything, so I got a T-shirt and tied off the arms and neck and put it in there." Matt placed the gift on the passenger seat and delivered it to the man later that day.

Often all-staff meetings concluded with a group exercise of some kind, meant to foster community or underscore core principles. On this day it was led by one of Lance's managers. Everyone would be asked to stand or sit, she explained, according to how they answered certain questions. When she asked, "If you found yourself without money, support, or housing, would you ask for help?," most of those present said yes and stood up, which was the response the manager was after. "If you are not able to accept help without judgment, you are unable to give help without judgment," she said. I thought that sounded reasonable. But Matt, generally aligned with La Puente's values, disagreed quietly. I was sitting next to him.

"No," he muttered. "That was the exact situation I was in a year ago. I've got my gun and my tent and the woods, and I'm going to take care of myself and my son. I like helping all varieties of people," he said, "but the target I like looking for is the people who help themselves, which most of my people do."

Recently a forest fire had started not far from where Matt lived, and I drove there with him to look around. The Spring Creek fire was centered in the mountains east of Fort Garland but had crept above the town of Blanca. Matt was prepared to evacuate himself, Joshua, and his animals, and meanwhile had been helping his "people" who had to get out now. Costilla County sheriff's vehicles blocked most of the roads to the affected areas, but Matt knew ways around and was able to get us closer. Billowing smoke from the fire was visible from practically the entire valley—it lent a low-level sense of alarm from where I lived (for a fire to spread widely across the flats would be unusual) but more palpable concern when you got close enough to see the occasional flame and the wide pillar of smoke that occupied much of the horizon.

Newspapers had reported that a man had been arrested for starting the fire. He was a fifty-two-year-old citizen of Denmark who had overstayed his visa—an undocumented Dane!—and had been living in his camper off-grid. He offered different versions of what had happened: in one, he had been burning trash and in another, he'd been grilling meat over a pit in the ground and had fallen asleep, and the fire had spread. In a press photo he looked stoned. Matt had met the guy at the Blanca RV Park and said he was a knucklehead. The man had shown Matt a vial of what he said was gold he had panned but Matt (who, as I've mentioned, paid close attention to such things) believed it to be only flakes of silica.

As we caught up on this and that, Matt told me that he had recently given a lift to James Worley, who'd been hitchhiking into Alamosa. He thought that James and Roxanne were living openly on their property again, Costilla County having backed off the threat to prosecute them for not having a septic system, at least for the moment. I had been trying and failing to reach them on the phone. But I had found a possible intermediary.

His name was Calvin. I had met him over lunch at the shelter—he had once stayed there for several weeks while recuperating from an injury that befell him on a farm near Crestone. He was a soulful, diminutive, long-haired man from Louisiana with bright blue eyes. He'd spent much of his adulthood camping, as he put it—living in the woods near Nederland, Colorado, or in the desert outside Tucson, Arizona, sometimes while holding down a job in town. He had made a go of selling clothing made of hemp for several months—he called the line Elfin. He was an aspiring writer, and I'd given him feedback on some of his personal essays. He lived on the edge of things, so I was not surprised to learn that he knew of the Worleys and, even better, knew a woman in Alamosa who was their friend. He would introduce me.

Soon I was on the phone with Vera. After asking me several questions aimed at figuring out how I looked at the world, she told me she planned to go see the Worleys for dinner that evening, and I could come along. I offered to drive; Calvin would come, too.

I picked Vera up at her weathered trailer in the Wagon Wheel trailer park, just outside Alamosa. I guessed she was in her late sixties. She unwrapped a small package of bread she'd baked (after grinding the grain herself, she said) and offered me a piece. As we went to pick up Calvin and then continued out onto the flats, she told me how she'd met James Worley. She was outside a store where she had bought a heavy bookcase that needed assembling. He was flying a sign that said something like "WILL WORK FOR FOOD." She'd taken a chance and found that she liked him, and that they had some things in common— in particular, devout Christianity. Her friendship with James, his wife, Roxanne, and their three kids had only deepened when the county came after them for code violations.

The Worleys had lived there for years when one day deputies rolled up and gave them papers that called them a "nuisance" for not having a septic system. They had eleven days to clear out or else they'd get fined $50 a day. "If you get a permit to put in a septic tank, you've got twelve months to complete it," Vera explained.

"I have been their advocate," said Vera. "I went with them to their little hearing date, and they were basically just read info and *Do you understand this?* I said, Couldn't they get a port-a-potty in the meantime? But they said no. I knew right away this means they don't want to cooperate with the people. I knew from when I owned a house in Costilla County that the whole county was corrupt. But the attitude back then and now is, This is our land and our place and we don't want white people coming in and telling us what to do."

Vera said she had appealed to the county commissioners on their behalf but was turned down there, as well. Afraid of the fines, the whole family had moved in with her for many weeks. Since they had joined in a lawsuit against the county, the Worleys felt a bit more secure. "They're back on their property now because they want to grow things and have a dog and a cat. But technically they could get fined for that."

We turned off a main road near the property of Vince Edwards, the man I'd seen the code enforcement officers harass—this area seemed to be a place they'd focused on. Our destination, Vera said, was the property of a couple from Poland named Ania and Jurek—the Worleys would meet us there. We continued for a mile or so up a hill on a road that soon became more of a track. The sun was just about to set—the time of day when the grasses of the flats all assume a radiant glow. We saw other cars and parked alongside them.

Ania and Jurek's compound was like others—it had some kind of a trailer as its heart and had expanded from there. One part of the expansion was a garage, where Jurek, a former computer repairman, worked on Jeeps. Another was a garden with clear plastic walls. We sat outside at a picnic table until the Worleys arrived. With sundown, it got too cold and Calvin started shivering, so we headed indoors.

The Worleys were an interesting-looking couple. James was tall, dark-haired, and handsome—except for a gash on his face; he had recently slipped and fallen on a rock, he explained. Roxanne's long skirt and head scarf made her look like a member of some conservative Christian sect; when I asked if she belonged to a particular church, she stared back at me suspiciously and said no. They knew I was there to talk about their experiences with the county and so went right to it, confirming all that Vera had told me. They had had to abandon their home as the winter came on, they added; when finally they returned to check on plants and animals, their chickens' feet were frozen to the ground.

Ania and Jurek were no fans of local government, either—or of any government, I soon found out. Recently they had refused to pay certain fees to Costilla County. Not long after, during a traffic stop in the town of Blanca that they say was a result of that refusal, Jurek had declined to show the sheriff's deputy his ID. In response, the officers broke a window and tased Ania. "It hurt, but I was so mad!" she said. The officer who came to his window, said Jurek, was Cruz Soto, who I had done the ride-along with. Another of the cops present, said Ania, was Andrew Espinoza, an undersheriff who was subsequently arrested in connection with poaching. "They are all corrupt!"

Ania and Jurek had many strong opinions. The more they talked, the more they lost me. AIDS, Jurek informed me, was, as everyone knew, a problem stemming from a wrong state of mind (and death from it was thereby easily preventable). The CIA, apparently, was run by the Vatican; and the Church of England owned the Pentagon. John McCain had given $800 million to al-Qaeda. The more I expressed puzzlement over these assertions, the more vehement Ania and Jurek became. How could I not know about admiralty law and the permanent state of martial law signaled by the flags you see in courtrooms? I kept asking what their sources were; where they had learned these things. The internet, basically, was the answer, delivered in a tone of shock that I would believe any differently. Where did *I* get *my* information, Ania demanded. I told her I most often got my news from *The New York Times,* prompting them to look at each other as though I were a type of imbecile they had heard talk of but never expected to meet in real life.

The Worleys appeared to agree with every assertion Ania and Jurek made and, like our hosts, conflated all levels of government into one corrupt whole. All American governments were secretly about making money, not about serving citizens. "So are you for the government?" Ania demanded of me. "Or let's say for the corporate democracy, because that's what we have now? I mean, don't kid ourselves—I can show you from the internet printout the United States Inc., where it's registered as a corporation. I can show you the Costilla County Corporation, the Zoning Department Costilla County Corporation, they're all incorporated, they're all for profit, nothing else."

Capital letters, moreover, were a code that signified enslavement—it has been that way since the Roman Empire. How could I not know this?

"It's called Dog Latin," Ania averred. "You can check it online if you don't believe me."

Roxanne said, "If you look at an ID, it's all in capitals. That makes you a corporation."

Their other obsession, in addition to the capitalization of letters, was flags. "How many people know," Roxanne asked, "that the American flag they fly now, a land flag, is really a sea flag?"

Ania jumped in: "It's really a sea flag, it's military. It's an admiralty flag, and the regular flag is a military flag." I tried to follow the significance of this point; it all seemed to boil down to a belief that the government was a fraud, that the real government had been hijacked by corporations. If you were clued in, you knew that meant that the government's power to collect taxes was void, and if you went ahead and paid taxes anyway, you were a chump.

Calvin, listening to all this, didn't argue, but neither did he agree. He did say, in a trenchant observation, "The people that try to say they don't have to pay income tax, they end up in prison or shot."

Ania and Jurek, both from rural Poland, had spent years in New Jersey and in Denver before settling out here. I wasn't comfortable in the presence of such avid conspiracy theorists, and I was particularly unsettled by seeing immigrants rejecting norms in this way. Didn't you come here to get away from something worse? I asked them. "I come from Poland, I was there when the Communist government was oppressive!" declared Jurek.

Ania shut that down, rather charmingly. "Jurek, you're lying," she said. "You were born in 1965" and weren't alive in the years just after World War II when the Communists killed so many. The point, she said, was that they had come for freedom and "what we need is to be left alone. I don't take nothing from government. Nothing. I want them to leave me alone because this is my right." Trying to find some common ground, I said I believed they had been mistreated. But I was having trouble squaring their anger over that with their complete skepticism about all American government institutions, their willingness to believe patently wacko statements, such as when Ania said, "Check your birth certificate—the paper it's printed on is actually worth a lot of money. And believe it or not, I didn't believe it, so I got my Social Security number, I went to this website, have you ever heard about CUSIP number? That's what your number is, either from your Social Security or your birth certificate. It's, how they call it . . . right now if you went to the Wall Street exchanges website and put your Social Security number or that red number from your birth certificate, you're going to find they're selling you as a commodity, in your name, because they copyrighted your name, that's why it's always spelled in capital letters."

James Worley, though not as articulate as Ania, had clearly been alienated longer. He and Roxanne had started their three kids in public schools but then switched to homeschooling, over religious differences he said he couldn't neatly summarize. But his rejection of the mainstream acceptance of government was at least twelve years old. "I went without using a driver's license or ID a dozen years ago . . . no ID. So it's hard to maintain a vehicle and keep it insured. So I lost my vehicle for no insurance, then I lost my job. It's kinda like a snowball effect. So I barter and trade with the neighbors so I can get supplies and live, but it's hard to come up with big piles of cash" when the county suddenly declares you to be in violation of its rules.

To be fair, they also believed in things that made sense to me. En route, I had picked up half gallons of iced tea and lemonade at a convenience store, so I'd have something to contribute to dinner. But they didn't want them because they didn't like plastic. And they said they believed in natural medicine. They believed in family and caring for those close to you—which I saw when I met Jurek's mother inside the trailer. We had a little chat. She was seventy-five years old, she told me, and had moved down here with them from Denver. She liked being out here, and they took good care of her.

When I went back outside, the talk had turned to the righteousness of the Bundy family and the FBI's "assassination" of one of the supporters of the takeover of the Malheur National Wildlife Refuge, in Oregon, not long before. Jurek raved about President Trump and his job creation policies. I thought I detected a hint of racism in somebody's snide comment about Barack Obama. But then Charlie showed up.

He was an African American man in his fifties, and he walked with a limp. One of his feet was wrapped in a bandage, and Ania immediately ushered him into a back room, where she, Roxanne, and Vera helped prepare warm water for him to soak the foot in. They added herbs to it that Ania said would help kill the infection. After a while I sat down next to them.

Charlie told me he was from Maryland and had bought his land out here a few years after leaving the navy. But the past winter he'd gotten frostbite, and lesions from it on his leg and foot hadn't readily healed. He'd spent four months in care facilities, he said, and only recently been discharged. I saw the sores that had been covered by his bandages—they were large and ugly, and his foot was swollen. "They discharged you before you were healed?" I asked. Charlie shrugged.

Yet another neighbor dropped by, and when he did the topic of conversation changed to the installation and wiring of wind turbines, which I found a relief. Nobody was angry at anybody else present, only at the government, and at some point Jurek produced a bottle of homemade spirits and small glasses and we all toasted.

On the drive back to Alamosa, Calvin snoozed in the back seat, and Vera allowed that I might have gotten a bigger dose of politics than I'd bargained for. I asked her if Costilla County's sudden, inflexible code enforcement had served to radicalize people. That seemed to be true of people I'd met. Had our hosts felt this strongly about all governments before?

Vera wasn't sure about Ania and Jurek, but she thought the Worleys had long held exceptional views. Soon after meeting James Worley, she'd learned that he considered a driver's license to be the "sign of the beast," or the Antichrist, and refused to get one. Vera had told Roxanne that a driver's license did not reasonably fit the definition of the sign of the beast—but Roxanne had pushed back and joined her husband in renouncing not only licenses but the use of Social Security numbers. Like James, she saw danger in numbers being assigned to people and was always on the lookout for 666, the sign of the Devil. This outlook meant, of course, that the couple couldn't legally drive or be legally paid when they found work. It effectively consigned them to the margins.

Vera said the couple had been under the sway of a Christian leader at one point, but no longer. She herself had been a member of the well-known New Buffalo commune outside Taos. Now that the Worleys were less fearful of living in their own house, their main concern was for their youngest child, a daughter, who was pregnant. But the daughter and her parents didn't always get along, said Vera, so "her choices are either me or La Puente." Someone else told me that drug use was part of the picture, and that the baby's father was rumored to be a sex offender.

I dropped Calvin off, then Vera. It was dark and it was late and I had an hour still to drive before I got home. I had a lot to process and was grateful for the quiet, which was good for that. A railroad tramp I had traveled with years before had brought me to the rescue mission in Spokane, where before we could have dinner we had to listen to a sermon, which he called an "ear banging." I felt I had just been through another ear banging.

But the other impression of the evening was of close community. These people, who had so little, were there for each other, united against enemies real or imagined. In the middle of nowhere, they shared food, drink, medicine. Unless you were a journalist (or, say, believed in science), there was a warm feeling in the makeshift home. Their aloneness wasn't so lonely.

Loneliness could happen anywhere, of course, even in big cities. But it struck me that the country I was driving through—the roads without streetlights, the huge distances between houses on the prairie—almost invited it in. To my way of thinking, you had to defend against it, just as you did against hunger and cold. They were physical dangers, and it was an emotional danger; I thought of it as an abyss.

I kept away from the edge of that abyss by planning things, most of which involved other people. I would check in on my prairie neighbors for La Puente. I would drive into Antonito, half an hour away, to do laundry. Or I would drive into Alamosa for groceries, La Puente meetings, or to get work done in the public library, with its good internet and pair of private study rooms. The absence of plans, for an extended period—for me, that meant more than a couple of days—was where it got dicey. I loved the open country. The emptiness was freedom. But too much of it could be a bad thing.

I had first learned this lesson in a different part of Colorado, where my family had a mountain house. I had tried to write my first book there and almost drove myself crazy. Writers need solitude to write, in my experience. But then, to stay sane, they also need to connect. I was at heart a social person, even if not always eager for conversation.

An email came from my New England friend who had lived alone in the prairie:

> How's your ammo supply? Have you considered a horse yet? Do you feel free and safe on your land? Is that western sky still big and full of promise?

These were nice questions to be asked—I felt that somebody understood and was reasonably concerned in making sure I didn't get isolated and stuck. Ideas of that were in my head: the snowbound writer played by Jack Nicholson in the movie *The Shining* ("All work and no play makes Jack a dull boy," he typed in his room thousands of times) or the forlorn trailer of the deranged murderer Robert Dear, who'd attacked the Planned Parenthood clinic in Colorado Springs. And then the singer Neil Young's thoughts on the matter: "My head needs relatin' / Not solitude."

Of course, with the Grubers around, it was hard to feel isolated. Always (and especially in summertime) there was a kid dropping by, a dog or five, something happening.

A few days later came a case in point. When I pulled into the Gruber place, I saw that something was different: the tail of a cow lay next to the driveway. Part of a leg and some hide were nearby. I parked, walked toward the house, and noticed that the open bay near the shop room had been turned into an abattoir. A partial carcass hung from a beam; Frank, Josh (still living at the Grubers' other property), and fourteen-year-old Trin all had knives and were carving away at big pieces of meat. They looked tired—cutting up a whole cow is a big job.

I said, "Wow" and left it at that for a moment. I knew better than to inquire into the details of the acquisition of this windfall. They knew I had worked in a slaughterhouse in Nebraska; I had also worked in one in Spain. I offered to help, but there wasn't really room. "How do you guys know how to do this?" I finally asked.

"It's a lot like dressing an elk," said Frank. Josh, I knew, usually carried a knife. I commented on the importance of it being a *sharp* knife, and they nodded.

"Wish you still ate beef?" asked Frank, who knew that I no longer did.

"Actually, I am tempted," I said. "I can see this is going to be delicious." A circle of dogs sat around the perimeter. "It looks like they already know."

Later I learned that the animal had been shot nearby with an AK-47. The shooter, who shall remain nameless, had picked an animal that was not fully grown, so that it could be lifted into the back of a pickup truck.

Now, shooting somebody else's cow might be seen as a bad thing. Cattle rustling, in frontier days, could be a hanging offense. But the cattle situation in my area of the flats was complicated. Cattle had once roamed freely across private land that was a series of ranches. Such land is generally considered "open range," which, as I said earlier, means that if I decide to live somewhere on it, it's up to me to fence cattle *out,* not up to ranchers to fence them *in.* But when those ranches were sold to developers who created giant subdivisions filled with five-acre lots, somehow the grazing didn't stop. The cattle no longer lived on the flats most of the year. Rather, they were trucked in by a couple of cattle companies, released, allowed to graze for free, and then rounded up (often by all-terrain vehicles, or ATVs, rolling across private land) and taken to market months later.

One problem with this is that cattle can be destructive, and among the things they destroy are people's gardens and their fences. Some locals had dogs that were good at keeping cattle away, but even then, the cattle might come at night when the dogs were inside. It was worst for residents who lived near a bank of the Rio Grande where the cattle might take a drink before stomping back to graze on higher ground. One of them was a neighbor of mine whose place was within walking distance of the Beach. One day he was out with his dog, heading for the river, when they encountered a wave of cows sent down there to get water; they fouled the riverbank and made things muddy. My neighbor told me he found himself shouting at them and waving his arms until their minder, on an ATV, rolled up and told him to knock it off. The men almost came to blows, the cowboy actually calling the county deputies, who, my neighbor said, arrested not the cowboy but him and took him to jail. Costilla County, I knew, had been trying to curb this grazing for years. Ben Doon, the county manager, told me he understood residents' frustration. When I hinted that occasionally prairie people, fed up with cows, were taking them for food, Doon said, "Good!"

It was summer, six-thirty a.m., and I was driving Trin and Meadoux to Antonito to meet the bus that would take them to a two-week summer camp. Frank and Stacy would have liked to do this but were short on gas money, and I was headed in that direction anyway.

About twenty minutes into the drive, we were waved down by a couple walking on the side of the road. The man and woman looked about seventy years old and were a bit frantic. "Can you give us a ride into town?" he asked. "We've been walking most of the night." I asked where they came from, and he said the Punche Valley. They were from New Mexico; they'd been on a pleasure drive, a loop from their home near Taos, when their Range Rover had broken down yesterday afternoon. "There's no cell-phone service at all back there."

"You must be cold," I said. "Let me make you some room inside." But we could see that this was going to require a lot of unloading—the small back seat of my pickup's cab was filled with the girls' camp stuff and boxes of La Puente supplies.

"Don't worry about it, we'll just ride in back," the man said. "It'll be faster." I sped off into town with the couple in the bed of my truck, sitting on knapsacks. The Punche Valley was the very definition of remoteness, a large tract on the other side of some mountains from the Grubers with some sparse ruins of human settlement. Lance Cheslock, I knew, was intrigued by its complete emptiness and a corresponding paucity of historical information. We had, in fact, made a date with a historian in Manassa, Loretta Mitson, to drive through with us and tell us what she knew. So far, though, I knew it just as a place where it might be easy to disappear. My fantasy of that involved a fugitive from the law intent on completely absenting himself from the modern world. But a more realistic version was presented by this couple, a living (thank goodness) testament to what could befall travelers in such a place. At their request, we dropped the couple in Antonito, at the Hometown Food Market. The man thanked me and said they would take it from there.

We met the camp bus in the parking lot behind the local school. Trin and Meadoux seemed nervous—the prospect of becoming part of a pack of kids must have been momentous for them. They recognized one kid and waved shyly. Soon they climbed into the bus and were whisked away.

My tour of the Punche Valley with Loretta Mitson and Lance took place a few weeks later. I'd invited Troy Zinn from the flats to join us, and he brought along his son, Jason. I'd been spending more time with Troy—the former truck driver was genial and human and deeply rooted in this place, and he liked to discuss history. And so as I drove to meet Loretta and the others in Antonito, my mind was on history, of which some was visible right where I was: one benefit of scarce trees and minimal development is that many traces of human settlement were in plain sight. From the Grubers' place, I drove a dirt road that paralleled the Rio Grande canyon for a mile or two. On the other side loomed the remains of an old mine that had produced bentonite, a kind of clay; yellow tailings ran down the hillside from the mine to the river. I knew that along the canyon walls, just out of view from my pickup, were petroglyphs scratched into the rock (human figures, a sunburst, a question mark sort of thing, a figure like a snake) as well as potsherds peeking out from the sandy soil and "bedrock metates," shiny concavities in the dark volcanic rock that show where ancients once ground grain and, perhaps, clay.

The road ended at the one-lane wrought-iron Lobatos Bridge, forged in Ohio in 1892. It was scenic, and always tempted me to stop in mid-span and look up and down the river canyon, and with little traffic on that road, I could usually get away with it. Once, a flock of cormorants passed under the bridge as I drove across it—the river canyon was a separate ecosystem from the arid prairie above. Beyond the bridge, on land belonging to the U.S. Bureau of Land Management, a zone of no houses, I passed a knob known as Kiowa Hill, or in Spanish as El Cerrito de los Kiowa. Frank Gruber, using his one bar of cell-phone signal, had searched the Web for information on this and sent me a pdf of a history journal from 1942 that contained an account of the battle that had taken place there, probably in the 1850s. Juan M. Salazar said he had often heard the story on the knee of his grandfather, an eyewitness. According to Salazar, a band of thirty Kiowa warriors from the plains to the east, apparently drunk, staged an attack on a party of Utes returning to a large Ute encampment nearby and killed their leader. Some two hundred Utes caught up with them at Kiowa Hill; the battle lasted most of the day, "until all the Kiowas were dead either from thirst or from well-aimed arrows. More than sixty Indians lost their lives on this hill." Another source said the stench of rotting corpses lasted for days.

I pictured the warriors on horseback (though they probably had not been), just because feral horses are today very much a part of the landscape. Often they could be seen in the vicinity of Kiowa Hill, usually in small herds, and in springtime with foals. Maybe some of them had ancestors who were there, as well.

In Antonito itself, history lives in empty buildings, among them the empty lodge of the Sociedad Protección Mutua de Trabajadores Unidos (SPMDTU, or the Society for the Mutual Protection of United Workers), a dance hall, and the mansion of a former sheep baron, which was about to be reborn as the town hall. A bit farther down the street, a former corner bar was enjoying a short-lived rebirth as a "dab lounge," where fanciers of hash oil vaporized with a butane flame could enjoy their vice. (The lounge, whose presence appeared to violate the law against using marijuana in a commercial establishment, forced every patron to sign a statement saying they were not a journalist.)

At the newish Family Dollar store—every town now seems to have one, or its equivalent—Lance and Loretta left their cars for mine and we headed off to the Punche Valley. (This was pre-Covid.) Both had long histories in the valley; their daughters had been good friends. Loretta had moved to Manassa from Fullerton, California, where as an anthropology student she'd met her future husband, Leandro Salazar, who had a master's in theology and had been headed for the priesthood. Both worked as community organizers for the United Farm Workers and César Chávez. Leandro was the oldest brother of Ken Salazar, who would become a U.S. senator and then secretary of the interior under President Barack Obama. Leandro died in a farm accident in 1992.

Our arrival at the top of the valley startled a herd of elk, which took off running. Troy and his son pulled up behind us as we paused to watch. Then we all drove a bit farther: the tour would begin at the most impressive man-made relic in the Punche Valley, a broken dam. On its completion in 1889, the dam created a reservoir, Cove Lake, which, though modest, was large enough that people had once fished in it in motorboats. The dam breached in 1974—Loretta and Troy had both heard that it had been intentionally dynamited. (While many locals agreed with this, a state water engineer in Alamosa would tell me that studies had later revealed that the dam sat on a fault line, and that the breach might have been caused by a small earthquake.) A ring of pale dead tree trunks showed where the shoreline had been.

The valley was so dry now that it was hard to imagine the lush garden it once had been. Cove Lake had been fed by a branch of the San Antonio River, which today has run dry. Loretta said it had irrigated more than two thousand acres of land, and farmers had grown lettuce, cabbage, potatoes, and other row crops, as well as alfalfa, and grazed sheep and cattle. Now we could see none of those.

Tona of La Puente had told me that her parents had farmed here; Loretta said it was once a place "where a Hispanic family might get ahead." As we descended a hill from the dam and, following a disused irrigation ditch, crossed an old barbed-wire fence that mostly lay on the ground, she told me that Ken Salazar had once been nearby with his father, who'd wept as he'd told of helping his parents put their fences up in the 1920s. The whole family would come from their main farm east of Manassa and spend their summers here, to meet the homesteading requirements. No grazing permits were required at the time, she added. "It was a free-for-all."

We were at the valley's north end, at a high spot. To our left were gentle mountains that defined the northeastern edge; straight ahead and to our right was a massive volume of space resting on an endless bed of yellow grass and shrubs. The valley extended south farther than we could see, fading out into New Mexico's Taos Plateau.

Of human dwellings, there were scant remains. We explored a row of small collapsed shelters made mainly of volcanic rock that Loretta theorized could have been a stagecoach stop, since they were situated alongside the trail. One still had part of its roof, and we could see the old vigas—stout timbers that had supported it. Finally, we poked around three larger, more complex houses that Loretta said had belonged to a sheep baron. They featured small porches, cedar shingles, and walls painted a faint green, most of which had crumbled to reveal the lath and plaster within.

The largest former settlement was a farm with a wooden barn close to collapse, a huge potato cellar with the roof gone, extensive foundations for what appeared to be animal pens, and the remains of pens and corrals. Two sources had told Loretta that German POWs had been interned down there and made to work on the farm. Troy was polite but skeptical—he said he'd fielded questions about POW internment camps his whole life but had never heard or seen evidence of any. Loretta, though, seemed persuaded: there had been hundreds of such camps during World War II, often sited where the prisoners could work in agriculture. "Branch camps" like this seldom had armed guards, said Loretta; she had been told that the extensive concrete foundation we could see had supported a horse barn that became a barracks, adding that prisoners had been paid twenty to forty dollars a month.

Loretta remembered that some young people from her town had taken a drive out here on a winter day in the 1990s for reasons that were unclear. One froze to death when their car got stuck and then ran out of gas. Later I tracked down two of the four survivors. Alcohol had been involved in the tragedy, they said. Both had suffered frostbite; one ended up losing some toes. The open country could be harsh.

On a warm summer day, though, it was heaven. I liked being out in the open valley, and I liked the way Loretta's knowledge invited us to imagine what it had been like in times forgotten. On a different day, she would lead me and Lance and a group from Conejos County further south to a circle of stones on the Taos Plateau. Nobody knew what the circle was for, but there were others like it in the region, and archaeologists guessed they were hundreds or thousands of years old. It was fine with me that nobody knew their purpose; the mystery evoked a time when people here saw God in nature and bowed before it. Historians could also raise awareness of aspects of the past that would seem to have been intentionally forgotten. On the same excursion, Ronald Rael, a professor of architecture at Berkeley with deep family roots in the area, showed our group around the early settlement of Conejos, just outside Antonito. Mexican families from Abiquiú, in present-day New Mexico, had started farms, built a plaza, and fought the Native peoples there beginning around 1854. Many of the residents, Rael mentioned, had likely been *genízaros*—Indigenous slaves, usually captured by other Indigenous people and then sometimes indentured to Hispanos and people like Lafayette Head, Colorado's first lieutenant governor, whose wife, from a prominent Mexican family, was one of those settlers.

I grabbed dinner with Lance after we said good-bye to Loretta. The restaurant, though called the Dutch Mill, served Mexican food. Lance had devoted his life to helping people. But he had other interests, too. An avid birder, he had pointed out a flock of horned larks near the stagecoach stop. He was intrigued by the idea of poking around ruins like the ones we'd just visited with a metal detector, to see what cool old things people might have thrown out. He was also one of many people I met in the San Luis Valley who never seemed to tire of looking at the sky, and sometimes photographing it. (Occasionally, on Facebook, prairie people would post photos of the same sunset, shot at around the same moment.)

The need to "put down" Tank had been a running topic in the Gruber household for months. The Saint Bernard was getting old and addled. He had become "food aggressive" and had bitten other dogs, and his weight had fallen from 227 to about 160 pounds. His ridiculous attempts to copulate with little Bear, the Chihuahua mix, were met with hilarity (and speculation over the sort of puppy that would ensue). But when he started growling at Frank and at Sam, I felt the end was drawing near.

My camper trailer had its own small water tank, and though I was far from the Grubers' well, if they connected together every last garden hose they had, it was just enough to reach me. One morning I needed a refill and so walked past Sam's snarling pit bulls to the main house. I saw that the Grubers' pickup truck was gone and realized they might not be home, but then I saw that the door was ajar and Frank, in the main room, was stooped over something. I walked in.

Frank, shirtless, was working on a small concrete mold he'd made from a pie dish. Impressed in the middle was a giant paw print. Around it, Frank was etching "TANK 9/2018." But Tank was lying on the floor next to Frank and appeared to be breathing. Sam and Nick sat on the couch, looking serious.

"Wait, Tank—" I started, confused.

"Today's the day," said Frank. He explained that after Stacy had gone into town with the girls, he'd given Tank an extra-big dose of the butter-mixed-with-CBD-oil preparation that the dog got every morning to calm him and relieve his aches and pains. As a result, "he's pretty well passed out," Frank said. He murmured to the dog as he worked on the mold. "You ate good this morning and last night, too, didn't you, boy?" Frank's face was wet. I'd never seen him cry before.

Sam came over to where Frank was crouched and spread a blanket on the floor. Frank hoisted the giant dog between his own two legs and started dragging Tank toward it. The dog started moving his front legs as though to stand up, but Frank persuaded him to stay down. I approached to grab the corner of the blanket next to Sam.

"Nick, would you grab that end?" asked Frank, when Nick seemed to miss the cue. Nick rose to his feet and picked up the third corner. Then we all kind of put our corners down and helped Frank drag Tank onto the blanket. The four of us heaved and staggered toward the doorway with Tank barely off the floor.

The part of the lot catty-corner from my trailer was an animal burial ground, and I saw that the grave had already been dug. Frank's bulldozer was parked next to the new hole. We lowered Tank into the ground. Sam, Nick, and I then stepped away, but Frank lingered, wrapping the blanket around Tank. He hugged him some more and wept—I thought how often the dog had joined him and Stacy on their bed, how many times I'd seen Frank wipe the slobber from his pet's face, the way that, now and then, he'd lovingly blow a little marijuana smoke into the big dog's mouth.

Finally Frank stood, turned his back to the grave, and walked toward the house. Nick and I joined him, but not Sam. Sam had his hand in his pocket, and as we passed him he pulled something out. Nick and Frank walked inside. I lingered at the door, watching Sam. He stepped down into the hole, tidied the blanket, and petted Tank one last time. Then he placed a pistol against Tank's skull. I heard the pop.

Sam came indoors and became emotional, too. He told us that killing his own dog, sick when it was only nine years old, was "one of the hardest things I ever had to do." I asked Sam where he'd aimed. "On top of the head so it goes into the brain stem," he said. "If you do it right, it's like a switch goes off." There was a little splash of blood on the dirt in front of Tank's head. If DIY euthanasia makes sense for people who can't afford a veterinarian, then Sam had done it right.

Frank went back outside and climbed up on his bulldozer. It started noisily, with a cloud of smoke. Sam handed him a joint, then held out a lighter for him. Frank used the dozer to push dirt atop Tank from several directions. It took about ten minutes. When it was done and he was walking toward the house, Sam put his hand on Frank's shoulder. It was the first time I'd ever seen them touch.

There was fun stuff on the prairie, too. In August, when the monsoons created a nearly impossible mudhole on a road we used every day, an old fiberglass motorboat miraculously appeared on its edge. And it hadn't floated there. The high jinks had Sam written all over it. He never confessed publicly. But one day when we were discussing the replacement truck he'd gotten after the gun battle with the "Shims," he told me how miraculous it was, on a recent evening, to have been speeding across the prairie, towing the red boat with a rope, only to feel a tug as the boat got stuck on something and then a shock as the vessel, airborne, landed slightly in front of his truck. "I almost hit it!"

Another day, in late morning, Sam knocked excitedly at my trailer door. "There's a guy on the road who could use some help from La Puente!" he said. I imagined an accident. "What happened?"

"I don't know, but there's a guy with no clothes walking over there. Do you think you could get him some clothes?"

I came out to see where he was pointing. Frank and Sam had been driving home and had seen the man in the distance; when they drew close, he moved off the road into the bushes and lay down on his back.

I had an extra T-shirt and socks. Nick offered to donate a pair of old pants, and we found some rope to use as a belt. Nick, Sam, and I headed out in my truck.

En route, Sam allowed as how he had showed the guy his gun during the previous encounter. But why? I asked. A naked man isn't carrying a weapon.

"We're close to a home with five girls in it," Sam said. "He needs to stay away." I asked Sam not to show the gun this time.

It didn't take long to find the guy, and he didn't try to hide. I spoke to him. He had clearly taken a lot of drugs—he mentioned LSD, meth, mescaline, and weed. I offered him the clothes and, with difficulty, he put them on. I asked if we could drive him to his destination and he said yes. He said he was staying somewhere near Troy's place, as good a landmark as any, and we started driving there. Nick moved into the bed of the truck to sit with him. They knocked on the window as I was getting close, signaled that I should turn right, and then later that I should turn left.

Frank's marijuana crop

Our destination was a camper trailer with a Prius and small pickup truck parked outside. Sam put his hand into his pistol pocket as he approached—he didn't know this place. A man emerged from the trailer looking bemused. "I wondered where you went," he said. The formerly naked fellow had wandered off the night before.

"You weren't worried about him?" I asked, a bit surprised.

"I figured he'd turn up," the man said. I told the guy he could keep the clothes. As we headed back to the Grubers', I asked Nick what they'd been talking about in the back. "Mainly about what he took," said Nick. Nick's parting advice to him had been: "Just do one drug at a time."

The ubiquity of guns around Sam set me a bit on edge, especially given his frictions with unpredictable others in the world. One day a guy known for drunkenness and belligerence turned up at the gate. Frank went down to speak to him. The man claimed that Sam owed him money for weed and that he'd regret it if he didn't pay up. Frank told the man that he knew Sam pretty well and that the man would regret it if he didn't go away, now. The guy drove away but said he'd be back.

Troy's son, Jason, liked to drive around at night with his truck lights off. Sam, not knowing who it was, followed him one night. The chase reportedly escalated into high rates of speed on Road G, with shots fired but no one hurt. Sam said he told Jason later, "Are you crazy? Coming around *my* place at night with your lights off?"

And then there was the property to the west of us, a trailer and a grow. One night it caught fire. Afterward, a dark-colored SUV would creep along the Grubers' road in a way Sam took to be threatening; I'd see him watching from behind a fence, AK in hand.

The people Sam and Cindy had left the property to during their boat odyssey had filled the Grubers' burn pit and left additional mountains of trash. One afternoon when I was resting, Frank and Sam decided it was time to burn it all. My trailer, alas, was upwind, and the pit was full of all kinds of noxious stuff—especially plastics, the smell of which filled my space. I took a nap anyway, hoping the wind might change. I was awoken by *BAM! BAM BAM!* and shouts. I walked outside. Sam said the sounds I'd heard were aerosol cans deep in the burn pit, exploding when they got hot. I was a little bit relieved, but not a lot.

Sometimes irritation builds on irritation. I found myself getting irked by the sound of Sam and Cindy's generator at night. They liked to go to sleep watching TV. To do this, they'd fire up their generator and then just leave it running until it ran out of gas, usually around five a.m. I'd gotten used to the noise of a generator in winter—you needed one if your batteries weren't sufficient to keep a furnace going all night. But in the summer? I mentioned it to Sam, but, cognizant of the fact that this was his property, I didn't pursue it. And then sometimes at night he and Cindy would argue loudly, or their dogs would get riled up.

Given that I was in the middle of so much space, I began to question the wisdom of living so close to the annoyances you might find in a crowded apartment building. Where once I had worried about loneliness, now I started thinking about where else I might live.

At La Puente, Matt was spending less time introducing himself to new people and more time responding to the requests of those he'd already met—his reputation had spread by word of mouth. Meanwhile, his personal time was mostly devoted to fixing up his new home at the foot of Blanca Peak. I drove up to see how it was coming on a beautiful afternoon with a warm sun and a moderate breeze. The gigantic sky above had room for several weather systems: to the east it looked like storm clouds, overhead it was high cirrus, and a different situation that had not quite declared itself was manifesting over the San Juans to the west, where most of the valley's weather came from. To me that sky said, *Wherever you are, you are not stuck. There's something different, new possibilities, new weather, a short drive away.*

Matt's new home was on a piece of land where, almost certainly, nobody had ever lived (though someone may have hunted or grazed animals there). And now it really looked like a homestead. The corral was done and the horse was in it, along with a foal he'd bought at a recent auction in Monte Vista for $500. ("I had to outbid some Amish.") He'd canceled his order for a big shed after learning of a gutted trailer at the Blanca RV Park that he could buy for a song—"It's basically the same thing"—and now this proto-home, a fifth-wheel-style trailer, was on-site.

Joshua came out of the trailer and sat on its step. "Can you say hello to Mr. Conover?" Matt asked him.

Matt at his homestead

"Hello, Mr. Conover," said Joshua.

We hung out for a while, talking mostly about the horses. I watched while Matt roped Mingo, the foal, after much effort, and got a halter on him, and tied it to a post—but then the horse broke free, the halter not being strong enough to resist his pulling. Matt was far from defeated. "Have you heard of prairie skiing?" he asked. I had not. "It's holding on to a rope as your horse drags you across the prairie," he joked. An aspect of prairie life he had not anticipated was the visits of feral horses who wanted to get to know Roxy Dancer and Mingo. Several times he'd returned home to find them with their heads over the fence. He worried that a feral stallion might break the fence down in order to get in—but all in all, he seemed more excited by the prospect than fearful. This was the adventure he had wanted to have.

While Matt's homestead was not aesthetically beautiful, it struck me that it was spiritually so. A defining feature of the valley was that a person, even a person of very limited means, could actually buy a piece of these vast acres of land—most of it undisturbed, primeval—for not too much money.

Even before my recent irritations, I had thought about that and about where I might like to buy. I couldn't entirely explain why: I wasn't going to move out here, and it wasn't my wife's idea of a nice vacation property. And yet buying and building was sort of the narrative of the flats. Being surrounded by so much beautiful and affordable land made it almost impossible *not* to think about it.

As the sun began to set, the prairie grasses took on a golden glow. The problem for somebody like me, who wasn't going to live here year-round, was the likelihood of theft: some neighbors were needy, and unattended property was a target. I knew from the many ruins I'd seen that almost everything was at risk, from the copper wiring in an old RV to the actual windows of a house. Solar panels would disappear in a flash. Matt had told me of an old mobile home he'd pass where the residents had moved out. A few weeks later, he saw that it had been tipped over: thieves had stolen the steel axles underneath, which he said were worth about $500 apiece. To tip the dwelling, they'd apparently thrown a couple of grappling hooks with chains attached over the roof, then pulled on the chains with a big pickup truck—he said he could see the holes where the hooks had pierced the aluminum siding and yanked it toward the roof. The only real protection, so far as I could tell, was proximity to a trusted neighbor, somebody who would notice if thieves tried a thing like that.

I'd had my eye on a property near Troy that, though seemingly abandoned, looked untouched. One day I asked him about it. It had a well, Troy said, and a septic tank. The trailer, long and light blue, was likely in pretty rough shape—it hadn't been lived in since its last occupant, a friend of his, had died four years earlier. How much would a place like that cost? I asked him. Troy was reluctant to say. There wasn't an actual market off-grid that made it possible to know. "Out here, it's worth what somebody will pay."

"Yeah," I said, pushing a little harder. "But what would somebody ask, and what might somebody pay?"

"Oh, it might be worth twenty thousand," said Troy. But he happened to know that it wasn't for sale.

"Well, let me know if you ever hear it is."

4

Raw Land

All of us can look back to the money-making opportunities we let slip through our hands. Now another such opportunity is knocking at your door. One you cannot afford to miss. It's your chance to invest in land located in one of America's most desirable areas, Colorado's magnificent San Luis Valley.

—"Only 50¢ a Day for Your 5 Acre Ranch," advertisement in the *Chicago Tribune*, 1973

WHEN TROY ZINN STEPS OUTSIDE his front door to smoke a cigarette, straight ahead of him is a mighty mountain range, the Sangre de Cristo. It forms the eastern horizon, extending about two hundred fifty miles from Poncha Pass, at the northern end of the San Luis Valley, to Glorieta Pass, near Santa Fe, New Mexico. San Luis, the oldest town in Colorado, established in 1851, sits at the foot of the "Sangres," its lights sometimes visible at night. Most of the highest peaks in the Colorado Rockies are on national forest land. But the mountains right in front of Troy, rising up on either side from San Luis, are an exception. They are part of a huge tract of land that is private property. The land, eighty-three thousand acres, is called Cielo Vista Ranch by its owner, an heir to a Texas oil fortune named William Bruce Harrison. He bought the property in 2017 after it had listed for $105 million.

Many others still call the land the Taylor Ranch, after Jack Taylor, a North Carolina lumber baron who bought it in 1960 from a group of Denver investors called the Costilla Land Company. The price then was $497,798. The Costilla Land Company had allowed locals to use the land for hunting, pasturage, and firewood collection for more than a hundred years. Taylor changed that practice, erecting long fences and detaining and even beating trespassers. Thus began an uproar and four decades of litigation. During this period, in 1975, while he was asleep inside, Taylor's house at the ranch was struck by an estimated ten bullets from a high-powered rifle, one of which wounded him in the ankle. Calvin Trillin wrote about the conflict the next year in a *New Yorker* article called "A Cloud on the Title." Taylor offered what Trillin characterized as "some mild attempts" at reconciliation with the locals, offering five thousand acres of recreation land in return for a guarantee of "law protection and some concessions on tax and eminent-domain disputes Taylor is having with the county." They turned it down. "It would have been a lot cheaper to pay someone off," Taylor said later, without specifying who such a person would be, or how such a payment could help resolve such a deep anger.

To locals the property is not known as anyone's ranch but simply as La Sierra (the mountains). To a significant subset of locals, among them Shirley Romero Otero, president of the San Luis–based Land Rights Council, the outsiders with jurisdiction over the land are not its owners but, rather, its "occupiers."

Just south of San Luis, hard up against the mountains, are several settlements that are very old and very Hispanic. Among them are San Pedro, San Pablo, Chama, and Los Fuertes. The residents of these places have a special connection to the mountains, which they have used for years for things like hunting and firewood. And they have a special connection to each other, including a dialect of Spanish unique to the area. The community is insular; outsiders often say they do not feel welcome there. Matt Little says the area generates few of the "calls for help" he gets in Rural Outreach.

An old bridge once provided direct access from a point just south of town to some of these villages and to La Vega, a meadow that has served as a communal grazing area for livestock belonging to generations of area residents. Starting in the 1970s, the bridge also began to be used by residents of a new subdivision atop Wild Horse Mesa, a rocky

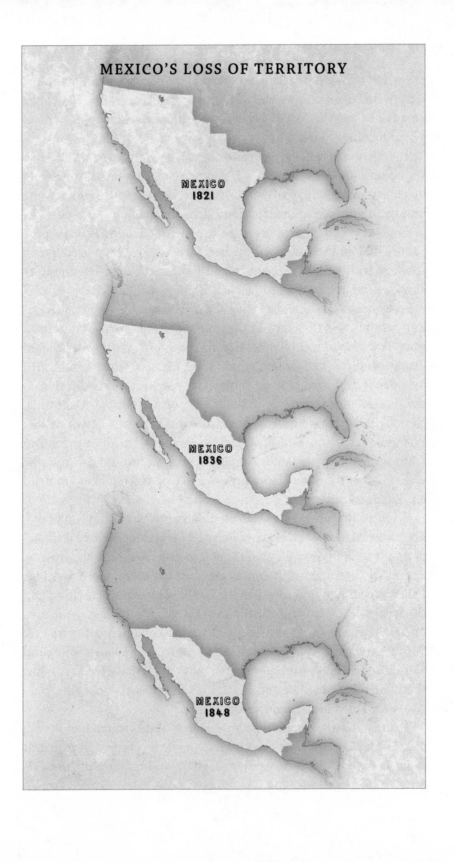

MEXICO'S LOSS OF TERRITORY

MEXICO
1821

MEXICO
1836

MEXICO
1848

pile south of San Luis. The county closed the bridge when it became rickety. But when they looked into getting state money for repairs, the board of La Vega said don't bother—they preferred that access remain a bit difficult.

The friction between those with long-term ties to the land and those with dominion over it goes back a long time. It seems reasonable to link it to a foundational dynamic of American history, in which white immigrants from Europe, and later their descendants, established a toehold and then control over vast expanses of land that other people considered their own. In the San Luis Valley, this played out in conflicts with Mexican, Spanish, and Indigenous people who either already lived in the valley or had laid claim to it.

Some of the story can be explained with maps. With the Louisiana Purchase in 1803, the United States expanded west across the Mississippi River, nearly doubling its size. Its continuing push west brought it into conflict with the young nation of Mexico, which established its independence from Spain during the years 1810–1821. Mexico, at the time, claimed territory including all of present-day California, Nevada, Arizona, Utah, New Mexico, Texas, and parts of Colorado, Wyoming, and Kansas. But it had little presence in these areas and scant control over the land. Hoping to keep the Americans out, the young nation continued a Spanish practice of making land grants to encourage settlement.

Seven of the land grants included parts of present-day Colorado. They covered more than eight million acres, and three of them included parts of the San Luis Valley. Of these three, one became known as the Sangre de Cristo grant. It contained most of the southern San Luis Valley, including the land where the Grubers and Troy Zinn lived and the Sangre de Cristo Mountains, which formed the horizon to the east. The grant ended up in the hands of Carlos Beaubien, a fur trapper born in Montreal who had married a prominent Mexican woman in Taos and become a Mexican citizen, after its original owners, Taos sheriff Stephen Luis Lee and Beaubien's thirteen-year-old son, Narciso, were killed in the Taos Revolt of 1847.

The map changed rapidly in those days. Texas, which had been a part of Mexico, declared itself an independent republic in 1836 and claimed some of the same western land (including the San Luis Valley) Mexico did. In 1845, President James Polk, a fervent promoter of manifest destiny, helped annex Texas into the United States. Polk then tried to purchase from Mexico its lands north of the Rio Grande and west to the Pacific. After Mexico refused to receive Polk's emissary, the United States invaded in 1846, with the object of capturing these very same lands, including present-day New Mexico, Arizona, Nevada, California, parts of Colorado, and more. With the signing of the Treaty of Guadalupe Hidalgo in 1848, the Mexican-American War ended. Mexico had lost more than half of its territory.

Hispanics who had settled in the San Luis Valley starting in the 1840s, encouraged by the land-grant system, found themselves unmoored. The terms of the treaty obligated the American government to honor all existing Spanish and Mexican land grants, but that didn't happen: only 6 percent of the land grants made in the New Mexico Territory were recognized by U.S. courts. The sense of dislocation and of subjugation to the United States likely deepened in 1861, when most of the valley was severed from New Mexico and became part of the new Colorado Territory. The border of this new territory (which would become the state of Colorado in 1876) made sense only as a straight line, and not in terms of the land (it lopped off the southern stretch of the San Luis Valley) or the culture. The ascendant culture of Colorado was white, European, and mainly Protestant—tens of thousands of prospectors, mostly white men, had arrived from the East and the Midwest following the discovery of gold in 1858.

"It's difficult to overestimate the level of disenfranchisement the valley's Hispano residents felt in the early days of Colorado's existence," wrote Robert Sanchez in *5280* in 2019. "Adding to their unease was the construction of Fort Garland, an army outpost created in 1858 to protect new Anglo settlers from Native American bands in the valley. Hispanos couldn't help but think the garrison was also a warning to them." At the time, some seven thousand Hispanos lived in humble settlements built around Spanish-style town plazas, in adobe rooms with thatched roofs along the Conejos and San Antonio Rivers. Native American tribes, especially the Utes, still traversed the region, trading with, fighting with, and occasionally enslaved by the Hispano settlers, but they were increasingly hemmed in and impoverished. In the eyes of Colorado's new territorial government, these non-white people were a "necessary nuisance," observed Sanchez—their numbers would be useful in gaining federal support for statehood, but otherwise they could be trouble.

In 1863, a dozen soldiers from Fort Garland arrived at one of the Hispano plazas, not far from present-day Antonito, to arrest two brothers, Felipe and Vivián Espinosa. A priest from Taos had alleged that the two had robbed and beaten a man hauling goods for him. The expedition was a fiasco, and the brothers escaped; soon after, they began a spree of attacks on white settlers, mostly north of the valley, eventually killing more than thirty. (Chapter 6 picks up the story about the Espinosa brothers.)

The valley was changing rapidly. Around 1864, the million-acre Sangre de Cristo land grant, which *had been* recognized by the U.S. government, was bought by former Colorado territorial governor William Gilpin and his partners. (In Denver, I'd grown up a block away from Gilpin Street.)

The investors promptly divided the massive property in two: the northern half would become the Trinchera Estate and the southern half the Costilla Estate. Gilpin asked Congress to confirm the legitimacy of the arrangement, and in 1870 it did so, explaining that the objects of Gilpin's new corporation were to promote and encourage "emigration and . . . settlements," to lay out wagon roads and "lease, sell, and mortgage any real estate," and to connect the valley to existing telegraph lines and railroads. In short, the San Luis Valley had moved into the development phase.

Whenever I asked people in my part of the valley who I might interview as an authority on local history, they said: Harold Anderson. Anderson was a farmer in Jaroso, a tiny town less than a mile from the New Mexico border, and his wife was the postmaster. I had first met him in the spring of 2018, when I went to request a post office box of my own. I saw "ANDERSON" across the front of the old building that contained the post office (it had once been a drugstore) and "ANDERSON" on a grain elevator a short distance away. Since it was around one p.m., I found that the post office, open from ten a.m. to noon, was closed for the day. But I wanted to meet Harold, so I knocked on the

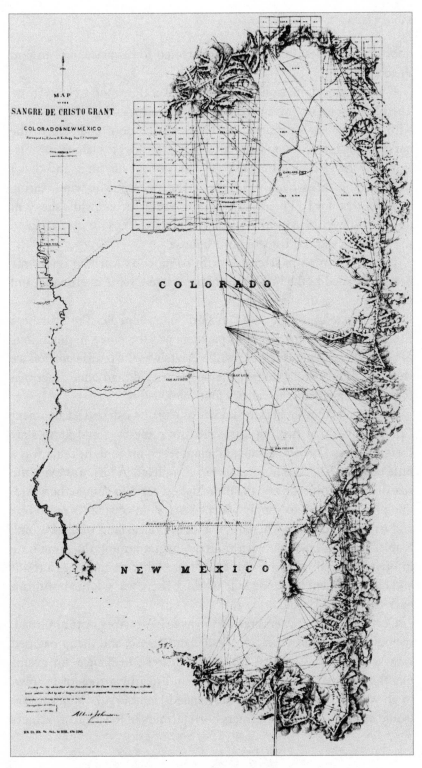

Sangre de Cristo land grant, just under a million acres, in 1880

ProQuest Congressional Record database

door of the nearest house and was directed to his place, just around the corner.

It was a handsome stone house with tall cottonwood trees in front. The big man about my age (60) in jeans, boots, and a western shirt, with muttonchop sideburns, who opened the door and said to the barking dog inside, "Don't bite him," was Harold. I explained my mission, and he said he'd be happy to talk history anytime, and that I should come back when I was ready. In the meantime his wife, hearing that I worked for La Puente, asked me to wait a second while she went upstairs. She returned with a stack of nice used jeans for me to take to the Rainbow's End thrift store in Alamosa.

Now, a few months later and with some book learning under my belt, I returned to the house. Harold answered, remembered me, and said he could spare some time.

His knowledge of the area was fairly encyclopedic. The Trinchera Estate created by Gilpin and his partners was the piney, mountainous area northeast of us, and the Costilla Estate was the prairie portion we were on. The Costilla County manager, he said, had once described this arrangement as "the valley's first subdivision."

The owners of what became known as Costilla Estates Development Company bet that two big infrastructure projects would jump-start their business. One was a dam and giant reservoir, and the other was a little railroad. The Sanchez Reservoir, completed in 1911, was twice the size of any in Colorado and the fifth-highest earthen dam in the world. The plan was for it to supply water to a system of smaller reservoirs and irrigation ditches, whereupon a lot of prairie land would become arable. The San Luis Southern railroad, begun around the same time in Blanca, would serve the farms and towns that sprang up as a result and connect them to the outside world. "There was a lot of optimism back then," said Harold.

Costilla Estates' owners created towns to be serviced by the railroad, including Blanca, San Acacio, Mesita, and Jaroso, and then imagined ways to attract "emigrants" from the Midwest. In Blanca, for example, they offered anyone buying farmland nearby a free lot in town to go with it. Mesita was originally called Hamburg, in hopes that it would attract a group of German-born farmers in Iowa; those farmers never came. But in 1913, some twenty-five to thirty families who were Seventh-Day Adventists moved to Jaroso, including Harold's grandfather. They established an Adventist school, with its own farm and dairy herd. But Harold said that the railroad, once envisioned to extend to lines in New Mexico, had never made it farther south than directly across the road from his house—thirty-one miles of track total. Today the path of the tracks is still visible, but everything else has disappeared.

On a summer trip to New Hampshire, my wife had visited a secondhand shop and bought a booklet entitled *The Fertile Lands of Colorado and Northern New Mexico.* Published in 1912 by the Denver & Rio Grande Railroad, it extolled—indeed, exaggerated—the agricultural opportunities existing in parts of Colorado for the very audience Harold described.

> The earliest American explorers of Colorado termed the San Luis Valley "an earthly paradise." . . . Today the San Luis Valley seems to have just started, both in the area of irrigated land to be developed and in the uses to which that irrigated land may be put. . . .
>
> The mountain streams that flow into the valley are all crystal clear and all teem with trout. The mountains on all sides are full of game. With a perfect out-of-doors climate, camping and fishing are favorite amusements of the San Luis Valley farmers. . . .
>
> In spite of the delightful climate, the good water and the many advantages, land in the San Luis Valley can be obtained at prices so low and on terms so reasonable that it is within the reach of men whose means would not allow them a foothold anywhere else. Every year hundreds of renters from the farms of the Middle West have flocked into the San Luis Valley, bought land and have started on the road to prosperity, and there is still room for thousands more and on the same easy terms. . . .
>
> A section of the San Luis Valley which in a few years has been transformed from a sheep pasture sparsely inhabited by Mexicans into a prosperous empire is what is known as the Costilla Estates. . . . Two years ago the original Mexican land grant was a vast sagebrush area, utilized for the ranging of cattle and sheep; today it is dotted with cultivated farms producing record break-

The cover of a promotional pamphlet
published by the Denver & Rio Grande Railroad, 1912
Copyright 1912 by Frank A. Wadleigh, General Passenger Agent, Denver

ing crops of wheat, oats, barley, alfalfa, field peas, potatoes, sugar beets, vegetables of all kinds and fruits.

Costilla Estates and the railroad "made good money" during World War I, said Harold, but "things went quiet" by 1920. In 1924 the railroad went bankrupt, and shortly thereafter Costilla Estates fired nearly all its employees. Today, said Harold, "we're down to the last two families that settled here"—his and one other. Shortages of water had been an ongoing problem, and continued to be: from 1933 to 1952, the water at the Sanchez Reservoir had averaged only 16 percent of its planned capacity. Farms that survived typically drew some of their irrigation from wells. Betting on that strategy, the Bankers Life insurance company, owned by John D. MacArthur, bought the land once owned by Costilla Estates around 1952. (Around the same time, MacArthur invested heavily, and much more lucratively, in southern Florida real estate.)* MacArthur and Bankers Life soon loaned $175,000 to new owners of the railroad, hoping it might get back on its feet.

Water from wells, used to grow potatoes, had taken on increased importance in the previous twenty years; farmers kept the potatoes cool by digging large cellars into the earth, many of which, defunct, still dot the valley. Bankers Life drilled its first one in 1956. In 1957 the potato market crashed. In 1958, the railroad finally gave up the ghost, abandoning twenty-nine miles of track and leaving only two in operation near Blanca. The rails were picked up and sold to the Climax Molybdenum mine near Leadville.

Bankers Life scaled way back, stopped growing crops, leased its land to cattlemen.

Troy and his family moved in.

History doesn't always declare itself in the American West, where there is so much emphasis on the present and the future. This is espe-

---

* Malcolm S. Forbes, another storied American financier, bought into the valley in 1969, purchasing what had become known as Trinchera Ranch, the northern, mountainous portion of the original Sangre de Cristo land grant. The land was, for a time, the largest private land holding in Colorado and included three peaks over fourteen thousand feet tall.

cially true of scarcely settled places such as the Punche Valley, where the internet will tell you practically nothing and the local library not much more.

But in the part of the flats where I was living, there was clearly a past to be uncovered. Every ruin of a homestead had a story, every disappearing track on a field, every tailing from a mine. The subdivision had a story and, before that, agriculture and ranching had theirs. The transience of local residents made these stories hard to uncover, but some of them lived on in the person of Troy.

Troy's dad had been a hard-living cowboy who sometimes wore a six-shooter and was no stranger to bar fights. He ran cattle in the area—Troy said his parents had owned various parcels of land and grazing rights on others—and had moved when Troy was ten, to a house catty-corner from where he currently lived. But his family's presence in the valley went back further. After I spoke with Harold, I gave Troy a copy of P. R. Griswold's *Colorado's Loneliest Railroad: The San Luis Southern*, recommended to me by Harold Anderson. He had never seen it.

The book had lots of archival photos, and as he slowly turned the pages, Troy was riveted. "That's Georgiana West. We called her Grandma Georgia," he said, "and there was her sister, Beulah." He had multiple connections to the book. In the end, I gave it to him. Later he offered to drive me around, describe how things had been, and try to explain to me the things in the man-made landscape that made no sense.

Our first stop was his three-bedroom, white-painted cinder-block house with a red roof, electrified and heated by a wood-burning stove. It had shrubs around it and the largest tree I had seen on the flats—a not-huge Chinese elm—which gave it a look of longevity. Extending out from one side was a series of small garages and many old trucks, mostly Fords. This house, said Troy, had belonged to the manager of the Bankers Life agricultural operation that raised cows, chickens, and potatoes and other crops.

The next stop was about fifty feet away, directly across the road—and like most prairie people, Troy drove everywhere, walked nowhere. We parked between two old buildings that had also been a part of the ranch. Both had the white masonry walls and red roofs, but they were in worse shape. The larger, a semi-ruin with no more doors or windows, had been a bunkhouse that held forty to sixty workers, depending on the season. The smaller one had held the kitchen and mess hall but was now a bungalow that Troy rented to his friend Bobby and Bobby's wife, Sonia, a couple he had known for years. Just out of sight to the northwest, he said, had been three potato cellars—large storage facilities that were mainly belowground and had once had roofs. Another one, now converted to his trash pit, sat behind his house. Matt Little's DIY Hunting Map showed "Sky Valley Ranch" superimposed over our exact location, though Troy said he couldn't recall the place having ever been called that.

Bankers Life had owned everything out here, Troy explained— about seventy-seven thousand acres that extended all the way to New Mexico. A lot of the firm's capital investment had been in the wells and irrigation ditches that could make agriculture possible in such a dry place. Almost all of these agricultural wells had since been capped, but he drove me to one nearby that "somebody was supposed to cap, but they never did." We got out and looked down into the bore—a pipe inside a sixteen-inch casing. When Troy dropped some pebbles into the well, we heard them ping or boing against the sides, then finally splash, faintly; the wells were nearly four hundred feet deep. Since we were off-grid, they had run on propane and on diesel. The land around them had been cultivated some fifty to seventy years ago, which was why the vegetation on it looked different from land that was untouched: mostly it was kochia, an invasive plant sometimes called "railroad weed." Cattle liked it, unfortunately, and would come to the area to graze. Troy told me, "The brush hasn't really come back."

As we drove around, Troy showed me another well that was supposed to have been capped but in fact still provided a small, illegal oasis for cattle a few miles away. Costilla County was a place where things like that could happen. For a time, water had been pumped from the Rio Grande onto fields, and there had even been a small dam in the river to serve irrigation, but it washed out in 1952. Taking water from the Rio Grande was now strictly forbidden, as I mentioned earlier, in part because the state of Colorado was obligated to send a certain quantity of water downstream to New Mexico.

Troy paused here and there to point out old ditches that had once been full of water. I had seen some of this land scores of times but never noticed the traces of the past until Troy pointed them out. "The soil is actually really fertile," said Troy. "The problem is keeping it wet." To try to prevent water in the ditches from percolating into the ground, some had been lined with plastic for a time, he said. And the amounts of water pumped from the ground had been prodigious—one year, he said, they actually pumped so much water that it lowered the water table below where his family's well could reach, with the result that their pump burned out.

A key characteristic of this land, one of the things that had originally intrigued me, was the huge grid of lines across it. The roads had not been there when Troy was a kid; nor did they exist when Bankers Life owned the ranch. They came in the late 1970s, when the land morphed in meaning from something that could be ranched to something that could be lived on—or, more accurately, something that could be sold with the *idea* that it could be lived on.

Residential land sales had boomed in the United States after World War II, particularly in Florida and California. Developers would buy a large piece of agricultural land and subdivide it into many lots. Subdividing could generate relatively quick profits; it was, in the words of one historian, "instrumental in opening the West." County governments were often in favor because subdivisions would increase their tax base. The more reputable developers would invest in infrastructure to make the place more attractive and livable: they would build roads, sewer and water lines, access to electricity. Some would go further and provide swimming pools, golf courses, or community centers; some would build houses. But other developers would not. With rock-bottom prices and creative marketing, often through ads in newspapers and magazines, they could find buyers for land that was only barely habitable or not habitable at all. The classic Florida land scam of the 1960s featured couples in the Midwest planning for retirement and buying a lot sight unseen, only to discover that they owned a piece of swamp.

I wanted to learn who had subdivided the prairie of the San Luis Valley: who had drawn those lines in the 1970s, etched them into the land, defiled it, in a way—and then basically walked away. I found that there had been many promoters of these low-cost subdivisions, so I focused on the one who was behind the roads in the area where I lived.

His name was Al Perry and he was a son of Italian immigrants who never finished high school. Perry, who died in 1994, owned or worked at different bars and clubs in Los Angeles, his son Tony told me. Al was a player, a "rounder," according to Tony, with many friends met through nightlife. One of Al's acquaintances was a big-time, down-market developer named M. Penn Phillips, perhaps best known for his efforts to create the Salton Sea resort in southern California—and for its marketing, in which potential buyers were flown in gratis for a "free vacation" and then subjected to high-pressure sales techniques. Phillips encouraged Al to get into real estate and he did, said Tony, selling land for Phillips in his Hesperia and Victorville subdivisions in Apple Valley, on the desert edge of Los Angeles (now part of metropolitan San Bernardino).

Overall, business was good, and Al started to wonder if he should go out on his own. Nevada was less heavily developed and regulated, and Al Perry got a lead on some ranch land for sale outside of Elko that he thought could be profitably subdivided. "My dad thought, *I could buy this grazing land and turn it into a jillion dollars,*" said Tony Perry. Al found partners and moved his family to Elko, where Tony finished high school and helped his dad with sales in his spare time. Al was selling through the mail, a novel strategy at the time, and business was good.

Tony Perry was seventy-two years old when I tracked him down in Grand Junction, Colorado. In the living room of a suburban house he shared with a fitness-oriented wife and their golden retriever, he told me that he had done a stint in the army after high school and came home thinking about doing more land sales. Though his relationship with his father was troubled—Al, a longtime alcoholic, had left him to be raised by his grandparents when he was a child—his dad was connected in real estate and would help him get started. The same real estate agent who had pointed Al to the ranch property in Elko had other ideas nearer to where he lived, in Alamosa, Colorado. The guy's name was Lonnie Brownlow. Al sent Tony out to meet Lonnie and assess the possibilities.

"We introduce ourselves, Lonnie is a good ol' Southern Baptist type guy, really nice, but Lonnie watched out for himself, too," said Tony. "Anyway, he gives us a tour of the San Luis Valley, we head south toward Antonito, we go east to Manassa, we go beyond that, and he takes us to this ground. See here it is, he takes us to this fence post, right along the Rio Grande River, and he says, It goes twenty miles south, it goes ten miles east." They were looking at the future Rio Grande Ranches, where Troy and the Grubers would live.

Tony was intrigued, but he was even more excited by parcels closer to Blanca Peak, as a photo of land with that mountain in the background would help with advertising. "I called my dad and Alvie Linnick"—attorney Albert R. Linnick, a partner of Al's—"and said we just gotta buy this ground, gotta buy it. But come to find out it's owned by John D. MacArthur, do you know who that is? He was one of the richest men in the world at the time! [But] MacArthur wanted out of that business—he was moving his stuff to Kissimmee, Florida," near Orlando. And so a deal was made. The venture was owned by the G-R-P Corporation, whose partners were Al Perry, Albert Linnick, and a marketing and advertising guy named Richard Greenberg. Tony Perry, his then wife, and their two kids moved to Alamosa to run the operation. Al Perry followed them a month or two later to help Tony get established and to keep an eye on things.

The first subdivision was in a northern part of the flats—San Luis Valley Ranches, close to Blanca. The last and largest, added in the late 1970s, was Rio Grande Ranches. In all, he thought, they created nearly forty thousand five-acre lots in Costilla County. Tony said his dad did the talking with the Costilla County commissioners, who were not sophisticated in the ways of real estate development but quickly grasped the tax revenue the subdivision could produce. As developers, the Perrys and their partners were minimalists. "Basically we built roads," said Tony. "Hired guys with graders and gave 'em a month." They also staked out the lots, so that anyone interested could see what they bought. But most never did—they bought through the mail, sight unseen.

The marketing was more sophisticated than it had been in Elko. Richard Greenberg brought in Lee Rogers, a direct-mail pioneer. Tony Perry told me that Rogers had schemed up "contests" in which readers

Land advertisement in *The Hartford Courant*
Historical Newspapers (ProQuest)

were shown an outline of Abraham Lincoln in profile or of the state of Montana and asked if they could identify it. "Do you recognize this? Send us your answer." "They didn't care what your answer was," said Tony. "You'd get a letter back saying, *You're a winner,* along with an offer to buy something cheap." He told me that Rogers was "one of the early ones to collect names and addresses in lists, of guys who bought rifles, or western novels, or subscriptions to *Field & Stream,* et cetera. We'd pay per thousand and could predict the response rate per thousand. And how many then would buy. Who would be a better potential buyer than somebody who loves the West? The advertising itself was the key" for these mail-order land sales.

I found ads the company had placed in *TV Guide,* the *Chicago Tribune, The Hartford Courant,* and *The Washington Post.* "Good Recreation Land IS Great Investment Land!" said one, under photos of people golfing, skiing, fishing, and snowmobiling. And "Claim Your Spread at RIO GRANDE RANCHES of COLORADO. Colorado Mountain Peaks Reach Out to You Like Beckoning Arms with an Investment Opportunity as Big as the Land itself!" And "THE SMALLEST RANCH IS 4 FOOTBALL FIELDS BIG!"

Typically, a corner of the ad was a form you could mail in for a "free 16-page brochure." Tony Perry showed me the packets they'd sent out. Glossy, colorful, and nicely produced, they included a map, a reprint of a 1971 article from *Reader's Digest* entitled "Colorado—'The State Nearest Heaven,'" and a brochure that struck the same notes as the ads. It told of rapid economic growth, healthy living, and recreational opportunities, and beckoned readers to a place that was "the Best of 2 Worlds / Western Leisure & City Luxury," though the cities mentioned (Denver, Colorado Springs) were hours away. The thirty-two photos in the brochure showed scenes of mountains, lakes, winter sports—and a single photo that might have been taken on the flats (a cowboy standing in a field with his horse).

I told Tony that I thought this marketing was deceptive. He countered by pointing out that, overall, his customers had been quite satisfied.

"We were selling dreams—you heard me say that before," he said. "Some guy living in Chicago with all the insanity, and I could live in Colorado with all this serenity and watch the eagles fly. We were not duping anyone—I want to reemphasize that. Our brochures said if you don't like this, we'll give you your money back."

People responded, and they bought. The terms for five acres ranged from $15 to $30 down, $15 to $30 a month, no interest, $1,950 or so total price. Tony set up a land office in Blanca for walk-ins and for mail-order customers who might want to see the land; he told me that "ninety percent liked what they saw." In-person sales, meanwhile, provided an opportunity for future real estate salespeople to get into the game. A brother-in-law of Geneva Duarte, mother of Angelo the fighter, made money selling five-acre lots for a 10 percent commission while he was a student at Adams State—and bought one himself. "People probably thought, *These five-acre lots, if we don't buy one now, we probably won't be able to afford it later,*" Maggie Duarte told me. His future boss, Chet Choman, sold them, too. "There was a mystique to owning a piece of Colorado that kind of lends itself to people from outside the area," he said. He remembered how the singer John Denver, originally named Henry John Deutschendorf Jr. came to Colorado from a childhood spent on air force bases in states including Arizona, Alabama, and Texas, and rebranded himself in the same spirit.

Choman, the owner of Colorado Realty & Land Company, in Alamosa, and the chair of the board of La Puente (he was also a cofounder of the group), told me that the land deals were what brought him to the valley. As a twenty-three-year-old living in Denver, he heard about five-acre tracts in a subdivision called Mount Blanca Valley Ranches, whose owner, he said, had probably copied Al Perry's idea. "It was my first experience in business or anything else. I came out here to look at it and I thought, *Wow, this is kinda neat! Mountain in the background and fifteen bucks a month.* So I went ahead and I told my friends about it." They were interested, too. "After I'd sold a couple of parcels, I got in touch with the company and said, Look, you're selling these for nothing down. If I could get a hundred dollars down, would you allow me to keep a hundred dollars? They said yes." Choman said he then told all his friends and relatives about the offer and in the first month sold twenty or twenty-five lots.

"Guy calls me up and says, 'You outsold our whole sales department.' He says, 'I'm coming to Denver, I got a proposition for you.' I said okay, go to lunch, and the guy says, 'You know we spent three thousand dollars last month on advertising and we sold some land. But you actually sold more land than our whole sales team did. I'd like to hire you.' I said, 'Hire me to do what?' 'Well, come out, sit in the office out there, and sell five-acre tracts.'" The company offered Choman $300 a month, but at the end of the summer the boss wrote him a bonus check for $10,000. "Well, ten thousand dollars to me was all the money in the world; this was 1972." Choman moved to the valley and surprised himself by selling more land.

Much of the work, he said, was driving people who were considering a purchase or had already bought lots through the mail out to the flats to see their land. The rest was sitting in the land office and calling prospective customers on the phone.

"We would use this rap on the phone: 'Do you smoke?' . . . The guy would say, 'No I don't smoke'. And we'd say, 'You know what? You're probably saving fifteen dollars a month by not smoking.' Or if the guy would answer, 'Yes, I smoke,' we'd say, 'Well, you know, for the same amount of money that you're wasting on cigarettes, you could buy a five-acre tract.' And the psychology was, what would happen, is that guy in Illinois would tell his neighbors, 'Yep, I just bought a ranch in Colorado. I'm gonna run out there this summer and check it out, see what it looks like.'

"A five-acre parcel was worth a lot more in Chicago than it was in the valley."

Mail-order land sales had been causing concern in the government for several years by this point. The U.S. Senate Special Committee on Aging's Subcommittee on Frauds and Misrepresentations Affecting the Elderly had held hearings on the subject in 1964; the senators' particular concern was that elderly people and those contemplating retirement were especially vulnerable to being gulled by land promoters. (A star witness was the historian Robert Caro, then a journalist at *Newsday*, who had reported on land scams in a series called "Misery Acres.") In 1976, the Federal Trade Commission took up the charge, aiming at Colorado land sales—in the San Luis Valley, mainly, but also in South Park. By sending materials through the mail that suggested that buyers were making an investment that was likely to appreciate in value, and by misrepresenting the value of the land being sold, the FTC alleged, companies like the G-R-P Corporation had been unfair and deceptive. (Bankers Life, which had financed some of the transactions, was also named.) The FTC claimed that the "lots are of little or no use or value to purchasers either as investments or homesites," that they have "virtually no use at present or in the foreseeable future," and that they are "not useable as homesites because of . . . the lack or unreasonable cost of utilities, the difficulty in obtaining home construction financing, the remote location of the property and the poor quality of the land."

Real estate people I spoke with said it was the suggestion that the land was a good investment that got the companies in the most trouble. Indeed, most purchasers of the land found themselves unable to resell it for anything close to what they had paid, if they could sell it at all. In 1979, the companies agreed to cancel debts and otherwise refund up to $14 million to purchasers of the land.

Tony Perry said that the episode had set them back but hadn't destroyed them. They did have to stop including Blanca Peak in their advertising, had to stop suggesting that the land was "similar or comparable to urban, metropolitan and industrial areas as well as to mountain resort areas and recreation areas." They also had to be more rigorous in their disclosures to buyers. "The FTC and others thought I was full of crap, but I believed in it," Tony said.

What was heartening, said Tony, was that so few buyers felt taken advantage of or robbed. Chet Choman and others confirmed this, that it was difficult to find many buyers whose sense of grievance was equal to the FTC's. "The fact is," said Chet, "when you're buying real estate, it's very, very unusual, almost impossible, to buy something with no down payment and no interest. The government suspected that there had to be something going on, that people must be getting ripped off. But the reality was, the last people to feel that way were the people who bought it." Most, as Tony said, had been buying a dream, and that's what they got.

Choman did not feel he had taken part in a scam. He told me that back when he was selling cheap lots at a steady clip, he had expected to see a city rise in the middle of the prairie "within maybe ten years, just because so many people were buying in. I really expected they'd be moving out there." Nobody felt that way by the time I got to the valley, in 2017. Most or all of the subdividers had sold out and moved on after the initial boom, because that was the subdivider way. One man who sold land in the Perrys' subdivisions after they'd left the area observed that middle-class people had seldom moved onto their lots. He thought that sometimes it was because they belatedly realized how much it would cost to drill a well and run a line to the nearest electrical pole, and sometimes it was because they realized that actually retiring in such a bare-bones place was daunting. Instead, it was mainly poor people, those who seldom had the money for a well or even a septic system, who came to live the reality of land ownership on the flats.

The FTC had been right about the cheap lots being of questionable value as investments. Most had scarcely appreciated in value over the thirty or forty years of their existence—a rarity in American real estate. The reason, evident to all, was that the subdividers had created a vast oversupply of lots—all without water, electricity, or sewer lines. Not only had some lots never sold, but many, many others had reverted to the county when buyers had stopped paying taxes. General real estate agents lost interest in selling single lots, by and large—it was hardly worth the gas money to show somebody distant land for a commission of possibly $180. Eventually land sales moved to the internet. What brought Matt and countless others to the valley was not a newspaper advertisement but searching online for "cheap land colorado." That would typically produce hits for 5-acre lots at sites like landwatch.com, landsofamerica.com, zillow.com, landandfarm.com, and landhub.com.

Lots for sale can also be found on Craigslist and on eBay. Amid various ads I found for San Luis Valley property when I first got interested was this one:

☆ **Caution--Cheap Desert Land** ⊠

This land is worthless and its only value is so you can tell your friends you own land in Colorado. You will get tired of paying taxes on it and it will be resold to the next sucker. You would be hard pressed to do anything with it as it is a oven in summer and north pole in winter. If you think you can leave something of value there and come back next summer and it will still be there---------Why do you think it is vacant?? Nobody except you has found it yet? People want to make a living off you selling you this stuff----over and over again. COSTILLO COUNTY IS OUTLAWING LONG TERM CAMPING ON YOUR OWN LAND----THEY DON"T WANT YOU THERE. Google it for yourself

• do NOT contact me with unsolicited services or offers

Craigslist

The sellers were often investors who'd bought a number of lots during a county tax sale. One prolific seller of land in Rio Grande Ranches had sold mostly on eBay, as "guatemike." Many of the residents of my part of the flats had bought from him. His long description of the land was enlightening and truthful, but the more time I spent on the flats, the less I agreed with the statement that it wasn't important to see the lots in person because they are "pretty much the same." A lot could be littered with trash from a previous owner or from a messy neighbor upwind. It could be all by itself (most were), or it could be next door to somebody with a lot of dogs running loose or tied up and barking. It could be in a low place where a well was less expensive to drill, or it could be somewhere elevated where drilling a well would cost thousands of dollars more. And it might have a decent cellular signal or none at all.

At the Grubers' first property, if I needed a good cell signal for an important call, I might drive five minutes to higher ground. That is how, one day, I found myself on Jerry Road. It was fairly close to the Grubers' place but significantly higher, generally affording me three bars of signal instead of one or two or none. As I finished a call that day, I sat in my truck with the engine off, felt the wind buffet it back and forth, and noticed how lovely and empty the area was. Neither houses nor junk were visible. The land had some little ups and downs—for purposes of cell signal, you'd want to avoid a ravine. But for purposes of a homesite, you might like that corner over there, or the cul-de-sac over here. I cruised around. The angles were irregular; it wasn't all a grid. There were some curves. The streets had funny short names, some visible on street signs: Tom, Dawn, Duck, Sot (Sot?!), Joe, Jerry, Ned, Fred, He, She. (The people who'd platted this land had clearly begun running short on ideas for road names at this point.) The sun came out as I idled on Jerry Road, and I saw something move. I got out and discovered that it was a horned toad—I hadn't seen one since I was a kid—still slow and easy to catch. That was a good omen. And Jerry was my father's name. I decided to look into buying land on Jerry Road.

On the Web I could find only one listing on Jerry Road—an unusual set of three adjoining parcels, pricier than what I wanted. Next I went to the county assessor's website. Here it was possible to learn the name and mailing address of the owner of every lot. Some were individuals; some were companies. I decided to do a small mail campaign, writing a total of fifteen notes to owners of lots on Jerry and nearby roads. In each letter, I explained that I was not an investor but a guy renting on the flats now looking for his own lot, and I asked if they were interested in selling. I gave my home address, email address, and phone number.

By a month later, three people had replied. Two did so by phone. I told both callers that I was a writer and interested in learning the story behind their ownership.

The first caller was a woman living just north of Los Angeles who had owned her five acres since 1993. Taxes on it were $49 a year. She had bought the land for under $3,000 and asked me if I thought it had gone up in value. I told her no. At the same time she bought, her brother, girlfriend, former sister-in-law, and cousin also bought lots. She told me she had always thought of retiring there, perhaps in a straw-bale house. She had also thought maybe she should fence the property so that nobody would get hurt on it and sue her. But her real hope all these years later was that the government would come in and offer her something better for it; that was what had transpired when her father had owned land in the Everglades. I told her I couldn't see it happening where her Colorado property was. *Well, you would say that,* I imagined her thinking. In any event, she said, she wasn't interested in selling.

The next landowner who called turned out to be a professional investor, Albert Jibilian, also in the Los Angeles area. He had traded a lot of oil leases, he told me, but also bought and sold some real estate. He didn't remember owning the lot I was interested in but said he owned more than a hundred parcels in the valley. He offered me the parcel I was interested in for $2,250—a fair price—and I said I'd think about it.

"I could tell you some horror stories," he said, when I asked how he came to own the land. I said I was all ears.

He'd come out thirty years before and visited with some Costilla County officials. "We have all these tax lien properties," they told him, explaining that the parcels brought in no income. "They made me a deal I couldn't refuse. They said, 'If you buy 'em all, here's a number.' My eyes lit up! They said, 'Not only that, we'll make sure nobody else shows up at the sale.'

"So when they advertised it, they put the wrong date deliberately. The sale was going to be a week before." At the sale, "the stenographers go item by item, two freaking hours though nobody's bidding, nobody's there but me."

Another year, "they held the sale in December. And it's snowing. I forget the name of the little motel half a block from the courthouse. Only two other people were there, so the day of the sale, we decide, *I'll bid on this, you bid on that.*"

Personal relationships with county commissioners had been key to these opportunities, he said. He named one he still remembered well. "I was teaching her son to do math, or was it her daughter? This is going back twenty years, the daughter was in the hospital, she needed two hundred dollars to get her out. I sent it and said, *No, I don't want the money back.*" As in, *Hint, hint.*

Jibilian told me that he had started writing a memoir, "The Wrong-Way Kid: How to Do Everything the Wrong Way." He said, "The first two chapters were mostly about Costilla County."

I had no way of verifying Jibilian's claims, of course, but they were of a piece with what others had told me about lot sales in the valley and the early days of the subdivisions. Back then, when there were few zoning restrictions, planning departments, or state regulations around subdivisions, especially in poor counties, the county commissioners had a great deal of power when it came to approving deals. Another person with a long involvement in valley real estate told me, "You'd buy land and plat it—you wouldn't necessarily even need to survey it or put in roads—then take it to the county. And sometimes they'd say, *How much for me?*"

One real estate agent told me about the time an aspiring developer invited a county official to the Cotton Club in Colorado Springs. "It was kind of a social club, but upstairs it had a bunch of rooms. And it was kind of a glorified whorehouse. Anyway, so they're wining and dining this guy, they get their deal accepted, and then they get a phone call. He said, 'You know what, I got a dose of gonorrhea, and gave it to my wife, and she's in the process of divorcing me, and you're never gonna get a subdivision done in Costilla County again.' That's what it was like in the early seventies.

"These guys would go in and buy the cheapest land that they could, and they'd go in and cut some roads, typically they're supposed to survey it. The survey methods at the time—and I hate to mention names, because it kind of casts a negative shadow on certain people—but there were two brothers that were surveyors, and they'd go out there with a chain, typically about a hundred-foot chain, and one would stick it in here and kinda measure it, and that was essentially the survey. And they'd do the first lines. It's not something you'd use today.

"And essentially they weren't paying anything. There was a guy by the name of Cochran who had a road grader, and he'd go out there and grade the roads. They were all supposed to be to county standards, and the county was supposed to make sure that they were, but the county, they didn't care particularly—they were getting money, they were getting this property on the tax rolls, and once it got cut into five-acre parcels, the valuation would go up quite a bit, so taxes went up quite a bit, too." And everybody was happy.

Before buying Albert Jibilian's lot for $2,250, I thought I'd see if I could get cheaper land by finding a lot with a tax lien on it, paying the taxes for two years, and then applying for the title. If it worked, I could become a landowner for $200 to $300.

The county records showed three lots near Jerry Road that were in arrears. I went to the county assessor's office in San Luis and said I wanted to pay the taxes; the clerk there was happy to accommodate me. But in the end, it didn't work out. All three landowners, notified by the county that they could lose their lots, paid their taxes. Costilla County dutifully notified me by mail each time it happened and sent me a check with interest added on. I told Matt Little about my experience one day when we were driving in the area. It had been fun to think I might become a landowner, I said, and now I was disappointed. Matt said he had done the same thing, with the same result.

In time, the county held a tax sale—but wanted $3,000 apiece for the five-acre lots in my area. None were near Jerry Road, and it wasn't a fire-sale price.

With my time at the Grubers feeling like it had run its course, I started trying to think more practically. Wherever I bought land, I'd want to leave my camper trailer when I was gone and not have it broken into or stolen. So I'd need a neighbor nearby whom I could trust to look after things.

The Grubers said they'd happily store my trailer. And Paul, the gay man I'd met early on, did, too. He was writer-friendly and told me how, years before, he had stored the trailer of a writer of self-help books, Rebecca Merriman, who was also a schoolteacher in Tennessee. She loved spending summers in Colorado and would drive out in her Jeep Cherokee. She referred to her camping and trailering experiences in books with titles like *Writing Out the Storm, Simply Happy,* and *Simply Free.* She found five acres not far from Paul by buying the lot off the tax lien list in San Luis. "I've been looking around for a tiny travel trailer, used of course, to take with me out to Colorado where I plan to stay the months of July and August," she wrote. Paul told me she'd found one, small and pink, that she'd leave on his land when she was away; when she arrived, he'd tow it to her land for her.

Merriman struggled with being bipolar and with social anxiety, as Paul did, too. "Sometimes bordering on agoraphobic, I couldn't bear the thought of interacting with people," she wrote. "It wasn't that I didn't love people. I did. But with people came noise and confusion and unpredictability. To a frazzled mind these are scary entanglements to be avoided at all cost." One summer she was involved in a car wreck near Colorado Springs, which injured both her and her dogs. Paul teared up when he told me that her husband called him later that year to say that she had killed herself with a gun.

Paul said he'd sold her trailer for $300 to a man who had lived within sight of Frank and Stacy's old place. The man later killed himself in it. The trailer ended up in the possession of a family Paul didn't like who lived across the road from him. "They used it as a shitter" before taking it apart for scrap, he told me. "I had to look at it every day."

Near Troy's little compound, maybe fifty yards to the east, sat a mobile home that had once been a modular office at the Los Alamos National Laboratory, outside Santa Fe. Its current owners, a retired couple from Mississippi, had added a front porch, roofed along its full length, and that's where Troy introduced me to Billy and Martha Jo Donaldson, whom he adored. They were summer people and loved the area.

The Donaldsons' five acres with a trailer

They owned a second property, about a hundred yards to the north of Troy, which had sat empty for the past five years. It consisted of a big old trailer from the 1980s and a couple of weathered sheds. From the road, I had seen the faded blue mobile home baking in the summer sun. A barbed-wire fence surrounded much of it, but sections had collapsed. There was a collapsed chicken coop, a mailbox fallen off its post, two burn barrels. The back side was harder to see, but there was a dog door, an obsolete satellite dish, and an old wind turbine on a short mast, still twirling.

A retired carpet installer named Terry, with whom Troy had become friends, had lived there for a time until he died, "basically from drinking," Troy said, in 2014. Not long after, the Donaldsons had bought it from Terry's family, thinking one day their children might want it. They didn't, and the place was in poor repair.

"It's a nice property, though," Troy told me. "It's got a well and a septic."

I found myself staring at it every time I drove by. It was not beautiful, but it was strangely intriguing. I suppose I was coming under the spell of land: it was hard to be surrounded by such beautiful, inexpensive land all the time and not imagine owning a plot of it.

But ownership itself was not enough, because what was the point? Without an additional investment of several thousand dollars for a septic system, I'd be forever vulnerable to county code enforcement if I tried to live on my land. I'd seen so many people come to grief on this point, have their lives turned upside down, that I knew I wanted a different path. To me, the property near Troy was a jackpot. Though I wasn't sure it was livable, it even had an old trailer on it. And every bit as important as those features, it had Troy next door—a steady person, a person I liked, a person whose presence might keep away prairie thieves who steal when people are away.

I asked Troy to call me if the place came up for sale. The call came about a year and a half later. Billy Donaldson had died; Martha Jo thought it was time to sell. She and I discussed it over the phone. The annual taxes were $48.74 ("We always laughed when we got the bill"). The neighbors were high-quality. She was asking $20,000. I offered $15,000.

Sold.

5

Ownership

The numbers were small, just a few thousand. But across the country the cause is extremely popular. They say—quite proudly—that they are the "sans-dents," the great unwashed, the forgotten majority from the sticks. And they've had enough.

—BBC World Service on discontent
in the French countryside, December 2018

• Number of the twenty least prosperous US congressional districts that are represented by Republicans: 16.
• Of the twenty most prosperous districts that are represented by Democrats: 20
• Percentage of statewide elections in the Deep South won by Republicans since 2008: 97

—*Harper's Index,* April 2019

THE SNOW WAS SHIN-DEEP and slushy when I returned to the valley in early 2019 as a property owner. I say property owner, not homeowner, because it was unclear whether the seventy-foot-long blue mobile home from the 1980s could become habitable. Troy Zinn had said he'd give me a tour, and so I climbed into his old Ford diesel pickup and we chugged across the road to my property, about a hundred yards away. Rather than stop and open the front gate, Troy just drove around it, through a gap between T-posts. We parked in front of the mobile home.

Troy trudged from his truck to the trailer—he had some trouble negotiating the unpacked snow with his prosthetic leg, which normally you didn't notice. The mobile home didn't look any prettier in the winter. It sat a few feet off the ground on cinder blocks, though its original axles and tires were still there. You could see them because the perimeter skirting—cheap sheets of wood known as OSB—that had once sealed up the space underneath had now mostly fallen off, so you could see through to the other side. I followed Troy up the rickety front stairs, looked up at the fake security camera as he found the key for the door, which wasn't closed tightly—you could see it had been kicked in before—and went inside.

As I had feared, it was a mess. Boxes of junk were everywhere, filled variously with old clothes, plumbing parts, VHS movies, dishes, credit card statements, and family photos. A bookshelf held jars of random screws. Rodents had partly unstuffed the couch. There was mouse poop galore and several sprung mousetraps with their victims' desiccated skeletons and little tufts of fur. Wooden paneling had popped off the walls and ceilings, there was water damage on the ceilings and floors, and some doors hung off their hinges. A red shag rug in a tiny bedroom might possibly have been the only original floor covering. "Frankly," said Troy, "it's hardly been touched since Terry died."

It was true: there were dirty dishes in the sink. The refrigerator hadn't been opened; I peered in with trepidation and saw a few eggs, a jar of mayonnaise, a carton of buttermilk. Old toiletries were still in the medicine cabinets, old cleaning supplies filled spaces under sinks. A calendar from 2013 hung on the wall—the space was a time capsule. You could consider it junk or you could consider it an archaeological site; I teetered between the two.

Outdoors, Troy showed me two decaying sheds, painted the same sky blue as the trailer. A third shed, the smallest, had the shape of a miniature Dutch Colonial barn and looked like it had been built from a kit. This was the power shed. It contained batteries and components for solar power that Troy told me had been state-of-the-art twenty years before, when it had been set up. Next door to this, the small wind turbine atop a tower supported by guy wires whirred fitfully; Troy said it had stopped producing electricity. I expressed surprise that it was all still here after so many years with nobody home. "Well, I keep an eye on it," said Troy.

We returned to Troy's house, where he filled me in on the story of the property. Tom and Melinda Wilkinson had moved there around 2000 and were responsible for most of the improvements—the trailer, the well and septic tank, the sheds, the fence. Tom had been a Green Beret sniper. Sometimes he'd set up a rifle on a tripod in a field and shoot faraway targets. Melinda was from Norway. They had kids near the ages of Troy and Marcie's, and the families would coordinate driving the kids to and from school in Manassa.

When the Wilkinsons moved to Texas, they sold the property to Troy and Marcie and carried the financing. Troy and Marcie used the trailer mainly as a study hall for their kids until their marriage went on the rocks, said Troy, and he started overnighting there. After two or three years, the couple fell behind on their payments to the Wilkinsons, who, unbeknownst to them, "sold the property out from under us" to Terry, to whom Troy had introduced them as a handyman when Terry was living nearby on his own property. "I found out about it when Terry Jr. knocked on the door and came for the keys," said Troy. He'd felt hurt that the Wilkinsons hadn't told him about the sale. But he didn't hold it against Terry, whose snapshot was taped to the fridge. On the contrary, he said, before long "Terry became one of my best friends."

Troy remembered noticing that Terry, who was heating the trailer using a wood-burning stove set up inside (as many do on the flats), was running low on wood just as it was getting cold. Between their two properties was a former staging area for Troy's family's cattle business: broken-down corrals, gates, and cattle chutes, a lot of old timber lying on the ground. He told Terry to borrow wood from it as needed; Terry did and was grateful.

Visiting Terry in the evening became part of Troy's routine. He'd bring in wood, make sure Terry had eaten, watch television for a while. Troy was lonely and found that Terry could relate. Terry's marriage had failed years before. His kids were leaning on him for help he couldn't always give (ditto Troy's). They did a lot of drinking together. They bonded. And when, in the spring of 2014, Troy found Terry in severe abdominal pain and noticed that he had basically stopped eating ("I'd take him food and he'd feed it to the dog"), he called an ambulance and rode with his friend to the little hospital in La Jara. Terry died soon after.

There was a knock on Troy's door and the neighbor known as Tie Rod Tony joined us. I told Tony I wasn't sure if I should clean up Terry's old place or just get rid of it and find something better.

"What I'd do?" said Tony. He pantomimed striking a match and tossing it under something flammable. "Whoosh!" he said, with a twinkle in his eye.

Truth be told, it was tempting. On the other hand, I didn't really want to send a lot of toxic black smoke into the sky.

While I figured that out, I relocated my little camper trailer from the Grubers' property to my own land. This was bittersweet, but they were very nice about it—made me promise to visit often (and I would; I was only moving two miles away) and said I could come back if I changed my mind. Stacy added, a little wistfully, "Now you have your own land," which I was indeed feeling unexpectedly proud about. My investment wasn't very large, but it did mark a big change in my status, at least in my mind, from frequent visitor to, well, neighbor.

Matt had pulled my trailer from Geneva's to the Grubers' first place, and Sam had pulled it from there to their second place. This time I decided to do it myself. Over the months I'd become more familiar with trailer tech, such as the need for one's truck to have the same size trailer hitch ball as the receiver on the trailer. Backing up was the hardest part, but I wouldn't have to do much of that. Slowly I drove the trailer over to my new place and parked it at the spot I'd predetermined, with an amazing view of the western horizon and a glimpse of Blanca Peak, something I hadn't had before. I positioned the door away from Troy's house, so I could walk outside in my skivvies and no one would know. The final step was making the trailer level on the uneven ground, but I now had experience with that and it didn't take long. After that, I just sat in the open doorway. It was quiet! I *owned* it. My newfound independence relaxed me.

That said, there had been some explaining to do. My reasons for wanting to own property were not immediately apparent back home. I tried to find words. My project was to understand life on the flats, and *ownership* was a major part of that. I could interview a hundred landowners (and probably had), but it seemed to me I'd understand them all better if I were an owner myself. If I had skin in the game. And it wasn't such a reach, to experience ownership on the prairie. One metric of a good life, in my book, is the number of interesting situations one can engage in, learn from, hang out with. For several thousand dollars, you might join an African safari, or a journey through the South American rain forest, or spend some time dining really well in France. Or you could, as the newspaper ads from the 1970s put it, own your own ranch and live in what was, to my way of seeing, one of the most beautiful places in the world.

Last, and probably the biggest thing, was the way I felt out here on the prairie. I felt good. I felt free and alive. I liked the weather even when it was bad—perhaps especially when it was bad, because it was so dramatic. I felt like taking notes on everything I saw and learned. When a place makes you feel like that, I think you should pay attention.

I walked around my new property, getting a feel for the land. Around the edges there was chamisa, chico bush, sagebrush, and some low cactuses—plants I had already gotten to know. There were also the scraggly weeds whose prickly seedpods Kanyon Gruber had first named for me: goatheads. They would stick to your socks and were a devil to get off. There were also half a dozen low, woody plants that I would have mistaken for just another desert shrub had Troy not told me they were lilac bushes planted by the Wilkinsons years ago. They had survived only because he periodically watered them. The land had something else new for me—the dark green kochia weed, which grew where soil had been disturbed by agriculture or building. Some of it was nearly a foot tall, some close to the ground. It was soft underfoot and I didn't mind it . . . yet. The lot across the road to the east, toward the Sangre de Cristos, also had a lot of kochia—this area had been the headquarters of Bankers Life's Sky Valley Ranch, after all. The lots just to the west had three collapsed potato cellars side by side. Most of the timbers that had supported the roofs had disappeared, but some pieces were still there. I loved these remnants of a bygone era, history living on in dug-out depressions and the long piles of dirt alongside them. Google Maps' satellite view showed the layout of the historic ranch, including some foundations and abandoned trails I hadn't noticed. It felt like my personal historic site.

During the course of an hour, I saw prairie dogs, rabbits, a mouse, and some kind of ground-dwelling raptor that would emerge from the soil when I entered its area and perch on a fence post. I kept an eye out for snakes. I noticed there were black widows in the power shed.

I still hadn't decided whether to keep the old mobile home, but I did want to empty it out, to parse its contents like an archaeologist. A bigger priority was to bring the power shed back to life and, hopefully, get the well to work again.

The need for a third project became clear on my fourth or fifth night in the camper trailer. I was deep asleep when the trailer shifted beneath me. It felt as though someone were leaning against it or intentionally pushing on it. I sat up in bed and listened: nothing. The movement stopped. I lay down and was drifting back to sleep when it started again, rougher this time. The sound came from the far corner of the trailer. My heart raced. I propped myself up on my elbows and wondered how I should confront my intruder. I peeked out the windows but could see nothing. Had it been a dream? I got back under the covers and was just drifting off once more when, about three feet from my head, there came a deep, loud, bellowing, directly outside. I peered out the window over my pillows. Something big was out there, mov-

Cattle fleeing my land

ing. I stood up, put on my headlamp, opened the door, and stepped outside: the beam caught a wide-eyed cow, leaning against the corner where I'd felt the pushing. "Hey!" I shouted. The animal started, possibly more scared than I had been, and then bounded off into the night. I followed it around the corner of my trailer and saw several other cows and calves trotting away. They had come up from the river for the kochia weed, and probably also for the bales of hay I had placed around the edges of my trailer to keep the wind out. And that was the genesis of the third item to my summer to-do list: fix the fence.

A few months earlier, before buying my place, I had published an article in *Harper's Magazine* about the flats and my time there. The photo editor, envisioning a modern version of Dorothea Lange's Depression-era photos of Dust Bowl migrants, had assigned a photographer skilled with an old-fashioned camera that required a dark cloth over the photographer's head and recorded her images using a nineteenth-century wet plate process. The Gruber girls loved her, and vice versa. A portrait of Stacy outdoors in jeans and cowboy boots, her long hair loose, was the issue's cover shot. I got her several copies and passed out at least twenty more to other folks I'd gotten to know on the flats. Other people read the piece online.

Most seemed to like it, but there were some unexpected reactions. Some noticed a mistake: near the beginning, I had written that the San Luis Valley spans approximately eight thousand square miles. But the article said it spans approximately eight thousand acres. A square mile is 640 times the size of an acre. I had described two people as African American who were *Creole* American. And my whiskery neighbor known as Camaro Jim felt that I had left out people like him when, in the article and in a podcast interview, I described some of the reasons that people move to the flats: the desire to own land, the desire to be alone (sometimes connected to PTSD, particularly among veterans), the desire to be self-reliant, the desire not to be noticed by law enforcement and other authorities.

"You didn't mention a situation like mine," said Camaro Jim when I stopped by to follow up about this. I was happy to find that he wasn't angry but, rather, just wanted to expand my awareness. "You didn't mention that some people are here because they tried to make it in the city but ultimately failed." Jim spelled it out for me. He was a navy vet. At age fifty-five he had lost his union job with a high-tech firm in Denver working on phone systems. It had paid nearly $80,000 a year. The country was in a recession and he had trouble finding a new job, followed by a quick cascade of other personal disasters: the passing of his mom, the overdose death of his son, the suicide of his wife. He lost his house and decided to relocate to the valley "for the economics"— he'd read it was the second-cheapest place to live in the continental United States, after somewhere in Alabama or Tennessee. Plus, there was a family connection: his mother was Japanese, and "my grandpa on my mom's side was a cattle broker out here" in the 1920s and 1930s. In the 1940s, tragically, the grandfather had been sent to an internment camp. But after he returned here, Jim and his family would visit him and stay with friends who were farmers. Jim, in second or third grade, "loved it to death," and he liked the idea of coming back. "It's almost like a river branched off into tributaries but then finally all came back together, and that's like my life."

Troy asked me why they'd put Stacy on the cover "when they've only been out here four years." Transiency was less the exception than the rule, and long-timers took pride in the years they'd endured. I joked that it was because she was prettier than him, but then admitted that I had no control over photos—magazines did what they wanted.

And then there was the interest of reality TV in my story. A producer in Los Angeles with a major company emailed both me and La Puente, asking to speak with us and requesting that we help him get in touch with the people in my article. This wasn't a complete surprise to me, as reality TV producers had several times approached me and other writers I knew about pieces we'd published—the reality TV genre had a big appetite for new material. But it was a double-edged sword: while the producers' interest could translate into income for those who became their "characters," it also could expose those people to ridicule and publicize parts of their lives they'd rather keep quiet.

Before responding to the producer, I checked in with La Puente. People there were wary. Research into this particular producer revealed that he had done some plausibly good work, such as a series on Black cowboys, but also the cringeworthy *Snow Cougars*, about divorcees in

Aspen. One clip showed a featured cougar saying that she had slept with all three of her husbands on their first dates. "Guess I'm pretty good in bed, huh?" This was not where La Puente wanted to go; the staff members would not participate, and they would tell Matt not to. Nor was it my thing to channel my subjects toward schlock. Yet we agreed that the people on the flats should decide for themselves—there could be money in it for them. I called up Stacy, who discussed it with Frank, then texted me that they'd be "interested to hear what the man has to say."

The producer flew out for a two-day visit. He spent time with the Grubers and with people they thought might be interested. A day or two later, Matt asked if we could talk on the phone about it, because "everyone is asking my advice."

Those who were in favor were excited about the money. Nobody knew exactly how much could be made, but they'd gotten the sense that the more time you spent on camera, the more you'd be paid. And they weren't naïve about the genre: for the past decade, the dominant depictions of rural Americans on television had been created by reality TV—*Duck Dynasty, Here Comes Honey Boo Boo,* and any number of gold-mining, prepper, and wilderness-homesteader productions. These series took viewers to the boondocks but, as everyone was well aware, they also required drama. Characters needed to clash, secrets to be revealed, somebody had to act badly. And not everyone came out of these shows looking good.

Some neighbors had legal concerns. One worried that celebrity might focus the county's interest on the fact that he lacked a septic system, which so far no one had bothered him about. The producer's answer: *You'd make more than enough to pay for a septic system from just one episode.* The system could be installed before the segment ever aired.

Matt said the producer had been intrigued by recent events involving a flats resident Matt knew. When a collection agent had appeared at the man's door, he'd fled by truck into the town of Blanca, where he'd caused a three-car collision. But insurance hadn't covered some of the damage he'd been responsible for; he felt certain that if anyone knew he was making money, he'd never live in peace. Others with vengeful exes or abandoned children or outsized marijuana grows also feared becoming famous (and being presumed rich).

Stacy, wisely, had gotten in touch with somebody who had experience: a miner of precious gems north of the valley named Brian Busse, who had been cast in a weekly reality TV series called *Prospectors*. She said he'd been enthusiastic—he'd told her that the attention he'd received had helped his gem and jeep-tour businesses and social media presence, and now he was preparing videos for a YouTube channel. But Stacy knew that absent a gem business, all the attention would be on her family and her acquaintances, and that she'd have only limited control.

Still, she was willing to give it a try, and others were, too. She started a Facebook group just for them, so they could share information and ideas. Not everyone she hoped to recruit was on board, alas—another family didn't want to get involved, and yet another family was unsure. "He seemed disappointed there weren't more families," she said of the producer. Still, he had taken a lot of video with his phone, she said, and had told her he'd show it to his team and let her know.

They waited and waited. The parallels with prospecting were clear: with luck, you might have a big payday. And yet the odds were against it. They waited some more. The producer said it was going to take some more time—he kept saying that. He wouldn't say no, but he never said yes.

In March 2019, I was having coffee in Alamosa with Matt, the first time we'd seen each other in a couple of months. I always tried to set up these get-togethers when I came back into town so that Matt could debrief me about Rural Outreach and things with La Puente and I could learn about what needed doing. I was still wearing my two hats, volunteer and writer, but Matt understood that going forward I'd also be spending time fixing up my place. And that is why Matt brought company to Milagros Coffee House, our usual meeting spot— his friend Luke.

I felt I already knew Luke a bit since Matt often mentioned him. Luke, he said, was a sort of genius who could fix anything electrical and many things mechanical. Since Matt was skilled in those areas, this was high praise. They had started out simply as neighbors on the flats at the foot of Blanca Peak who helped each other out on construction projects, engine work, and the like. As the friendship grew, they became partners in some gold-mining claims, mostly on Blanca, and interested in the idea of lost treasure. Both had other moneymaking schemes, as well. Matt's included allowing an application to take over his smartphone's processor when he wasn't using it, in order to mine Bitcoin. His take from this was pennies a day "but it adds up," he said. Both loved raising animals and tried to monetize that: Matt's latest scheme was shipping horse manure to buyers who found him via eBay. It was organic, the product of alfalfa feeding; he sold it dried, wrapped in plastic, and packed into a flat-rate postal service box. He'd made several sales so far at twenty-five dollars a box, of which about half was profit. He chortled about it: "Cash for my horseshit!"

Luke was interested in the possibilities of selling milk from goats—between them they had several—and making cheese from it. Luke also believed there was money to be made in heirloom tomatoes, and he gave me his business card. "KUNKEL FAMILY HOMESTEAD FARM," it said. "NATURALLY GROWN HEIRLOOM PRODUCE. NON-GMO."

Both were also preppers and had realized that between these various pursuits, they might have enough going on to start up a YouTube channel. "The problem is neither of us wants to be on camera," chuckled Luke.

Luke was forty and overweight, frumpy and energetic, with reddish hair and an unkempt beard. Matt was older and leaner. Luke wore a sweatshirt over a dirty yellow T-shirt with the logo of a cement company. The conversation turned to Asperger's syndrome, something Luke brought up. It was a main reason he lived "in the desert," he said. Being around more than one or two people could make him nervous, stressed. "My nervous laugh gets a lot worse! Lots of social situations make me nervous."

I noticed that eye contact wasn't a problem for Luke and commented that he seemed to have good awareness of what made him different. "Well, I been living with it for forty years," he said. He had monthly appointments with a psychiatrist in Salida, about an hour and a half from where he lived, because there was not, at present, a psychiatrist in the San Luis Valley. I asked Luke if he might take a look at my energy shed. He replied that he'd be happy to.

A few days later, when Matt was in the area, he and Luke stopped by. Luke was eager to look inside the shed and, once there, seemed perfectly at home. As he explained to me what everything was, I wasn't sure whether to take notes I could refer to later or try to concentrate on the concepts that filled his head—voltage, amperage, wattage, serial and parallel wirings, and distinctions between hardware such as monocrystalline versus polycrystalline solar panels, deep-cycle lead-acid versus lithium-ion batteries, and the virtues of efficient new maximum power point tracking (MPPT) charge controllers versus the older, cheaper sort, like what I had.

Of particular interest to me was making the wind turbine work. Luke confirmed that it was no longer generating any current and suggested I might want to buy a new one that we could mount on the same pole—it would cost $300 or $400 and would generate ten times the power of the old one. He would text me a link to a company he liked. I loved the idea of harnessing some of this monster force that was such a fact of life in the valley; having a working wind turbine would be a reason to *appreciate* the wind.

Could I pay him for his help? I asked. Luke had already thought about that, but not in the way I expected. "Would you trade me for that?" he asked, pointing at an unused switch box resting on the floor of the shed. "Once I've done some work, I mean." I told him yes and asked if there was anything else. Well, he said, if I didn't want it, he'd also take the old wind turbine and see if he could do anything with it—but only when I felt he'd earned it. Later he pointed to a rusty old barrel, one of three or four around the property that had been used to burn trash. "Do you think you're going to use that?"

"I doubt it," I told him.

"Well, it's a good size and hard to find." Matt nodded in agreement. "Take it," I said.

A few days later, I was driving with Luke from Alamosa to my place with four new batteries we'd bought at Walmart in the bed of my truck. Luke, it turned out, was often available if you could give him a lift. His car situation was ever-changing; like the Grubers, he seemed to be without one fairly often. Matt had brought him into Alamosa when he came in for the La Puente all-staff meeting; later he'd handed him off to me, and our day had begun.

The drive was good for talking. Luke pointed out an electrical substation and transformer yard west of Alamosa, which I'd never noticed; I commented that it looked like a big version of the one next to the La Puente wood lot.

"Yes, but that one is hardly used—maybe one-quarter," said Luke.

"How do you know?"

"Well, I noticed that only one part of it is buzzing," he said. "And the switches for the rest of it are turned off." I mentioned that it's unusual to pay such close attention to an electrical substation and its barely perceptible sounds. He told me that he liked figuring out wiring and electronic systems, making sense of them—which is exactly what Matt had said. He said it was his Asperger's. Another symptom of the syndrome was evidenced by his notebooks. He had a lifelong habit of filling notebooks with possible solutions to problems he'd been working on, such as how to compress alcohol and concentrate its energy. He was from rural Oklahoma and had taken some courses at the University of Oklahoma but never finished his degree. In Oklahoma, he had worked for a company that did weather forecasting. In the valley, where he'd arrived only three years before with his third wife and his support dog, Yuna, he had worked for a guy installing ATM cash machines. But for some time now he'd been subsisting on a monthly payment of $217 from the state to single men out of work; he supplemented this with odd jobs when he could find them.

His interest in electricity, he said, dated from when he was a child. "My mom gave me an old TV I could take to the basement," so he disassembled it and "started figuring out how everything worked."

I recalled a day when Matt had come into La Puente's outreach office upset that sheriff's deputies, responding to a call about something else at Luke's property, had noticed a pistol in his trailer. "And now he's in trouble, might get arrested," he said.

"But why?" I asked. "Why can't he have a gun?"

"Well, he's a felon," said Matt, who doubted the rightness of gun confiscation.

I asked Luke about that. "Well, yes, I am," he said; in his youth he had passed bad checks and done seven years for it in prison. But he said that seemed like another lifetime. He'd been a bit of a hell-raiser back then; now he was just trying to stay alive. Among his health challenges: high blood pressure and, especially, heart problems. "My psychiatrist said people like me have an average life expectancy of forty-eight years old," said Luke. He wondered if he'd make it even that long.

While Luke seemed affable, and his nervous laugh conveyed a sense of self-deprecation, he allowed that he could be difficult to live with. His third wife, whom I had briefly met a year earlier, had recently left him. He said that was largely "because of my quirks." A big one was testiness. He hated to be interrupted when he was engrossed in one of his notebooks or a mechanical or electrical project—"I'll snap at somebody for asking an innocent question."

I saw this a week or so later when Luke brought his son, nicknamed Maverick, along on one of his visits. Maverick—twenty-one, portly, good-natured, and wearing a cowboy hat—was visiting Luke for a while, he said. He would later explain that he was on the lam: his girl-friend had complained about him to the authorities, and because she was underage, he'd been charged with statutory rape. Luke was short-tempered that day: Maverick kept trying to hand him a wrench or screwdriver only to get berated by his father for selecting the wrong one. In his frustration, Luke even yelled at me—he later apologized, but it was a vivid illustration of his social deficits (and a window into the challenges Maverick faced having him as a dad). One of his daughters, he had told me, was pregnant and staying with her boyfriend at the La Puente shelter. Another daughter who had been staying with him had used a phone app to hook up with a guy at his trailer when Luke was in town, but the guy had been abusive and she had called the sheriff. There was a lot of drama in Luke's life.

Things were simpler in the straightforward world of electricity, where practically everything, with some creativity and effort, could be understood and made to work properly. Little by little, Luke got everything in the shed working, replacing several components with rock-bottom-priced units made in China—but encouraging me to keep the outsized old inverter I had inherited, as its broken relays were fixable. In fact, he decided, the most economical way forward with those would be for him to take the unit home and replace the relays himself. As ever, when I asked him the cost to do something like that, he would quote only the cost of the parts. And for his labor? "Just pay what seems right" was his mantra. He helpfully suggested things he was interested in (a spare breaker panel, old batteries, some tools) that I didn't need and he could accept as barter; when those ran out, I went to cash and we estimated hours.

By early summer the power shed had two new solar panels attached to the roof and was supplying all the electricity my little camper trailer could use. But still the well wouldn't work. Although it hadn't been used for years, once the shed was producing power again, Luke didn't understand what the problem could be. For weeks he kept trying: the pump seemed to be on, and occasionally we'd get a trickle of water from four hundred feet in the ground. It came out of a hose connected to a pipe inside the shed. Finally, one day in midsummer, *whoosh*— something that had been stuck came unstuck, and water gushed onto the floor of the shed. I'd felt as though we'd struck gold or oil: something free and plentiful, pouring forth from the earth onto my land.

The next big milestone would be the wind turbine. Slowly we had lowered it to the ground, removed the old turbine from atop the mast, and examined the mast and the wiring. Over a couple of weeks the replacement turbine and other parts had arrived, delivered to Troy's house (since, for reasons unknown, my address just a road away from Troy did not appear in delivery databases). Now it was time to put the new turbine up.

This was an operation best accomplished with several hands, and so I asked for help. We would need to start early so as to finish before the afternoon winds began. Luke arrived with his truck, carrying Maverick and his dog with one blue eye, Yuna. Troy came over with his truck and a teenager, Joseph, who had a tough life at home and stayed with him and his wife, Grace, and her two kids, on weekends. We convened outside the power shed for a strategy session. A winch would have been helpful for lifting the tower back up, but nobody had one. Luke had brought a come-along, which could accomplish the same thing, but very slowly. I had added an extension to the top of the pipe, so that the new turbine would be farther from the ground and, I hoped, less noisy. As a result of this, we had to make longer guy wires; since we knew the height of the new pipe, and the distance from its base to the long metal stakes that would hold the wires to the ground, I realized

Raising the wind turbine

you could figure it with the Pythagorean theorem (the mast formed a right angle to the ground; the wires would be the hypotenuse of the triangle). I asked everyone to hang on a couple of minutes while I went into my trailer to calculate numbers on my phone. Troy had his doubts about the whole setup and my motley crew and quipped, "A former truck driver, a college professor, and a juvenile delinquent decide to set up a wind turbine," as though it were the beginning of a joke. Luke and I laughed while Joseph, the designated delinquent, scowled. (Troy and most others knew that I taught at New York University.)

Finally I came back outside with my numbers. We set to work adjusting the cable lengths. Maverick, meanwhile, helped attach the turbine to the tower and, doubting that its carbon-fiber blades could be as sharp as they looked, ran his finger along one and cut himself. Finally, four of us started lifting the mast while Luke ratcheted away on the opposite side with his come-along, to negligible effect. Then Troy had a brainstorm: we could lift it faster if we used his truck. He had me drive while he and Joseph stood in back, pushing up on the mast. As I inched toward the mast, the turbine moved higher and higher.

Maverick held a guy wire from the side to keep the mast from tipping sideways. Finally it was in position, and the wires tightened. There was little wind, so we couldn't test it yet, but once the turbine was spinning it would help keep my batteries charged on cloudy days. And if I ever had a hot water tank in the mobile home, the wind could keep the water hot.

Troy and Joseph headed back to Troy's place. I had picked up lunch for Luke and Maverick at Subway in La Jara earlier and asked if it was a good time to talk more about their lives. We cleared a space inside the big blue trailer and sat down, me with a notebook.

Luke seemed exhausted. I asked about it, and he said it was mostly due to being overweight and having a weak heart. But he blamed Asperger's, too, "because of the anxiety and stuff" that Asperger's brings: "it just wears their body down so much quicker in their life.

"I've noticed that, as I get older, emotional stuff hits me harder," he continued. "I see how I take things harder and I get aggravated about things a lot quicker. I kind of had some woman issues this last month. And it seemed to hit me a lot harder than it should have. And I mean I didn't really want to get out of the house, just stay inside." His doctor, he added, "has me on antidepressants. I'm on an anti-anxiety med. You know, that kind of stuff. I think it helps."

I asked Maverick how much his father's autism had affected him growing up. He told me it hadn't directly—Luke had been in prison when he was born, and he was given up for adoption. After Luke got out of prison, he checked in on Maverick occasionally without letting Maverick know who he was. Then came a day when he was sixteen, Maverick said. "I still did not know that he was my father until . . . I mean literally that day I figured it out. He said, 'Oh, I guess we'll figure out who I am when you turn eighteen' and it just kind of clicked in my brain: *This must be my dad.* But yeah, we lost contact for a while until I turned about eighteen or nineteen and then we started talking again."

Maverick said that in addition to his legal trouble, he'd been getting into fights with his adoptive dad. "And Luke was like, 'Well you know I have property up here if you want to come up here and work on the farm with me.' I was like, 'No problem.' So that's when I moved up here to get to know him a little better. It's been a little over a year and a half, almost two."

Maverick said he'd never met his "real mother," and Luke said she wasn't one of his three wives.

Luke told me that he himself had never known his father. I asked whether he wanted to meet him. "Not now. There was a time, yeah. Then once I got to about twenty, I got to the point where, well, not sure if I want to, you know, hug him or kick his ass. I'm at a point now, well, he still ain't showed up so I just want to kick his ass!" Luke laughed nervously. "You know, I guess that's why I tried so hard to try to somewhat keep tabs on my own kids."

Maverick had helped Luke with various projects, including the heirloom tomatoes, but Luke said that was now kaput. There had been a frost in late June—not terribly unusual, actually—that had damaged most of the tomato seedlings beyond usability. He had had hundreds, kept alive by a huge investment of daily trips to get water at the spring. A few potato plants remained near his tiny trailer, chicken coop, and goat pen. But it was hardly enough to call a "farm," as Luke liked to do.

Later that afternoon, I felt a breeze rock my trailer gently and looked out the window: the turbine swiveled atop the mast so its blades would face the wind. And then, a few seconds later, it began to spin. A gust came up and it whirred, the wind now mine.

Spring and early summer had been eventful for my other new neighbors, and not always in a good way. Jack, who had followed through on his promise and gifted his horses to the Gruber girls the summer before, was diagnosed with bladder cancer. Frank and Stacy had been driving him from the RV where he lived alone on an austere plot of land into Alamosa for medical appointments. I offered to help, and learned that Jack was a fairly extreme Christian fundamentalist. The town of Antonito had murals painted on some old buildings, and as we drove by them, Jack muttered that the paintings of Indigenous people were immoral.

"What do you mean?" I asked.

"Well, look at her, the one next to the campfire—she's naked on top." The woman depicted was about forty feet off the ground, and I never would have noticed. He didn't like the way the littlest Gruber girls were allowed to run around naked, and he didn't approve of the mess they lived in. To my surprise, he told me that he was planning to fight his cancer with cannabis suppositories, which he would prepare and administer himself.

What Jack didn't know was that in January his horses had died. They'd run out of forage on the Grubers' land, but their friend Josh, who was staying with them for a few months, had found work on a ranch called the T-Bone and would bring home hay to augment the horses' diets. Only when Josh got fired, the free hay ended. The last time I saw the horses, late in the fall of 2018, they looked gaunt. Where their coats had bare spots, the girls told me, was where dogs had bitten them. Stacy said she planned to move them into a shed to protect them from the winter wind. But then in midwinter, within two weeks of each other, the horses died. This was a big deal. Jack hadn't yet been informed, though he was sure to take it badly. Trin told me that one of them had died of a stroke, but an acquaintance who had had success with horses said they may have died of starvation. "It takes money to feed a horse," he said. "You don't have any business owning a horse if you're on food stamps."

Frank and Stacy had some good news, however: they had finally sold their old trailer and the land it was on. The buyer was a friend, Lori, who lived in Greeley, just north of Denver. She was in her early sixties and had a homebound daughter in her early forties. During the first Christmas I'd spent with the Grubers, the biggest package under the tree had come from Lori—she had sent tablet computers for the girls, and needless to say, they'd been thrilled. She had also paid the service for three of the family's cell phones.

As Frank and Stacy explained to me, two years prior, Frank's painting business had been doing well, and at year's end they'd decided to paint one needy family's house for free. Lori had been the grateful recipient; the families had bonded over the gesture.

Lori had been intrigued by the Grubers' decision to move to the valley and to the flats and had once visited. Ever since the family had moved to their new place, they had been trying to sell the old one. Lori had been interested, and finally they had come to terms and signed a contract.

There was a lot of cleaning up and other prep to be done before Lori and her daughter arrived in March 2019. I joined the Grubers a week before the women were set to arrive in their U-Haul, and watched as Josh and Frank installed a new tankless water heater while Stacy and the girls swept and tidied. The house and its immediate surroundings were a bit of a disaster area, so there was a lot to do. Trin confided to me her doubts that Lori was going to last out here. "She likes to keep things really clean, but she's gonna have a dog"—one of Trin's puppies—"that goes indoors and outdoors, and so it's gonna get dirty."

I wasn't there when the two women moved in. Suffice to say that the experiment lasted less than forty-eight hours. Apparently it was cloudy on their arrival, the batteries weren't fully charged, and during the night the power ran out. At 5:07 a.m. Lori posted on Facebook: "We have no power. The inverter is alarming and the Genny is not recharging nor is it powering the house. Help. Please who sees this first. Call me, I can come get you [to come help repair things]. This is urgent."

Josh, who was still living in his camper trailer on the property, responded and got the generator working. But he and Lori had already clashed—he said she was burning trash in the burn pit while the wind was blowing, setting fire to adjacent weeds. Meanwhile, Lori's daughter called the sheriff's office and requested a "welfare check"—she wanted somebody in a position of authority to check in on her. Later in the day, the two packed up the U-Haul and returned to Greeley, never to return.

Lori would later post to her Facebook friends:

I was seriously scammed. Months of pouring money into the house, none of the work was done, what was done was done wrong.

It was a nightmare. I was still going to bull through it, until last Sunday when it started raining in the house. It was supposedly roofed last November.

The final nail in the coffin for the deal was when the police came out. Sarah had called for a welfare check, worried about us. I have NO problem with that.

The police informed me that I was dealing with bad people, dangerous people.

I am not going to go into all the details, but this picture is of the "shed" built for battery containment. $350 in materials. . . .
I feel like a fool.

The journalist in me wanted to contact Lori and fill out the picture she had sketched of her dealings with the Grubers. On the other hand, I knew that if I did and it got back to the Grubers (as it likely would), it could permanently spoil my relationship with them. So I held off.

What, then, to say? The Grubers never once cheated or tried to take advantage of me. For more than a year, when I rented space from them for my camper trailer, I would leave it unattended, and often unlocked, and never was it touched. Frank and Stacy sold me two solar panels and a rudimentary inverter for a modest amount of money, and Frank spent many hours helping me get my solar power set up and helping me troubleshoot other things. In their dealings with me, the Grubers were always honorable; I had found them completely trustworthy. But in Lori's case, I can't say. I'm just relieved that I don't have to watch it repeated on television.

I liked to stop by and see Sam when I was at the Grubers' because something was always up with him; Sam was never dull. As usual, my arrival that fall was announced by the frenzied barking of his chained-up pit bulls outside the tiny camper trailer he shared with Cindy. Sam came outside, yelled at the dogs to shut up, and limped away, where we could talk.

Sam usually limped, due to a motorcycle accident that had damaged muscles in his calf years before. But today he limped even more, and his hand was wrapped in a bandage. Sam always had a bit of a grin (being toothless added to his charm) and was generally keen to find the humor in things, and today that included the battering that had resulted in his current state of injury. His soreness that day, he said, was to some small degree left over from the nighttime battle with the "Shims" down at the Beach the summer before. But to a greater degree it was because he had recently driven, at a high rate of speed, into a snowbank at the end of the road. At night. Nick had been with him. They had been unable to move the car out just then, he continued, though whether this was due to the state of the SUV or to their own lack of sobriety was unclear. His biggest regret, he said, was that somebody had reported the accident to the county sheriff the next day and, improbably, some official had sent a wrecker to tow the vehicle away; to retrieve it would have cost $500 or $600, which was also the reason he had a "new" SUV now.

As for his hand: No, he said, it was not the same injury I recalled from before, when the reciprocating saw he was using underneath his trailer to install a new water tank unexpectedly jumped back and sprained his wrist. That had mostly healed. This time his hand had gotten crushed inside the wheel well of his truck when the vehicle rolled off its jack (a peril of working on uneven, unpaved ground). It might require surgery to repair the tendons.

Sam's injuries were almost always self-inflicted. My favorite was when, in midwinter, he had spotted a big, full diaper sitting in the driveway, dragged from the trash pile by some dog. In a moment of careless bravado, he had walked up and given the diaper a swift kick— only to discover that it was fully frozen and stuck to the ground. The diaper did not yield, only his foot.

Sam's cancer was still around. But the bigger challenges at the moment appeared to be problems for an orthopedic surgeon. And he'd had some inner-ear issues lately, he confirmed, identified after an MRI as Ménière's disease, which causes dizziness.

None of this, however, had dissuaded him and Cindy from preparing for their winter road trip, which would take them to Arizona for some gold prospecting and then possibly on to the Slabs, in southern California—a legendary off-grid desert community adjacent to a military bombing range. "What you get tired of after a while," Sam said, "is the cold." They wanted to go somewhere warm in the winter, just like other retirees do.

One of the people most welcoming to me on the flats, since my first visit, was Paul. When he was in his right mind, which was most of the time, he was like that to everybody. Though slight of stature, he was fearless about approaching strangers; he'd drive up in his car (an old Mercedes wagon when I first met him, then later a compact Nissan), introduce himself, and ask if they were sure they were camping or building on the right property (it was easy to make a mistake) and if they were aware of county code regulations. He was unabashedly nosy, and usually funny about it—"I'm the Gladys Kravitz of this area," he liked to say, referring to the meddlesome neighbor character on the sitcom *Bewitched,* which both of us had grown up with. His friendliness often had a flirtatious side when the new arrival was a man. On the first day I met him, with Robert from La Puente, he had shown us the binoculars he kept by the window. He used them to keep track of "all activity" in his "jurisdiction" from his living room window, he said. From his kitchen window, he added later, once I had moved onto the Grubers' property, he could even track my movements, from more than a mile away. I must have looked alarmed at this news because he added, in jest I think, "You look good in shorts."

He often invited me over for a meal; once he promised that the brunch he was serving would be "so good you'll want to leave your wife." I appreciated the neighborly gesture. Anyone arriving at his house would find their cars swarmed by "the girls," his four or five female dogs. Though they barked, they never bit, and likewise you didn't worry upon approaching Paul's place that you might get shot, because, as Paul freely confessed, he didn't have a gun. Paul's five acres had two weathered mobile homes on them, articulated in an L shape, but one was used only for storage. Two testaments to his longevity on the property—twenty-five years, during which the land had possibly not appreciated in value one cent—were the Chinese elms he had grown from saplings. Paul explained that they'd survive on their own if you could get them past the first four or five years. He'd watered them several times a week to get them through the summer heat, and gradually their roots had grown deep enough that they could keep themselves going. So they were a sign of constancy. (I would later hear Frank Gruber say he'd pay several thousand dollars extra for Paul's place, "just to have those trees.")

Occasionally Paul would ask me to pick up something for him in town—a bag of ice if I was going through Manassa, because it was fifty cents cheaper at the gas station there than anywhere else, or Pepsi or RC Cola from Family Dollar in Antonito, where a six-pack cost only

$4.75, or a propane refill from Gibson's in La Jara, or dog chow from Tractor Supply in Alamosa (both at rock-bottom prices).

Sometimes after I'd delivered the goods to him, we'd sit in the somewhat protected space inside the L formed by the two trailers, where Paul had built a deck with a small table and chairs. One day his dogs suddenly took off as a group against an intruder of some sort; their run ended with them yawping near a faraway fence post where no trespasser could be seen.

"What got into them?" I asked.

"Oh, it's the crows," said Paul. I hadn't even noticed, but a pair of black birds were flying away into the distance. It actually might have been the same pair of ravens the Gruber girls had named Coo and Caw. I had never seen dogs chase birds like that. Another day, when it was windy and the dogs were inside, Paul identified a small tawny bird that looked as though it might be hurt—it was cowering near the base of a tuft of grass.

"That's a horned lark," said Paul. I asked if he thought it was okay. "Yes, it's just escaping the wind."

The bird's predicament had a resonance with Paul's, I knew. He was greatly affected by wind, and not in a good way, as anyone who followed him on Facebook knew: "This storms WINDS Have been brutal. Blowing all night @ 28–35 mph. Woke me up every 2–4 hour's . . . I'm highly agitated . . . oh and it blew off a section of the chicken run area. . . . 😣 😣 😣 😣 😣 😣." Or, a week after that: "Oh Jesus lord if you exist Please make it stop Make it stop." Or: "Would some 😩 one please hear My Plea. . . . STOP THE WIND. . . . Now On its 6th Day Arggggggggggg 😵." When the wind picked up, it would sometimes lift some of his neighbor's trash and drop it on his property, and he became obsessed with this, and with them.

Paul no longer drank alcohol, but he did sometimes use other drugs, and he told me that sedatives and pain relievers sometimes helped with the wind. He would take these for other things, too, such as a scheduled extraction of several of his teeth in Alamosa, which would pave the way for him to get dentures. I agreed to drive him into town for the appointment.

He seemed a little loopy when I picked him up; he told me he'd taken "some Valium." But the dental clinic, once we were there, feared he'd had too much and refused to perform the procedure (which he had waited months for). Paul ranted and complained, not entirely coherently, and demanded to speak to the director, who was unbending. Finally I got him back out to the car. I knew he loved Taco Bell, so we went there before returning to the flats.

The springtime winds, the abortive appointment at the dental clinic—these and other factors beyond my ken were the prelude to a slow emotional breakdown for Paul. I knew he loved making shopping trips into town with two neighbors, Tamera and Grace—he enjoyed referring to the three of them as the Prairie Bitches and the journeys as Bitch Trips. But he started having fights and disagreements with them, and during the summer the group journeys ended. His social media posts and text messages became so garbled that sometimes it was hard to figure out what he'd meant to say. One day in June he posted pictures of his living room in disarray; it seemed that something had fallen but then, in frustration, he'd trashed everything, including his small TV. He asked if, via La Puente, I could help him get mental-health counseling. I learned that in the short term it would be easiest to take him to a drop-in center in Alamosa and volunteered to drive him there.

Not too long after, in early fall, Paul sent me an inscrutable, hard-to-read text that sounded despondent. I told him I was away but to get himself to the drop-in center. Soon I received a series of worried texts from his neighbor Tamera:

> Can you tell me where is Paul
>> I can't find him
>> I don't know where he is and I've checked every wher,
>> He left his dog in the car
>> And his power on he don't do that
>> This is not like him
>> If he walked his dogs would have followed him right
>> They were out side except Clio was in car window was all up
> except one was down a little

I called her; she said Camaro Jim was on his way over to look for Paul.

It was not until the next day that the emergency seemed over. Paul, back home, told me he had called 911, fearing he would kill himself. A deputy came and kept him in a squad car until an ambulance arrived and took him to the hospital. There he was admitted, sedated, and kept under observation overnight. Now he was back home but afraid of what might come next.

I discussed matters with my supervisor at La Puente, a longtime social worker who knew her way around the valley's mental-health offerings. She put me in touch with a manager at a network of clinics, and over the phone I pled Paul's case. The next day this got results: they wanted to schedule him for evaluation. This turned into a regular counseling session for Paul that I still regard as a signal achievement of the time I spent as a La Puente volunteer. It didn't mean Paul's trials were over—it would be several months before he seemed dependably happy and stable again, and terrible incidents would follow, including the one where he tipped over his refrigerator, dumping all its contents onto the floor, and threw a tea kettle through the two panes of his kitchen window.

Other trouble was quieter. Early in my days doing La Puente outreach, I had stopped at the home of a young man named Sundance to introduce myself. His was a simple, fairly crude one-room wood-and-cinder-block structure he had built himself at age nineteen, five years before. His parents, he told me, who were hippies in Vermont, "wanted me to have an unusual name." As it happened, he loved to ski, and had taught at Mad River Glen in Vermont. He had a black diamond trail marker posted at the end of his driveway that said "PARADISE" and a fence around the front with old skis as pickets—the kind of thing you'd find in ski towns in the 1970s. These skis, he told me as I entered the dark of his house from the bright outdoors, had been discards from a shop at the Red River resort area in New Mexico. As we spoke, I sensed movement nearby, and saw somebody sit up who had been lying on the couch, draped in a blanket. This was Jon, a.k.a. Little Jon, and he looked like he had a bad hangover. "We had a kind of a party last night," said Sundance. I'd noticed that in lieu of the decorative gravel a house might have around its front door in the suburbs,

Sundance's house had what appeared to be hundreds and hundreds of crushed beer cans as ground cover.

I had an easy, laid-back conversation of half an hour or so with the two of them. Sundance, I would learn, had a reputation as a hard worker—he often held several jobs—and a good guy. Local opinion about Little Jon was mixed. A small man, he didn't seem to work, often didn't have a car. If he needed to get somewhere, he asked Sundance or others for a ride. Stacy said that when her family arrived, Little Jon was living in a borrowed yurt near them on land that belonged neither to him nor to the owner of the yurt. He came over one day when she was outside and, drunk, tried to light his cigarette by leaning a bit too far into a campfire, singeing his facial hair. A bit later, he had bought land and built his own place, as basic as that of Sundance but colorfully painted on the outside. I remembered him pushing a lawn mower in front of it one summer day, an unusual sight on the prairie. I brought him firewood; he asked if I wanted a DVD from a substantial collection of them he once bought and sold, stored on shelves in a part of his dwelling that had an earthen floor. Troy recalled being summoned by Little Jon one day to help kill two rattlesnakes that had slithered into his house. I remembered him coming by Troy's Fourth of July barbecue, open bottle of wine in hand, then held to his lips, almost like a parody of an alcoholic.

And then later, one midwinter day after three or four days of driving by his friend's place and not seeing wood smoke, Sundance stopped to check on him. He found Little Jon dead, frozen. Had he passed out, thus failing to stoke the wood-burning stove in his place? Had he been killed by gas from a burner of the stove? Reports differed. Sundance told me that, according to his mother, Jon had died from a heart attack. Not long after, Sundance posted a picture from a river trip the two had taken on his Facebook wall. He wrote, "A couple years ago we paddled this river together. . . . I'll never forget it! Rest easy Jon, make sure to have some good music ready when I join ya!"

I stopped by to see Sundance on another occasion to talk about something less sad. Troy and Grace had first described it to me: they'd been sitting outside as dark was falling when they heard engines roaring on the main road down the hill. A truck had just crossed the one-lane bridge over the Rio Grande at a high rate of speed, pursued by several police cars. They watched as the cop car closest to the truck got right behind it and delivered a strategic bump, sending the truck into a roll. When finally it came to a stop, the driver, a man, jumped out and ran. The passenger, a woman, was arrested. Police cars, perhaps a dozen in all, combed the surrounding area as it got dark and failed to find the man.

News reports said the truck had failed to pull over for a traffic stop in Antonito. Instead the driver had struck a state trooper's car and then fled civilization by heading east, onto the flats. The police were on his tail and later said the chase had reached speeds "far above the speed limit."

Sundance was three roads away from the action. He told me he had seen the sky lit up by the many police cars but hadn't really known what was going on until he heard about it the next day at the liquor store where he worked. That day he went home as usual. The next morning he got up, hungry, and decided he'd cook himself a big batch of spaghetti with meat sauce.

It was while he was cooking, he said, that he realized someone was standing outside his door, "about ten feet back." Sundance opened the door and said the man in his mid-thirties standing there started right off by saying, *I'm the guy who caused all that trouble.* "He told me straight up!" said Sundance. The man hadn't heard what had happened to his female companion; Sundance told him she'd been apprehended. The guy said he'd been doing 120 miles per hour up to the bridge, then 80 miles per hour over it. He had hidden for two days alongside the river and claimed that he wasn't hungry because he'd recently killed a fish with his knife and eaten it. "He was totally straight with me, one hundred percent, except for that fish," said Sundance. Wasn't he a bit worried by the sight of a fugitive at his door? I asked. A fugitive who'd admitted he had a knife?

Sundance said the only thing that really would have worried him was if the man had a gun, and he thought he didn't—he'd become skilled at sizing up whether people were carrying or not from his work at the liquor store.

The spaghetti was almost done, so Sundance offered the guy a bucket to sit on and a plate. He accepted, gobbled the food down, and then asked if Sundance could give him a ride. Sundance explained that his car was unreliable. The guy asked to borrow Sundance's phone so he could call a friend for a ride. He did, and after a while the friend called back, saying he couldn't figure out where Sundance was. Meanwhile, a neighbor stopped by on a social visit. He told the guy he'd take him to Colorado Aggregate, an easy-to-find landmark at the bend on Highway 142. After they left, Sundance called the state police in Alamosa. Three days later, the man was captured in Denver.

While they'd chatted, said Sundance, the man had made reference to coming back to the area later to pick up some stuff he'd stashed. Sundance felt he must have been referring to meth and admitted to having walked the river looking for signs of the stash. Interestingly, the Grubers, who had had no contact at all with the man, conducted an independent search for things he might have left behind—in the area of the rollover. Stacy told me that she and Frank had scoured the location the next day with a metal detector. They had come up with some socket wrenches and a small digital scale, the kind useful for weighing drugs.

Sometimes living on the prairie felt like taking blinders off. I heard that a couple in their seventies were fixing up one of the few stick-built homes in the area, a humble place that had been vacant for years. Don and Sherry Bosdell had moved from Oregon, where they'd met Ken Hershey. Ken owned at least three properties, including the one down the road from Paul whose inhabitants perennially drove him crazy. Ken, according to Paul, had a long history of renting to *anybody,* with no regard for the integrity of the community. Case in point: Phillip Quinn, from Alabama, whose trash would blow onto Paul's land and who was ultimately convicted of charges of sexual abuse of a disabled young woman who lived with him. The next couple, from Missouri, penned their wolf-dogs in tiny enclosures that Paul felt offered little shelter from the sun and the wind.

Don and Sherry seemed different. They came across as humble, polite, self-effacing. I'd met Ken at Troy's; when he'd heard that I worked with La Puente, he'd suggested I stop by and introduce myself to them. Initially I liked Ken, a mustached man in his late sixties who seemed intelligent, outgoing, and resourceful. He had joined the history tour of the flats offered by Loretta Mitson, where he'd informally talked up the idea of some kind of property owners' association to combat the abuse of land by cattle companies. I doubted it would get much traction in this region of cash-strapped, libertarian-leaning mavericks, and it did not. But apart from its going against the cultural grain, I thought it was a smart idea.

(When I met Ken, I was playing with some blue heeler puppies—also known as Australian cattle dogs—that one of Troy's dogs had recently given birth to. Ken asked how much Troy wanted for them, paid him the twenty-five dollars, and left with a puppy under his arm.)

Ken happened to be at the Bosdells' when I dropped by. A generator was running, and power tools were strewn about—Don, seventy-two years old and with one eye squinting, was fixing up the house. It was a lot of work, and my heart went out to him. He was rehabilitating walls, floors, and ceiling. The kitchen would get a small island. He had just repaired the bedroom window and the front door. In lieu of a regular vapor barrier, some of the ceiling was getting covered in aluminum foil. A leaky utility area had been sealed up and would soon be home to lots of baby chicks. The bones of the house were good, he told me—it had been engineered to withstand strong winds.

He took a break outside, and Sherry served us all sodas. They had met Ken in a church group in Oregon, they said. Don had held many jobs, including work on an Indian reservation. He and Sherry had recently wed and were looking for a new situation. Ken offered them "lifetime tenancy" on the property if they'd fix it up. Don even said he might be interested in starting up a new congregation at the old stone Baptist church in Mesita. "Only costs forty dollars to rent," he said. Speaking of church, I asked Don if one of the church work groups that visited La Puente during the summer might be useful to him and Sherry, and he said yes. I also offered to help them apply to some programs designed to help low-income homeowners with energy and weatherization costs, and they said absolutely.

It was a month or two later when Matt arrived with the work groups. The chickens had grown large. A barbed-wire fence was mostly in place around the property, and the front gate had a flagpole. Atop it was an American flag with the face of Donald J. Trump superimposed, as well as the words "MAKE AMERICA GREAT AGAIN."

The church volunteers were mostly adults from New Mexico. Trump had been president for more than a year at this point, but many people still weren't used to the fact. One woman came right up to me and asked, "What's with the Trump flag?" I told her she needed to ask the homeowners, so she asked Sherry.

"It was the least expensive flag for sale at Walmart!" Sherry said in her defense. But then Don weighed in, saying that America was already better off since the election of Trump, and something had to change, the way Obama had left it. The volunteer questioned this. "Do you mean leaving us with universal health care?" she asked.

While the volunteers unloaded a horse trailer packed with tools and building supplies that Don had driven down from Oregon, moved around fencing and pallets for a future outdoor chicken coop, and assembled a great pile of trash out back, my talk with Don and Sherry turned to dogs. Specifically, the Grubers had a dog, Stormy, that was pregnant, possibly by Jack's Great Pyrenees or possibly by the Bosdells' much smaller dog, Warrior. (Most dogs wandered freely across the prairie; only a few were tied up.) Don and Sherry were pretty sure that Warrior was the dad: "We used to call her 'Mrs. Warrior,' she was over here so often," said Sherry. I knew the Grubers were hoping that Jack's Great Pyrenees was the father, since the big white dogs were prized out on the prairie, but I didn't say anything; time would tell, and I told them I'd keep them apprised.

I stopped by once more to check in. Don wasn't there, but Sherry asked me in. I told her that the puppies' father didn't appear to be Jack's Pyrenees, so Warrior it was. She said that Grace, Troy's wife, had recently been over for Bible study—would I be interested in joining? I confessed that I wasn't very religious. We talked about her family in Arizona and also, briefly, about her husband. I admired his industry. Sherry worried about his eyesight and his heart. Sherry said she was his sixth wife, which I found surprising. Then she went further: "He has ten kids and not a single one will talk to him. Period. What do you think of that?" I asked her what might be the reason for that, and she said she didn't know, though she suspected there might have been too short an interval between wife No. 4 and wife No. 5. I said I couldn't really say. But I thought, *There's a warning sign.*

Don started preaching at the little church in Mesita. Grace attended the first couple of services, and she sat on the new congregation's board of directors, along with Ken. Then, on a Friday, not long before he was set to preach, Don got arrested on a felony warrant out of South Dakota. The county sheriff's office posted his mug shot on their Facebook page, with "CAPTURED" superimposed on it. The post read, "Boswell [*sic*] was wanted on a felony warrant out of South Dakota for sexual assault on a child. Boswell was located in Mesita, Colorado and was arrested with out incident. He is not facing any charges locally and will be held pending extradition."

Many commenters called for his head—sex offenders are uniquely hated. One commenter wrote that "he was claiming to be a Pastor at the Mesita church." Others took the anti-prairie line, such as "Good job costilla county there are a lot more out there in the prairie" and "Some of these nasty squatters are probably coming here because of shit like this nasty old piece of shit that hurt kids and only God knows what else they did and come here to hide and they are in my community I don't think so." In response, somebody wrote, "I'm not a squatter but I did relocate here, but I have noticed there are a lot of people running from the law here." This was certainly true: a lot of people on the prairie seemed to be running from warrants.

In the end, Don was not extradited but released. It seemed that he had, in fact, already been convicted of assault on a sixteen-year-old boy, and that his current offense was in not registering as a sex offender in Costilla County. Anyway, that was the end of his pastorship.

I stopped by the Bosdells' a bit later in the year—I felt that, in fairness, I should allow Don to say his piece. But this time the gate was closed. There were vehicles inside, suggesting that someone was home, but nobody came out to greet me. I got to thinking about how the needy are not always the good.

Just over a year later, in June 2020, law enforcement raided the Bosdells' place and removed "more than 100 dogs and puppies," as well as dead dogs. Ken Hershey wasn't mentioned in the county press release, but the operation appeared to have been his brainchild: as the unhappy current tenants at his other property, across from Paul, had noted months before to anyone who would listen, their landlord had a long history of legal trouble over animal abuse, particularly in running puppy mills. Oregon had an open case against him for thirty-two counts of animal neglect, most involving dogs. In Florida he had been charged with animal abuse and with selling sick dogs with forged pedigree papers. Six years earlier he had been convicted of cruelty to animals for killing a neighbor's German shepherd and hanging it in a barn in California. And there were other charges in other states, such as the time he had let seven cattle die for lack of water and had starved horses, who had resorted to eating the bark off trees.

Costilla County charged Ken with 107 felony counts and one misdemeanor. A majority of the dogs recovered were heelers. That, of course, was the very breed of puppy I had seen Ken buy from Troy.

Into the great openness of the flats flowed not only those seeking freedom in a good way but those seeking the freedom from their bad deeds of the past—or even freedom to do more bad.

It was time to excavate the mobile home. On Troy's suggestion I hired Joseph, the seventeen-year-old who stayed with him and his family on weekends, to help me, as there were mountains of stuff to carry out. We wore disposable masks. It was pre-Covid, but mice had been everywhere. I thought of them and of the pack rat metaphor as we sorted through Terry's endless piles. I'd seen my first actual pack rat nest the year before, at the Grubers' old place. Frank had discovered it near the burn pit, a midden several feet across that was filled with shiny pieces of the girls' toys—a bit of lamé from a Barbie dress, some neon-colored mane from a My Little Pony doll. Terry had collected not the eye-catching but, rather, the potentially useful, in a way known to generations of those raised in a time when screws and nuts and bolts were sold by the piece, instead of in packets hanging in plastic packages in big-box stores. There were cans and jars and boxes of hardware.

Though I'd asked him to help me carry everything outside, Joseph kept getting distracted and looking a little too hard for stuff he wanted to keep for himself—a vinyl gym bag, a frame backpack, a fleece-lined denim jacket. (I said yes to everything.) Troy, meanwhile, was being hugely helpful, his prosthetic leg no impediment to his work as a moving man. We hefted the disgusting couch outside and onto a flat trailer behind his pickup truck, and then took on the refrigerator. Once we had it outside, we paused. Troy wisely treated it as a Pandora's box and

The derringer found under the mattress

had no interest in peering inside. Unfortunately, my approach was different. Rather than describe the details of everything I opened, let me just say that if you ever find a six-year-old bottle of buttermilk, leave it alone.

Joseph had been quiet for about half an hour when I heard him practically scream—I thought he must have uncovered a rattlesnake. I jogged to the main bedroom, where he was holding up the mattress— and pointing at the pistol that had been secreted between mattress and box spring. It was a silver derringer with two barrels. "I bet it's loaded," he said as I picked it up. I opened it and he was right. We took it outside to show Troy.

He looked surprised but said it was definitely Terry's. He asked if he could return it to Terry's daughter in Colorado Springs. I said okay. In addition to having trouble deciding whether to keep the big trailer at all, I was having trouble deciding whether I wanted a gun.

We sorted a large volume of stuff and hauled it away: flammables, including clothing, to my burn pit; items ranging from Kentucky Deluxe whiskey bottles to ancient toiletries to Troy's big potato cellar burn pit. I paid a place in Alamosa to recycle the refrigerator, and I donated a few things to Rainbow's End, La Puente's secondhand store. I gave Troy an album of Terry's black-and-white family photos—he said he'd return it with the pistol—and gave Joseph an old Polaroid camera kit, complete with flashbulbs, that he had excavated and longed for. I thanked them both and then, alone, puzzled over what to do with some singular relics I just couldn't throw out because they seemed to belong in a Terry time capsule.

These included Terry's dentures, which had been resting in their case atop the stove's exhaust hood; a Western Airlines ticket folder from 1974 (Denver to Phoenix round-trip); a 2012 notice from the Jefferson County Sheriff's Office ("deputy attempted to contact you"); a couple of sheets of S&H Green Stamps; practice targets for marksmanship, including one that pictured a bad guy holding a knife to a woman's neck; a paperback book from 1966 called *Flying Saucers—Serious Business;* bumper stickers that read, "YOU'RE A GREAT CURE FOR HAPPINESS" and "STEAL HERE DIE HERE"; and business cards and installation invoices from Terry's carpet service.

The calendar from 2013, the year Terry had moved in, had pictures of classic cars in front of McMansions and scantily clad women. It also had notations on various days that I realized were not to-do's but, rather, accomplishments. For example, April 2013 included: "Put large heater in. Removed propane heater from liv rm, cut a little wood, cut firewood all day, hauled water, Went p.o. and bought food. Gathered paint and VHS tapes. Got ready to do dishes." (Those dishes! Rather than wash the dirty dishes from 2014 that were still in the sink, I put them in a trash bag.)

Behind that 2013 calendar hung a mystery: a hardware store calendar from 2002. Puzzled, I asked Troy about it when he dropped in. He chuckled. "Terry was the cheapest person in the world," he said. "He knew that calendars repeat and if he kept it, he wouldn't need to buy a new one." Vaguely I had understood this: calendars are on a cycle, and every few years, the same days fall on the same dates. "So you're saying Terry saved his 2002 calendar for eleven years?" Troy thought he had. We looked more closely and saw that March 1, 2002, was marked "2013." "I think partway into the year, somebody gave him this calendar with the cars on it," said Troy, referring to the new one. "But he still didn't want to throw away the old one."

I sat in a plastic chair as the sun fell low and contemplated the vibe. Overall, the place had a nice smell—sort of woody. Terry had been a smoker, but with all the clothing, upholstered furniture, and carpeting removed, that smell was hardly noticeable. I suspected that Terry had not had a particularly happy life. By the time he'd moved into this place, he'd been sixty years old, about my age, but had probably seemed older due to his alcoholism, smoking, and life of physical labor. Troy said that Terry had never gotten the well working and tended to keep his lights off so as to conserve as much electricity in the aging batteries as possible—the priority was keeping the television powered. At his first property on the flats, two roads away, he had built a small house and a shed, and his handiwork had caught the attention of the Wilkinsons, the couple who had brought in the mobile home and made most of the other improvements. They had hired him to help with some projects and later, of course, sold him the property. But it appeared that by the time he'd moved in here, he was spent. He made few further improvements, and mostly seemed to be living out his last days. I pictured the time passing slowly, as it does when you have nothing to do.

To burn the trailer down, as Tie Rod Tony had suggested, or to fix it up? It wasn't an Airstream, something of beauty that could plausibly be refurbished and take on new value. It was, rather, the cheapo dwelling version of all the ephemera I'd been sorting through. I could dispose of it, but did I really want a new trailer on the site, attracting burglars while its plastic fixtures off-gassed into my living space? The good thing about this trailer was that the plastic stuff was mostly gone. Replacing windows and doors and the ugly green bathtub would not be a Herculean task. Already I had a lead on a couple of locals with carpentry skills who might give me a hand, and, should they not be available, there were always the Amish builders who everyone said were good. And for whatever reason, I've always preferred renovation to building from scratch.

From the chair in my living room I could see that it was shaping up to be an exceptionally dramatic sunset. (Two of my neighbors would post photos of it on Facebook.) This was the time of day when the valley looked its best, the most like a painting, the least visited by human-kind. I thought of the writer Barry Lopez, an early hero of mine whom I'd met once in Idaho. He was deeply affected by landscapes, especially the Arctic, and extolled the beauty and power of natural places. I loved this place and how I felt in it. But I wasn't sure that its beauty brought out goodness, our better selves, as Lopez suggests. The Arctic world of Barry Lopez didn't have alcoholic, burned-out carpet installers drinking away the last weeks of their lives; it hardly had people at all. Put people on the land and things change. A friend of mine who, after graduating from Stanford, spent her working years as a waitress in Aspen, wrestled a lot with the despoliation of a beautiful valley and the gentrification of a funky old mountain town, which she saw happening around her. She might have been quoting a friend of hers when she shared one of her mantras. "The problem with paradise," she said, "is you bring yourself to it."

6

Love and Murder

Motherfucker, you just made me fall in love with you.
—ZAHRA DILLEY to her future husband, a white man

I'm Jewish, he's from Colorado.
—MY WIFE, explaining us to friends

THE WIND TURBINE had blown over and lay on the ground, in pieces. Troy thought it had happened in December, three months earlier, on a day with gusts around seventy miles per hour. Clearly it had needed more support for the additional height I'd added. It was springtime 2020, a year after I'd bought my place. I walked around the still-snowy ground beneath the turbine, picking up shards of the carbon fiber blades, which had shattered. "I'll be back," I muttered to the wind, but not loud enough for it to hear.

There was a lot to catch up on in the neighborhood and with La Puente. Matt Little had started seeing somebody in Blanca, Willow. Before long the two of them had bought a used trailer out on the flats and moved in together, along with Willow's preteen daughter and, for a while, Matt's son Joshua. The place needing fixing up but it had a well, which was a huge advantage. Over the course of many trips, they moved all of Matt's animals over. His wolf-dogs had to start living mainly outdoors, because inside was reserved for Willow's two Pomeranians. I was very happy for him.

Then Matt, heading toward town on the dirt roads of the flats, hit an elk with his pickup truck. The truck then hit a pole, rolled, and was totaled. The elk was killed. Matt broke his femur.

Paul was doing much, much better. The weekly therapy sessions were helping to ease his anxiety, and his mental health turned a corner. On Facebook he started asking friends what they thought of the colors he was considering painting his rooms. He posted photos of dishes he cooked. He asked friends over for meals.

In June he invited me to join him on his daily walk with his dogs. Our route led past a house on a corner lot that I had passed many times. It looked decrepit, but it was hard to tell for sure from the road; Paul walked me around to the other side, where I could see that the house was kind of ingenious: most of it was situated below ground level, where a room two stories tall let in sun through big windows. We walked inside; the place was abandoned, but clearly it had once been nice. A staircase led up to a loft, situated at ground level. "This is where Zahra stayed for a few months with her kids," he told me. I recognized the name and knew she was a Facebook friend of Paul's, but I didn't know the details of the story.

"But you've seen her picture, right?" Then I made the connection: the pdf my sister had shared with me from her visit to La Puente more than three years earlier had included a photo of an African American woman standing near a table with several little kids. "That was Zahra, and that was here," said Paul. Later, over a dinner of spaghetti and meatballs, salad, and garlic bread (I brought a pie), he told me more.

Zahra Dilley had come to the valley from the Chicago area in 2014. She was filling her car with gasoline in La Jara when Paul first laid eyes on her. "I saw that car stuffed with kids and everything tied to the roof and I thought, *She's headed for the flats.*" He was right. Her tenure on the flats was only a few months, but it was tumultuous. Paul shared the basic outline of the story and then put me in touch with Zahra so that I could ask her questions myself.

She met me on a weekend morning in June in Alamosa's grassy Cole Park, which adjoins the Rio Grande and is ringed by cottonwood trees. Animated and bright-eyed, Zahra, thirty-seven, wore jeans with combat boots, hoop earrings, and an orange scarf over her hair. We sat at a picnic table—I had bought us both iced coffee—and over the next two and a half hours she shared her epic American story.

Zahra Dilley, or Ankhzahra Soshotep as she then called herself, had left Michigan City, Indiana, in a rented car with her six children three days before Paul saw her and driven west. She had never spent time outside cities and got confused when she passed through tiny Eads, Colorado, late at night before she reached the San Luis Valley.

"I had just got past the Colorado border and the time zone changed and I'm like, 'What is that?' It was the first time I ever seen stars so close. I thought they were trees with lights. So I pulled over and they were stars, but we were so close that they looked like they were moving. And I'm like, 'But it can't be trees. They're moving.'" She called Leroy, a member of the African nationalist group who had moved to the valley as a pioneer and was hosting her. "I asked him and he said, 'No, those are stars.' Because coming from Chicago, man, I've been looking at the same star all my life. All my life. And I had no idea that Earth could look so freaking beautiful."

Zahra was seeking a new life dedicated to her ideals. She considered herself a Pan-African—"I'm about the liberation of Black America." As a schoolgirl on Chicago's South Side, she said, she'd grown up with the idea that the history of her people began with their enslavement. So when she heard her manager at the Clarion Inn in Michigan City, Indiana, a white man, talk about the history of African people *prior to* enslavements in Europe and North America, it opened her eyes. And, she said, "I got angry. Because I'm like, this was information that I felt like should have been taught to me [before]. I have a white man talking to me right now that knows more about my history and my culture than I do. That's not right. So I was angry. I was angry with the government because I'm like, these are things that you guys are purposely hiding from us. Like, why is it that he's learning these things in his school, in his area, but it's not a curriculum in our schools? We're taught that we started off as slaves. That's what we grew up thinking."

The missing information, said Zahra, was that "before then we were kings and queens. We did have our own land. We did live on our own, you know, then slavery came into the picture. So, yeah, I was very angry. And then I got into these groups and I let them talk to me. And it's like my anger turns into hatred now. Now, I don't even like the smell of you," she told me, meaning white people.

In seeking out her past, Zahra discovered Kemetic science, a religious practice based on Egyptian polytheism. People she knew were part of the group, which traced Black Americans' roots back to Egypt.

"I had noticed that a lot of the people that I talked to either went by Kemetic names or Muslim names," Zahra said. "Because in another group that I tried to get into, my name was Kamaliyah Shakur." (Shakur is one of the ninety-nine names of Allah in Islam.) "So that's when I learned that even in Black-conscious communities, they have their battles, too, about where we started. And that's really what the battle is about. Was we Muslims, Moors, or was we Egyptians that *captured* the Moor people and enslaved them?"

Casting her lot with those who claimed Egypt as their homeland, Zahra had a revelation that led her to choose the new name, Ankhzahra Soshotep. Rediscovering Black identity meant claiming new names and words and, soon, the idea of establishing new communities as well. Members of her group had become intrigued by the concept of Earthships and aware of the cheap land in the San Luis Valley. They began a pioneer effort, with the ultimate goal of establishing a sovereign state. Zahra signed on; at a moment in life when most people are settling down, she wanted to break her old life and mind-set and start something new. The group member named Leroy was building a house and looking for other settlers. He welcomed Zahra and her family on the condition that they help him get established—and that eventually, they would establish their own place and sponsor more settlers. "So me and my kids were one of the first to come here, all six of them. Yep. The youngest girl was two." Her oldest, Damian, now twenty, was fifteen years old.

At the same time Zahra was seeking a new physical environment, she was also seeking a clean break from her ex, who she said had abused her. They had been together and apart for years; the physical abuse, she said, had left her bruised and shaking, and had terrified her kids.

It was November when Zahra arrived in the valley. Her rental car needed to be returned and Leroy helped her, after which she was completely dependent on him for transportation. His house, three roads over from Paul's, was less than had been advertised: though Leroy had told Zahra the house was finished, it was not. "It's like a fourteen by sixteen box of plywood. Half the floor is not done. There's no roof. There's not even a wood-burning stove." There was a big gap at the bottom of the door that "we had to stuff a blanket into at night so the coyotes couldn't get in." Leroy promised the shack could be quickly completed with the help of Zahra and her kids, and Zahra tried to stay positive "because it was for a greater cause, a greater good. Like something good was gonna come out of this."

But then Leroy got distracted. His girlfriend arrived in the valley; she picked him up in her car, and they left to spend some time in a motel. "So, of course, he wanted some time with his boo. So I understood that—you know, when you're out here, sexually deprived. But we still didn't have a roof. Oh, my God. So it started to rain. Everything got soaked. While in the rain, me and my oldest boy is trying to climb on top of the car to slide plywood over the top of the house so we could stop the majority of the rain from coming in.

"But by the time we were able to get everything somewhat okay, all the blankets were soaked, all our clothes were soaked. We were soaked, like, the floor was soaked. By the time [Leroy] came in to check on us, I mean, the house was already pretty much flooded."

Then "his girlfriend comes and all of us are living in that little bitty box. All six kids, me, her, and him. And it's super cold. And that was the first time I ever made a Thanksgiving dinner on the back of a trunk of a car." Zahra laughed. "I learned how to use a propane can with a grill that goes on top. And on the windiest day to be trying to make a Thanksgiving dinner for my kids. But I made gravy, I made stuffing, I found some little canned greens. It wasn't my usual, but I think my kids appreciated it because I tried to bring a little bit of normalcy to the situation."

Torn between her anger at Leroy and the group's insistence that "we are submissive to our men," Zahra lasted two more weeks, into December. That's when Leroy announced that *another* woman and her son were due to arrive. "And this is where things started to click for me. I said, 'If you're looking for pioneer families to start building, why aren't you bringing any men out here? Why is it all women or us with children?' So I'm like, 'I'm starting to think you're a polygamist and this is your way of getting us out here, isolated, with nowhere to go and only you to turn to.'"

Her defiance enraged Leroy. "He said, 'Well, I'm not going to deal with your aggression and your attitude. So you can pack your shit and get out.'" As he left to drive into San Luis on an errand, he told her, "By the time I come back, I want you gone."

Zahra decided to walk to Manassa, the nearest place with a phone. It was some twenty miles away, but she didn't know that "because he's the one who was always driving." Uncertain how to go, she started marking her path down the dusty roads with Z's "so people would know Zahra had been there"—and so that she could retrace her steps if necessary.

But then she spotted a house whose occupant she thought she knew. It was Little Jon, Sundance's friend. He had stopped by soon after she'd arrived and had given her a pot brownie as a housewarming gift. "And by the time I get to his house, I'm in tears. I'm breaking down. 'Cause at this point, I don't know what to do. I'm like, I really fucked up. And that's all I kept saying in my head. *I fucked up. I fucked up.* I can't believe I put my kids in this situation again. Like, I don't know what the heck is wrong with me. I'm just like, I just keep making bad decisions, just, like, really coming down on myself really hard. So he asks me what happened and I told him." Little Jon didn't have a car either, but he welcomed her in. And while they were talking, like a Christmas miracle, Paul and his neighbor Tamera drove up with a paper plate of Christmas candy for Jon.

(Here I felt that my own prairie story had finally intersected with Zahra's, because Paul had given *me* a similar paper plate of candy the Christmas before, and the one before that.)

Zahra laughed to recall it. "And that's when Paul walked in the house and he's like, 'What the hell? You're that Black girl that came in with all that stuff on the top of your car!' And I'm just like, 'Yes, sir.'" Zahra quickly sketched out her crisis. "And he said, 'Well, Leroy's back now, because we tried to drop off a thing of candy and he acted like we were trying to poison your kids.'"

Paul and Tamera had an idea for where Zahra could stay. They took her back to Leroy's so that she and the children could gather their things, and then, as a snowstorm moved in, they drove them to an empty dwelling where they could be safe, warm, and dry. That's where they still were in 2015 when Robert, La Puente's first Rural Outreach worker, dropped in during his "point in time" count, and took the photo my sister had shown me before I ever came to the flats.

The family lived there about six months, which Zahra describes as one of the best periods of her life—and certainly the best of her five years in the valley. But in the meantime, much drama ensued. Leroy, said Zahra, reported to the group that she had "run off with a white man," by which he meant Little Jon. This was not true, but it was like an excommunication: the group's ideology was all about African women not becoming the "bed wenches" of white men, as had happened during slavery. Angry and isolated, Leroy fired a rifle at Tamera's SUV as it drove by one day, according to her and Paul. And Zahra said that once Leroy figured out where she and her kids were living, he called the county's child protective services and claimed she was keeping her children in a state of deprivation. But when the authorities came, she says, they found a warm house with plenty of firewood outside, plenty of groceries inside, and children who were attending public school—Paul, as it turns out, had arranged for the school bus to stop near Tamera's and pick them up. Finally, when Leroy learned that the property Zahra and her family were in was up for sale, he scheduled a showing with an agent—and that, said Zahra, is what finally prompted her to move into town. They stayed at La Puente's shelter (she later worked as a volunteer there). When her ex showed up and also checked into the shelter, Tona, the shelter's director, stepped in, encouraged him to leave, and ultimately helped Zahra file for an order of protection.

Around this point in our conversation in the park—nearly two hours after we'd begun—a handsome man in a cowboy hat sauntered up, asked Zahra if he could get her anything, and nodded shyly at me. "This is Jeremiah," said Zahra. I had seen his photo on Facebook when I'd first friended Zahra and knew they were in a relationship. She told him we would be a while longer and he said he'd be back.

Zahra gave me a quick catch-up on her life since leaving the flats. She now was working the phones for the regional health-care company, but for a while she had made money as a bartender. That's where she met Jeremiah, who had grown up on a ranch in the valley and clearly liked her. She put him off, but he kept coming back. One of her passions was roller derby; she had joined a team in the town of Salida, and Jeremiah came along to watch her practice. Afterward they'd go to a bar for beer and tacos.

"One day we went to play pool. At that time I always wore the same thing—combat boots, jeans, and these RBG bandannas around my ankles."

"RBG—Ruth Bader Ginsburg?" I asked.

"No, so, RBG just stands for red, black, and green," said Zahra.

"Oh, the color combination, like Africa, like on your tattoo?" I gestured at the tattoo of the African continent in red, black, and green just below Zahra's collarbone.

"Yes," she said. "And it was just one of them things. I don't care what I did or who I knew, you gonna know who I am and what I stand for. And I showed it proudly and I didn't care. And I still don't."

She had just that day gotten another tattoo, and a friend wanted to see it. "So I had to take off the boot and pull up my pants leg and take my sock down and I showed her. And then as I'm putting the plastic wrapping back on my leg, Jeremiah kind of like swats my hands away and he puts it back on. He rolls my sock up, pulls my pants leg down, ties my boot up the way I always tie up my boot. And then he tied up my bandanna.

"And I looked at him and he looked at me and I was like, *Motherfucker, you just made me fall in love with you.* Like that freakin' easy. And we've been together ever since."

Actually, she went on to explain, there was one more step. "At the time I was also a part of the New Black Panther Party"—Zahra was the representative for Colorado. "So when they found out that I was with him, I got a call from one of my generals, in North Carolina, and he gave me an ultimatum. He straight up told me that I could not fight the fight for my people while I'm laying with the oppressor, is what his words were. And I said I would have to think about it, 'cause at this time I'm head over heels for Jeremiah already." She asked him to clarify their commitment. "I texted him and I asked, So what are we doing? Because, you know, I'm about my people as a Pan-African. I'm

Zahra and Jeremiah Dilley
Photo by Zahra Dilley

all about the progression. So I asked him like, I need to know, I don't want to be a fetish (because he's never dated a girl of color before). And I said, What I don't need is some white boy that's never been with a Black girl, got a little taste and now he has a little fetish. I need to know, are we going to go somewhere from here? And he texted me back and said, Well, babe, I actually thought that we were already together. And I'm like, Well, we never actually like *said* it." He reassured her via more texts—texts she would later memorialize with a special-order blanket that reproduced them. "So when he sent those, I called the general back and told him I'm done. 'So you really gonna leave over a colonizer?' he asked. 'This is what it is,' I replied.

"And at this time, we still hadn't, like, he never stayed the night at my house. He rarely came in. He was so respectful. After coming from a man that chokes you on the regular, you know—"

Jeremiah was sitting at a nearby picnic table with an iced coffee, waiting out of earshot so that he wouldn't disrupt my interview with Zahra. She'd been through a lot of hell, she said, and could have done without the whole Leroy part. But in retrospect, "I was blessed." Living in the box with Leroy "was just a means to get me here." Without it, "I'd probably still be in Chicago struggling, still trying to get away from my ex." Prairie life, she said, had been of a piece with the education she'd sought. "Being off-grid, you learn that there is things that you need to be prepared for in order to be off-grid the right way." She'd thought a lot about self-sufficiency, about spending thoughtfully. "When I finally moved to Alamosa people was like, 'You been off-grid for six months? You don't smell like it!' I said, because I didn't buy gallons of vodka—that's why I don't smell like prairie. I got six kids. I can't afford to have that. I got to pay for water and take care of them, that's why. Whereas others, they spend their money on the wrong things because that's what make them feel better."

She had started growing vegetables, and learning from some neighbors who raised animals. She wanted to make sure those lessons stuck with her kids. "Because they can go to the store and buy bacon and eggs. But do they know the process to get that meat, those eggs? So, no, I want to teach my kids from the very beginning because I feel like you appreciate things more when you know the roots of it."

Speaking with Zahra left me energized. Hers was an unexpected update of the stories of generations of Americans who had headed west in hopes of a better life. The San Luis Valley had some of the political conservatism of many rural places but little of the dullness: interlaced with familiar tales of ranch and farm life were the stories of seekers, dissenters, people willing to risk everything in hopes of finding, or forging, something better. The availability of so much cheap land was foundational to that.

Of course, it didn't work out for all who came. Early on I'd met a woman who had moved to the flats with her partner and a dream of starting a community of people committed to permaculture—agriculture designed for sustainability by adopting arrangements observed in nature. Costilla County, during its repressive era of code enforcement, had essentially kicked them off their land. A few months before, I'd sat at a picnic table twenty feet away from where I'd sat with Zahra, having lunch with a young family who had come west from

Maryland, having bought ten acres sight unseen. The online seller had illustrated the property not with photos from the arid flats but, rather, with photos of Cole Park. They had expected green grass and cotton-wood trees. Instead, in despair, they eventually found themselves in La Puente's shelter, and then in a subsidized apartment in Alamosa's seedy Walsh Hotel.

But the stories of hopes and dreams, both realized and dashed, were a valley constant, and I couldn't get enough. Most of my other research for books has been based on a concentrated period of immersion, whether on freight trains, in the company of Mexican migrants, or in a prison. The longest of these, for my book about roads, extended over a period of two years. All of the experiences were invigorating but, especially in the case of prison, they'd been difficult, and when the time came to finish, I was ready.

This experience in the San Luis Valley was different. This time I wanted the immersion to last. The longer I was there, the more I learned—it had taken three years, for example, to hear about Zahra, get introduced to her, and arrange to meet her. Perhaps if I'd had to report over one solid block of time, I'd feel differently—finding stimulation and healthy living over a long winter on the flats would be a real challenge. But I didn't have to do it like that. I could spend time in the valley, leave for a spell, and then return for more. My beloved wife and my teaching job were back East, but both were forgiving and flexible enough that my periodic exits to Colorado were fine. (I had more than a few Zoom meetings in the front seat of my truck, having driven to a place with a strong cellular signal. Once, when I needed a quiet space with a table in order to spread out papers for a Zoom meeting, I found a motel outside Antonito where the manager let me use a room for a couple of hours for twenty dollars, as long as I didn't mess up the bed or bathroom. It turned out that, years before, she had spent time at the La Puente shelter and was very pro–La Puente.) As I write, I can count more than twenty trips to the valley since the spring of 2017, when I first met Lance Cheslock, Matt Little, and so many others.

New York was the busy, stimulating, social part of my existence; the valley was the quiet, big-sky, inexpensive, and, frankly, more relaxing part. That's not to say it was more comfortable. I often had a chill in the winter, and it could get too hot in the summer, particularly inside my camper trailer—I tried really hard to finish everything I needed to get done inside by nine or ten in the morning, because after that it just became too hot in there to think. After Luke got my well working, I had running water during the summer (the pipes would freeze in the winter if I left it on). Life without running water was certainly doable: gallons of artesian well water cost only seventy-nine cents each at Walmart and wouldn't freeze if I kept them in my living space (or, at least, wouldn't freeze very much). I'd gotten used to buying a day pass (ten dollars) at an Alamosa gym, where I could exercise and then shower a couple of times a week. But still, it was an hour drive to take a shower. After my well came back to life, I discovered a good alternative: my place had come with two or three hundred feet of old garden hose. At the end of a sunny day, the water inside it would be quite warm—easily hot enough for a sponge bath or, if I screwed the end into a garden spray nozzle and tied it to the ladder that went up the back of my camper trailer, a five-minute outdoor shower.

A highlight of that second summer as a property owner was the day when my handy neighbor Woody and I connected well water to the house (re-creating what had been there years before). Hours of fixing leaking pipes ensued, but the payoff was a working toilet! I paid it a visit the next morning, where it functioned exactly as a toilet should and I felt almost guilty, it was such a luxury. (Since my arrival on the prairie, I had used an old drywall bucket that Stacy Gruber had fitted for me with a toilet seat. I'd kept it outside my trailer, sealed shut except for when I needed it.)

One of the greatest challenges of prairie life for me was the havoc wreaked on my sinuses by the dry air. Trouble typically didn't start until the fourth or fifth day. I guess my nasal passages dried out little by little until—well, until their distress caused me to sneeze, get bloody noses, and have trouble breathing in my sleep as the passages swelled shut. It was worst in the spring, when the airborne allergens that bothered me reached their peak.

Woody, who had lived in the area for a long time, was bothered by allergies, too, and said he had even submitted to skin-sensitivity tests from an allergist, who'd pronounced him allergic to tumbleweed. Woody recommended running a humidifier at night. Once my solar panels and batteries could supply enough power, I tried that and saw improvement. My internist back in New York also helped by prescribing some allergy pills.

In truth, I was happy when I was in Colorado, glad to be in New York. New York was the cure for loneliness, among other advantages. Still, I remembered the winter past in Colorado and how, on an unusually warm day in November, I'd gone to try to make progress on my barbed-wire fence. The day had gone well until the very end, when an off-the-mark swing of my hammer on a corner post landed on my thumb. Under my thumbnail, the next day, the skin turned purple. I kept an eye on the thumbnail as winter came on—it was both a fitting souvenir of the flats and a sort of timer, a way to measure how long I'd been gone. By early March 2020, when I returned again, the bruise had made its way to the tip of my thumbnail, and one morning on the front step of my little camper trailer, I happily clipped it off.

A couple of months later, I was ready to jump back in. Building a fence, you lay things on the dirt, pick them up, put them down again: T-posts, wire stretcher, hammer, staples, wire cutter. In preparation for the final push on my fence construction, I'd bought some new T-posts and also collected a handful of used but still functional metal and wooden fence posts from around my five acres. I'd made a small pile of these alongside my utility shed. While sorting everything out one day, I dropped a wooden post near the pile with a thump. I was about to reach down and pick up the one next to it when a sound stopped me in mid-motion. It was a sound I'd never heard before but one I had been expecting to hear, frankly, since I'd started spending time on the prairie. It was a sound my brain stem knew; my body responded with adrenaline. The sound went, *Hissssssssssssss.*

It took me a few seconds to see the snake—more specifically, the rattle, the part that was moving. It was shaking madly. Then I saw the snake, alongside the pile of poles, start to move toward a hole under the shed. Most of the poles were six feet long; the rattlesnake was about four feet. It was a pale green with a repeating pattern on its back. My guess was it was a Mojave green, though I couldn't be sure. The snake slowly slithered under the shed. Then only its rattle was visible, shaking away.

The truth is, I had long expected to see a rattlesnake out here but after four years had largely forgotten about it. My neighbors, I knew, invariably killed rattlers they saw on their property, or even on the road. Rattlers could kill your dog and probably your child; Mojaves were especially venomous ("known for its particularly powerful neurotoxic-hemotoxic venom, one of the most potent in the world," notes the Wild Snakes: Education and Discussion website). People would hit them with shovels or hoes or stones, even with cans thrown at their heads. (Stacy told me that Trinity Gruber had recently stunned one near the river with a can of spaghetti sauce.)

Over the next couple of days, I told a handful of neighbors I had seen a rattlesnake. The response was invariably *Did you kill it?* I had to admit I had not. This, of course, prompted them to look at me like an idiot or, as likely, a New Yorker. The snake, truth be told, was right out of my nightmares, and yet I had not wanted to kill it. It wasn't coming for me, after all; it just wanted me to leave it alone.

I wanted to look at the snake some more and found that most days, by midafternoon, it was back around the same spot by the shed. Sometimes it was stretched out in the sun; sometimes it was coiled. If I stomped my foot, I could make it rattle. I'd be leaving in a few days and considered just ignoring it—recently it had dawned on me that I hadn't seen a single rabbit lately, whereas on previous visits they'd been all over the place. That was fine with me.

But I also knew that my neighbor Woody would be doing a little carpentry for me in the coming weeks and would kill the snake if he saw it; he was bound to see it, since he used the shed. (A diamondback rattler had killed his family dachshund a couple of years before, he had told me, adding, "It died in twenty minutes.") So I decided I would try to move it.

As with building the barbed-wire fence, I consulted YouTube on how to do this. The internet is full of videos of brave (and macho) men catching rattlesnakes. I watched everything, from a guy doing it with one hand to a Texas snake-removal expert showing his technique with a long-handled snake clamper. My inspiration, though, was a guy whose goal was just to protect his dogs by relocating the rattlesnake he'd found near his woodpile. He showed how he turned a length of PVC tube into a crook by heating it near the end with a propane torch, then bending the bottom five inches or so ninety degrees. I had some PVC in my shed but lacked a propane torch. However, it occurred to me that one of the old burn barrels, still full of kitchen cans and whiskey bottles, would make it easy to build a small fire. It took only about five minutes for the fire to get hot enough to start melting the PVC. I placed the warm end of the plastic pipe on the ground and rolled it out at ninety degrees using a short length of metal pipe I had around. Next I found a ten-gallon plastic bucket and lid; apparently, this was the complete toolkit.

The operation commenced the next afternoon. I wore leather gloves, a long-sleeved shirt, jeans, and boots. My PVC crook was about six feet long; my aim was to get the bent part under the snake and then lift the creature up and drop it in the bucket. The snake's clear goal, once I began nudging it, was just to return to its den underneath the shed, but when it slithered, it slithered over the crook. I lifted. The snake was heavy, and less flexible in its midsection than I had guessed. It flopped off near the bucket, tried to head home. But I placed the crook ahead of it and, when it slithered over, lifted again. Again I missed, but the third time was a charm: I succeeded in dropping it in the bucket. I tossed the lid onto the top, tamped it down. The bucket hummed and hissed with the snake's angry rattle.

Next up: the drop zone. The YouTube guy had placed the snake-in-a-bucket on the passenger seat in his car. Had he not seen the movie *Snakes on a Plane*? I strapped my bucket onto the bed of my truck, outside the cab. My destination was an unpopulated spot several miles away where I had seen the ruins of a shed: the snake would need a place to live. I drove there and parked. I carried the bucket away from the road and toward the ruin. I loosened the lid, worried about a jack-in-the-box scenario where the viper leaped out, fangs bared. But the snake stayed low. When I peeked in, it was simply coiled, rattling. I knocked the lid away. The snake made no move. I tipped the bucket over. Again the snake made no move. Finally, gloves on, I lifted up the bottom and gently shook the snake out. Unlike before, it clearly had no idea where to go, but then it began to move. Its destination: away from me.

———

I suppose that murder and venomous snakes engage our interest in similar ways: fear of violent death. Out on the prairie, there's quite a lot, both in history and today, to make you think about it. Driving past Kiowa Hill, for example, put me in mind of the bloody Ute-Kiowa showdown there. Just outside the valley, there was more. In the Sand Creek Massacre of 1864, on the plains east of Colorado Springs, a 675-man force of the Third Colorado Cavalry slaughtered some 230 Cheyenne and Arapahoe people, mostly women and children. And just over the Sangre de Cristo Mountains from my place, in Ludlow, Colorado, soldiers and private guards killed twenty-five people as they razed a tent colony of twelve hundred striking coal miners in 1914.

The story of the thirty-two (or so) murders committed by the Espinosa brothers in 1863 begins in the valley, then spreads north. Like the others, the killings appear to have followed social upheaval. Fifteen years earlier, the Espinosas' land had belonged to Mexico. With the end of the Mexican-American War, it was situated in the New Mexico Territory of the United States. Then, just two years before, it had become part of the new Colorado Territory. Longtime Hispanic residents no doubt chafed under the authority of a new white government— including the construction of Fort Garland in 1858, the stationing of soldiers there, and the stream of immigrant prospectors headed west. Different by virtue of language and culture, Hispanic southern Colorado must have felt like a land apart. Certainly it was viewed that way from up north: a Denver newspaper reported in 1862 that "Mexicans of Costilla and Conejos counties are holding secret meetings and organizing for an armed resistance to the collection of taxes."

Brothers Felipe and Vivián Espinosa lived with their wives and children on the Conejos River, not far from present-day Antonito, when they were accused by a priest of robbing and beating a man who had been hauling goods for him. In January 1863, a dozen soldiers from Fort Garland arrived to arrest them. But the extended family responded with a flurry of arrows, resulting in chaos: one soldier dead and others wounded, the families' dwellings set afire and burned to the ground, their livestock and other property (beds, blankets) confiscated. And the brothers escaped.

The unexpected sequel to the raid on the Espinosas was a series of murders of white settlers. Most were killed in settlements to the north of the valley. Hidden assailants shot white men one or two at a time along remote roads, at a sawmill, at camps, and in a gulch, often mutilating the bodies afterward. A posse eventually surprised Felipe and Vivián at their camp and killed Vivián Espinosa. But Felipe escaped and, it is said, recruited his sister's teenage son, about fourteen, to help him continue his vendetta. By fall of 1863, at least eleven more killings were attributed to the Espinosas. In a letter Felipe supposedly drafted to the territorial governor shortly before he and his nephew were shot and decapitated outside Fort Garland, he claimed to have killed thirty-two.

A strong argument can be made that the Espinosas had been incited by the oppression of Hispanics by white Americans, and by the violence done to their own households. In the 1970s, Chicano activists hailed them as resistance fighters. Reyes Garcia, a retired philosophy professor whose great-grandfather, a famous sheriff, was a boy during the Espinosa era, told me there were still many descendants of the Espinosas in the area; the quirky and contentious artist Cano Espinoza, whose giant folk-art towers in Antonito are a local landmark, claimed to be one of them. The Espinosa brothers, Garcia said, "were part of a resistance who took it to the extreme."

Murderous violence had lost its political nature by the time I made it to the San Luis Valley—though people still like the apocryphal quote by the judge who sentenced Colorado's most famous cannibal, Alferd (also known as Alfred) E. Packer, a prospector who killed and ate his companions east of Saguache in the winter of 1874: "There was seven Democrats in Hinsdale County and you up and ate five of them." Less well known was the story of Carolyn Gloria Blanton, an Alamosa woman who killed and ate her boyfriend in 1994. (The headline in the *Valley Courier:* "Woman Has Friend for Dinner.")

Much closer to me and not at all funny was a lonely grave marker, surrounded by black wrought-iron fencing, off the road to the east of my place. I passed it every time I drove into San Luis. This small but conspicuous monument featured a candle, a small statue of a skeleton in robes seated at a throne, and a metal cross about four feet tall with letters that spelled "Torrey Marie Foster."

Locals and the internet filled me in. Torrey Marie Foster was one of at least five victims of a serial killer named Richard Paul White, who

Memorial for murder victim Torrey Marie Foster

grew up in Mesita. (White's nephew was Junior, whose RV occupied the space near the Grubers' old mobile home before mine did.) They were identified by the police as prostitutes. White raped and tortured at least three more women who survived. In 2002, White had picked up Foster at a bus stop in Denver, taken her to his house near there, and strangled her. He was captured in 2003 and escaped the death penalty by showing police officers where he'd disposed of his victims. He'd buried Foster where the marker now stands, west of Mesita.

In addition to three life terms for the murders, White received 144 years for the rapes and torture.

One day when I was at the Grubers' with Junior, the topic of his uncle came up. Junior didn't want to talk about it, but a cousin of his later told me that their grandfather—White's father—had made the shrine.

My friend Paul Andersen, whom I met when I worked at *The Aspen Times,* had visited for a few days during the previous summer. We went backpacking in the San Juan Mountains. Paul reminded me how he'd moved from Chicago to Gunnison, Colorado, to go to college and then spent time editing the newspaper in Crested Butte. It was the beginning of the mountain-biking era, and Paul became part of that scene and friends with one of the new sport's leading figures, a cycle maker and bike shop owner named Mike Rust.

"He was an artist, he was a craftsman, he was smart," remembered Paul. "He had a beard and longish hair. I wouldn't call him a hippie, though—he just didn't want to shave. He was immersed in the excitement of creating the technology he loved, and it was bicycles. And he was a great athlete, very strong and agile." Rust left Crested Butte after a while for Salida, just north of the San Luis Valley, where he started a new shop. But he didn't like it when Salida got "discovered," and he's said to have decided it was time to leave "when you had to look both ways before crossing the street." In 1995 he moved onto eighty acres in Saguache County in the San Luis Valley, where he built a house by himself.

Rust had been living there for several years when, at seven p.m. one day in March 2009, he called a friend to say that somebody had come into his house while he was away and stolen a .22-caliber revolver. He set out on his motorcycle to follow two sets of vehicle tracks leading from his house. He was never seen alive again.

Rust's family offered a $25,000 reward, but it led to nothing. In 2015 a documentary film came out about Rust's life and disappearance, *The Rider and the Wolf*. (I watched it and caught a glimpse of Paul on a group ride with Rust.) Not long after, Michael Gonzales, twenty, the son of Charles Moises Gonzales, contacted law enforcement to say that he thought his father—already imprisoned on weapons and burglary charges—might have been involved in Rust's disappearance. Specifically, he thought Rust's body might be in a hole on his grandfather's ranch, about five miles from Rust's place. He told police that he, his brothers, and his dad had once planned to make an underground clubhouse there, but the hole had been filled in with trash and covered with tires in a way that made him suspicious.

Sheriff's deputies dug up the hole and found human remains identified as Rust's, as well as "73 items of evidence," including "a unique belt buckle, in the shape of a bicycle gear of the type worn by Rust." Months later, Charles Gonzales was found guilty of killing Rust.

Perhaps remoteness was a factor in the burglary and murder. Where there are no close neighbors, breaking in is easy, and murderers might escape the consequences. (But while the valley is immense, in another sense it is small: not long after Gonzales was convicted, Geneva told me that her daughter and he had once been an item. Gonzales was the father of her granddaughter, whom I know.)

Isolation seemed to have made possible another murder, one that took place in 2018, when I was living with the Grubers at their second place. It was summer when news broke of arrests for murder in Amalia, New Mexico, about twenty miles from us in the San Luis Valley. Sheriff's deputies, acting on a texted tip that people were starving, had raided an off-grid compound where two men, three women, and eleven children were living. The kids, aged one to fifteen and malnourished, were taken into state custody. The adults, all Muslim people of color, were charged with felony child abuse. Police found evidence that a twelfth child, who had been three years old when he was reported missing by his mother in Georgia, months before, had been there previously. His decomposing body was found not long after, buried in a tunnel on the property.

Authorities later said that those arrested were religious extremists who believed in faith healing. One of the men, Siraj Ibn Wahhaj, eventually charged with kidnapping, was the dead boy's father. The boy had a seizure disorder and required medicine. Prosecutors would say that after he'd returned from Saudi Arabia in 2017, Wahhaj and one of his wives, a woman from Haiti, had concluded that his son actually suffered from demons. They believed that once the demons were expelled from his son's body, he would become Jesus and he would instruct the adults in the compound on which "corrupt" military, law enforcement, and financial institutions they should eradicate. According to the FBI, Wahhaj trained the other men and some of the older children in the compound in firearms and hand-to-hand combat techniques. He took the boy off his meds, then hid the body when he died.

All sixteen people had lived in the same small travel trailer, surrounded by stacks of tires and plastic sheeting, as well as lots of weaponry and ammunition. (Reuters would later report that "the two men and three women are all related as siblings or by marriage. Three are the adult children of a New York City Muslim cleric who is himself the biological grandfather of nine of the children involved.") A local couple who owned the site had told the police that they'd thought they'd spotted the missing boy months before, but the police had not acted. Though the child-abuse charges were dismissed when state prosecutors missed a procedural deadline, months later federal terrorism-related charges were added, alleging that the group had been preparing "for violent attacks against federal law enforcement officers and members of the military."

This part of the world is a good place for fugitives or others who want to disappear; neighbors tend not to be intrusive, and law enforcement sometimes seems barely there. Some of those who like to disappear are run-of-the-mill criminals, but for focused dissenters like the members of this group seemed to be, seclusion is just a first step toward bringing down the established order of society at large.

It was at one of Troy's Fourth of July potlucks where I first heard of AJ. Bobby, Troy's friend and tenant, was telling someone how he had stumbled across the body. It was mostly hidden under a door lying on the ground, at a property just two roads away from me that had been abandoned by Terry when he'd bought my place from the Wilkinsons. Bobby hadn't known whose body it was—even after he found the head, which was a few yards away from the rest, a detail Bobby seemed to enjoy. "Looked like the coyotes might have been at it."

But Bobby and everyone else had a hunch who it was: AJ White, also known as Anthony White, Brother Anthony, Anthony Ferrer, and Gerry White, who had been a notorious figure on the flats until his disappearance in 2013. He had been missing for two years. Six months after the discovery, DNA tests confirmed that the corpse belonged to AJ. But the police never identified a killer. A longtime resident of Jaroso told me, "The joke was always 'Anybody killed Anthony yet?' And then somebody did."

That the murder of AJ might have been viewed as desirable, or even inevitable, was due to his long history of abusive behavior on the flats. Mostly this involved his large herd of horses, but also it had to do with his treatment of individuals. Most people believed that AJ had

Feral horses

once been in the Catholic Church and was possibly a defrocked priest. Most also believed that he was a pedophile who had been convicted in either California or New Mexico and had chosen to escape his past on the flats. Troy, who was friendly and widely liked, said to me of AJ, "I pretty much detested him from the get-go."

AJ's herd of horses was said to number some two hundred, mostly paints and ferals. They did not stay on his property, where he lived in a trailer. Rather, they wandered—some might say marauded—in search of food, water, and sex. This was legal, in the same way that free-ranging cattle were permitted to roam, but it could be massively more impactful. Some of the horses were big and could bring down fences. Particularly alarmed were people who owned horses themselves. Among AJ's herd were many stallions. If you had a mare and the stallions got interested in her, you were very much at risk of having your fences busted (whether they were made of wood or wire) and your horse impregnated by a big, aggressive stranger.

A neighbor of AJ's who had her own small herd told me that his horses, thirsty, broke down her fence ("or maybe he did it himself") and helped themselves to her water. When she complained to AJ about it, "he threatened me with a gun."

Woody, helping me fix up my trailer, told me that AJ was interested in his twelve-year-old son and offered to give him a horse. Woody's daughter then asked AJ if she could have one; according to Woody, AJ said, "I don't give horses to little girls, I only give horses to little boys."

AJ's life intersected with that of Demetrius, a young man of color who appeared on the prairie and stayed awhile with various people. He'd been living with AJ for some time when one day he showed up at Troy's on horseback, soaked by the rain. Troy and his then wife, Marcie, took him in, and Demetrius stayed on Troy's couch for several months. He eventually went back to AJ's.

When AJ disappeared, I was told, so did Demetrius, and a rumor was that Demetrius had done it, after having been abused in some way by AJ.

Pat Crouch, an investigator for the Colorado Bureau of Investigation, was intrigued by the valley and its crimes. In retirement, he turned his interest to cold cases. He played a role in bringing Charles Moises Gonzales to justice for the murder of Mike Rust. In 2019, I heard he was visiting my neighbors, asking about AJ. (One of them, upon hearing that Crouch was hoping to talk to him, disappeared for months.) I called Crouch up.

He wouldn't go into the state of his investigation. He did say that he thought he had found a record for Demetrius in California, where he had been charged with a home invasion, taken a plea bargain, and ended up on probation. Crouch spoke at length about spending time in the valley.

"You tell other people this is how people live [on the flats] and they look at you like you've got three heads. Because it's the twenty-first century now." Crouch had recently been to Mesita (which he rightly identified with the "White serial murder case"), where "there was an old sod house—it had a wood-burning stove, bed frame with wood slats, and a dirt floor. If you were standing in there, it was like the 1800s.

"It's a learning experience every day you work down there because things are not what you expect 'em to be. You get past San Luis and Mesita and it's another world. The income they have is not even an income, yet they make it on the barter system, they're trading water, everything—that's the image of the true frontiersman back in the 1800s." And for better or worse, he observed, "they're their own law enforcement" out on the flats. "They don't believe in calling the sheriff's department."

Late in 2020 I noticed a headline in *The New York Times* about three bodies found buried in the San Luis Valley, the murders possibly the work of an Alamosa man nicknamed "Psycho."

The mutilated bodies had been discovered on two properties in a sleepy Hispanic village fourteen miles from my home that I drove through on days when I felt like taking the scenic route into Alamosa.* The little settlement, called Los Sauces, was perched alongside the Rio Grande River. It had trees, some old adobe buildings, irrigated fields, and picturesque fences made from dead branches.

Regular updates followed, in local and Denver media, complete with photos of Adre "Psycho" Baroz, twenty-six, who had lived in the run-down Walsh Hotel in Alamosa. Baroz was heavily and scarily tattooed, including all over his face. He was said to be a member of a southern Colorado gang related to the Sureños of southern California. He already had a long criminal record full of drug, weapons, and assault charges. An arrest warrant for two men, including Baroz's brother, who lived upstairs in the hotel, suggested that Adre Baroz had been selling drugs in his apartment when a deal went bad. The Baroz brothers pinned one man to the floor and cut his throat; his companion appeared to be cooperating with the police. The other buried bodies were thought to belong to two young women—one of whom happened to be waiting in a truck outside the hotel during the murder,

---

* My regular route, through a sleepy little town called Romeo, had its own recent murder. From the local paper: "In one of the more bizarre homicides currently in the court system, Michael John Robinson, 32, is accused of bludgeoning his step grandfather James H. Sprouse, 77, to death sometime between June 3 and 12, 2016 at the residence they shared for a time behind a small former grocery store in Romeo, wrapping his body in plastic and stuffing the body into an unused freezer and taking off with Sprouse's vehicle. After Sprouse's body was found this spring, Robinson was arrested April 28 of this year [2017] in Indio, California on first-degree murder and related charges."

and another who was believed to have been murdered by Baroz a couple of months earlier. On November 25, 2020, police executed a search warrant at the Walsh Hotel and found blood under the floorboards of Adre Baroz's apartment. That night the Walsh Hotel (which had recently been condemned) burned down, leaving its residents homeless and, one presumes, destroying evidence. Officials suspected arson. Psycho was eventually charged with murdering five people.

I discussed the tabloid quality of this violence with my sister in Santa Fe. That town, of course, was associated with art, adobe architecture, and Indigenous culture dating back hundreds of years. There were spiritual seekers there, and fitness buffs, and well-heeled retirees. But there was a darkness and violence to New Mexico culture that we'd also talked about. One of America's bloodiest prison riots had taken place just a few miles south of Santa Fe in 1980 at the Penitentiary of New Mexico. Though it wasn't as famous as the Attica uprising nine years earlier (and many locals had not heard of it), it was more grisly: men were butchered, dismembered, decapitated, hung up on walls, and burned alive. Thirty-three prisoners were killed, one more than at Attica. Scores were injured. Of the twelve officers taken hostage, seven were seriously beaten or raped.

Was this a legacy of the American invasion of the Mexican-American War? Of the Spanish invasion of the conquest of Mexico? Who could know? The story of Psycho reminded my sister of the young man from the area who had methodically killed five people west of Taos in 2017, then fled north in his car, as far as Antonito. Along with all its beauty, said Margo, the region "has this weird darkness."

Of course, while murders make headlines, homeless people dying of exposure often do not. The workers at La Puente, however, were keenly aware of them, since often the victims had stayed at the shelter or used other services. Indeed, deaths from exposure in Alamosa had been one of the main spurs to the founding of La Puente and the shelter in 1982.

Lloyd Jim, thirty-six, recently out of prison and hoping to stay with family members, was rejected when he told them he was transgender. After a few nights in the shelter, and emotionally "in a very dark place," according to Lance, he had checked himself out; he was found frozen under a bridge in Alamosa soon after, in late January. I've already mentioned Sidney Arellano, a frequent patron of the shelter's free lunch, who was found frozen in his car just prior to the Christmas party. There was also an older guy who Matt had noticed living in his van at the base of Blanca Peak and asked repeatedly if he needed anything, like blankets. Matt was stunned (and seemed, unreasonably, to feel some responsibility) when the man was found frozen in November. A shelter guest about thirty years old who had been beloved by staff froze to death in his trailer in New Mexico just after Christmas. La Puente would hold a candlelight vigil the next month for him and other unhoused victims of the cold.

Matt was an action-oriented guy deeply skeptical of his doctors' claims that it took six to eight months to heal a broken femur, and that in the meantime he needed to stay home. La Puente tried to reinforce the medical advice by insisting he take time off, but Matt found reasons to get back behind the wheel, even when it was painful to do so. And as springtime turned to summer, he suggested it was time to visit one of the mining claims he worked with Luke.

Mining law allowed people to stake claims on public land, provided they invested a set amount of money and labor in them every year, and Matt and Luke did so with enthusiasm. They had claimed three different sites on Blanca Peak they believed had deposits of gold and silver. These doubled as possible locations to retreat when the "shit hit the fan," as doomsday preppers would say; Matt told me they had stashed enough food at one site to survive for at least six months. And he said they'd be well situated to defend themselves: "With binoculars, from up there I can see almost to Highway 142 some days," a distance of maybe twenty miles. Like many others, Matt believed that the most likely spark of this doomsday scenario would be urban unrest that spilled over into rural places, with city people both escaping chaos and looking for things to eat, presuming the collapse of the food-distribution system. I asked Matt, somewhat facetiously, if he'd shoot me if he saw me coming up the hill to join them. He took the question seriously: "Naw, I wouldn't do that. You could join us. You'd just need to do your share of work is all."

Matt and Luke called themselves the Lost Mountain Miners; they made business cards and created a YouTube channel that assembled videos of interest, such as *How to Find Gold Claims Online* and *The Cheap and Easy Way to Find Gold in Rivers and Streams*. In his pickup truck Matt kept a small vial filled with gold flakes he had found on his claims; he loved to show it to people. This DIY wealth creation struck me as the same impulse that had driven waves of prospectors some 160 years earlier. You had to be canny and indifferent to physical hardship, and that described Matt and Luke.

I questioned whether we should save the expedition till fall, when Matt's leg was better, but he was insistent. "I can't stand it!" he said of the forced sedentariness. "It is totally driving me nuts. Even when I cut my toe off, I was back to work the next day." (The toe had been lost to a lawn mower when Matt was a teenager.) The logistics for the trip came together in fits and starts due to poor cell-phone service at the new place on the flats he'd moved to with Willow, his sweetheart. And we had to coordinate with Luke. But finally we had a plan. I would drive to Matt's place after breakfast, and from there we would head up Blanca Peak, picking Luke up along the way.

It was only my second visit to Matt's new place, which in the interim had become more farmlike than any other five-acre plot I knew on the flats. For one, it was fenced—barbed wire around the entire perimeter, and other fences within. Behind the trailer was a small marijuana grow, the gate to it closed with a padlock. "But all that lock does is keep honest people honest," said Matt. Around the front, a tall fence of wood and wire kept his wolf-dogs from ranging too far. A smaller fence protected some ducks and turkey chicks from dogs and other animals—but not, Matt told me, from a great horned owl: when chicks had turned up missing lately, he'd checked his security camera and seen the big bird swooping in at night to prey. His horses were in a corral nearby, and his goats, including at least one sold to him by the Grubers, luxuriated in fresh bedding next to them. A donkey lay in shade near the goat pen; Matt's wolf-dog Allie tried reaching through the goat pen fence to gnaw on the horns of the billy goat, who seemed to like it. Matt told me how one day the donkey had broken in through the outside fence. "I thought, *Okay, sure, a donkey*," he said. "He can help at the mine—help carry stuff." He fed and watered it and the donkey seemed happy.

"Two weeks later, a guy drives up, says, 'You took my donkey.' I said, 'If you really cared about him, you wouldn't have waited two weeks.'" Matt thought but didn't say, *And if you cared about him, you would have trimmed his overgrown hooves.* Matt said, "You're welcome to him" and thought but didn't say, *And you're welcome to pay me for the fence he broke on his way in.* The donkey didn't want to leave, but "the guy and his family rope him up, start pulling him behind their truck." Matt said he stood in the road behind the dragged-along donkey, miming, *What the fuck?* "They gave up but said they'll be back. I'm worried it might be today." Willow said she'd call Matt if they returned.

Matt finished drinking a can of Mountain Dew, lit a cigarette, and picked up a backpack containing walkie-talkies and a holstered pistol ("for mountain lions or bears"), and we were off. I realized that his piece of countryside was, as we say in the city, in a bad neighborhood as we passed the dwelling nearest to him. All the windows in the small stick-built house had been broken, the place vandalized. It was a distinctive-looking ruin because once it had clearly been nice; Matt said he thought it was probably a former meth house. He said people still came by semi-surreptitiously and drove away with stuff. He suspected neighbors in a different direction were also up to no good— they would never meet his eye.

Near the intersection where he had hit the elk, the sandy berm was destroyed and there were splinters in a utility pole where the truck struck it. Matt didn't appear to be suffering from any PTSD over the incident. And he told me that, in fact, in January he'd hit some deer when they'd crossed in front of him at dusk, damaging his truck only a bit. "Elk are much bigger—like, as high as the hood."

I was happy to see Luke, dressed in overalls and heavy boots, though he revealed that he'd recently suffered some health setbacks. Mainly he was worried about his heart: "Do you remember I had a pacemaker put in in January? Well, it's been going off a lot." Most recently, it had zapped him at the spring, when he and Matt were filling their tanks with water. "It's like being kicked in the chest by a mule." He had packed two small bottles of nitroglycerin alongside his bottle of Snapple, and told me, "Good for you to know in case I need them." He settled into the back of Matt's truck, took out an inhaler, and breathed deep.

Among the topics of conversation, as we headed toward a rough road that would take us up the side of Blanca Peak to the mining claim about two thousand feet above, were Luke's two recent brushes with officialdom. The first was an unannounced visit from a Costilla County zoning code inspector—though Luke's property sat in Alamosa County. Luke said the man was new, a white guy from Denver, and didn't realize he was in the wrong county. He demanded that Luke open the gate and let him in. Luke refused—and called police dispatch in Alamosa, which, he said, sent over three cars. He said he'd filed a complaint against the errant inspector.

Luke had also had to call law enforcement recently when a truckload of hunters, chasing elk down the slopes of Blanca in an SUV, followed the elk onto his property—and began shooting their rifles at them. "On my land! The sheriffs came and arrested them."

The road up was very rough. Matt was a skilled driver and his truck had all-wheel drive, but we pitched and yawed, sometimes violently, as we wound through a dry piñon forest, over rocks and dips, sometimes squeezing between trees. (My passenger-side window was cracked slightly open, which must be how the wasp that ended up stinging my finger got in there.) There was evidence of recent tree cutting, which Matt and Luke said was illegal, and probably the work of somebody looking for free building materials. At one point, a substantial cedar blocked the road. We all got out and strategized over how to move it. Oddly, whoever had sawed through the trunk with a chain saw had not finished the job. "Maybe they got scared," said Luke. The fallen tree was too heavy for the three of us to push out of the way, and we didn't have a saw or a rope stout enough to attach to the trunk and pull. But Matt found a hatchet in his trunk, and after half an hour of taking turns whacking away at the tree, we had enough room to squeeze by.

During this pause, Matt took a call from Willow: the donkey's owners had returned and were on their property, "chasing it all over on their ATV." She was stressed; he told her to keep an eye on them.

We drove on until finally Matt parked at a small clearing, just past a collapsed miner's cabin. Luke ventured that it probably dated to 1880 to 1910, when gold was worth $18 to $20 an ounce. Now, though, it was around $1,700 an ounce, which was why it made sense to revisit these claims. At any rate, we weren't the first prospectors to come this way. As we bushwhacked across steep hillside, we passed various old diggings, broken timbers, and metal fittings. Matt, "taking point," as Luke put it, bounded ahead like a mountain goat despite his sore leg. Luke lagged, huffing and puffing; but the friends used the walkie-talkies frequently to keep track of each other. Both carried loupes for identifying minerals. Our destination was a small waterfall on their claim; the whole way there, Matt, especially, kept picking up rocks and breaking them open. They found various kinds of pyrite, possible copper, and occasional crystals. Matt frequently added samples to his backpack, which I knew would quickly make it heavy, but this only seemed to energize him.

Finally, we reached the falls, which were actually more a small stream of water running down a rock face and into a pool. There was shade near the pool, and we all paused for a drink of water. After that Matt, mostly, poked around the silt along the edge and started panning it, looking for gold flakes. Luke helped for a bit but then retired to the shade. The claim was one of three they owned on Blanca, Luke said. In his exacting numerical way, he explained that each was "twenty-point-sixty-six acres, six hundred feet wide by fifteen hundred feet long." The

Luke panning for gold at the mining claim

claim where we sat was owned by Luke; directly above was one owned by Matt. The third claim, which they shared, was a ways distant—and the location of the prepper stash that they hoped would sustain them when the apocalypse hit.

Luke used his inhaler, then lit a cigarette. It was restful and cool where we sat, and we could see way out over the flats. "Sometimes I like to come up here just for the serenity," said Luke. "I'll come up here and just hide." There was a big healthy milk thistle at the bottom of the falls, in bloom and beloved by bees, but it would make cows sick, said Luke. Lining the little pool at the bottom were chokecherries with little red berries; the word in local Spanish was *capulín*. They were in Matt's way, and he said he'd like to clear them out.

Matt stopped for a smoke and opined, "If I want to take five days to get the gold out, I will. If I want to take five years, I'll do that. It's good just to come up here and know we own it. We've pulled an ounce total so far—it's my bank."

By the time we returned to the truck, Matt was really limping. Partly it was the fifty or so pounds of rocks in his knapsack. But mainly, I thought, it was his broken femur. He immediately popped Tylenol once he was behind the wheel. But not until I asked about the pain did he say where it hurt: in the muscle of the inner thigh, in the knee. "Sometimes I feel the bone healing."

One of the pleasures of returning to the flats after being away was seeing what had changed. Most obvious were new arrivals: a tent or an RV or even a new dwelling going up, especially in the warm months. But the ebbing away of something previously built and then abandoned was also interesting. Part of the interest was aesthetic, as with the gradual collapse of a prominent stockade fence of slab lumber, eight feet tall. It encircled and kept you from seeing a roughly roundish space, maybe thirty feet in diameter, just off a main road. Most often these walls kept eyes off a marijuana grow. I kept expecting somebody to begin dismantling it, to steal the wood, once it was clear that it had been abandoned, but over the three years I spent watching, that didn't happen. Then, in year four, it began to slowly tip over, like a wave or dominoes caught in freeze frames, an inch or two more of collapse every week, until a person on the outside could peer inside through the breach. Nothing of value lay within, just some discarded junk.

From where my trailer had been parked at the Grubers' second place, my front door had afforded a view of a similar but more intriguing structure, about half a mile away. From the trailer, it looked like a medieval fort. The tall slab-wood fence was rectangular and encircled an entire abandoned compound. It was perched on a rise, and the remnants of some kind of fabric fluttered in the wind from the top of one side—in my mind, like pennants or banners of a long-lost cause.

One day I stopped to explore it. I don't think anyone could see my truck where it was parked, but I knew this was a somewhat delicate thing to do in the prairie community. The existence of abandoned stuff raised a question of ethics: If you were just giving a second life to slabs of wood (say) that had been definitively abandoned, that might be okay. People who "helped themselves" too soon, however, got a bad rep in the community. But if you waited too long, somebody else would beat you to it.

The padlock on the compound's front gate had been clipped, so somebody had already gone in. The first thing I noticed was maybe a hundred used butane bottles rusting in piles around the property. Most often this was an indication that people had been manufacturing hash oil or shatter from marijuana there. It looked as though several vehicles had once been parked inside; one of them, a camper trailer that was itself covered in slab wood (as insulation?), remained, but it had been ransacked. Near this was a large partition made of wood that had once been covered in a tarp that was now in shreds. I realized that it was the source of the medieval-looking flags I could see waving from my trailer.

In the spring of 2020, as I'd driven down to pay a visit to the Grubers, I had passed the compound for the first time in a few months. To my surprise, much of the wood had disappeared. I asked Frank and Stacy about this when I got out of my truck, and they told me that, yes, a longtime local had returned from out of town. He'd been living nearby and had decided the time was right to collect that wood and resell it if he could. He was a prairie rat—a person who could probably get a minimum-wage job somewhere if he wanted to but preferred just to hang out, subsist, keep a low profile, and do the drugs that made him happy. Prairie rats weren't all bad. But because they were often young, and often had addictions, and often lacked a real stake in the place (or any other significant property, except perhaps an old vehicle), and might have an outstanding warrant or two, they were often blamed when things went missing.

Nick had departed the Grubers' a little while after I did (back to Denver to own up to a warrant, he told me). But as I sat in the living room with Stacy and Frank, most of their five daughters, and a handful of favored dogs, a boy about seven years old appeared from the back room. This was Tommy, said Stacy, the son of a friend of Frank's who now was living here. Tommy, short, chubby, and extroverted, said hi and went to play outside with Kanyon.

The Grubers filled me in. It was a long story that started "back in juvie," said Frank, where he had lived during periods of his misspent youth. During one memorable stay in particular, Frank had become friends with Tommy Sr. "even though I only had forty-two days" as a sentence "and he had two years." They engaged in mutual protection, which was very important at the time. Tommy Sr. had a reputation as an enforcer; he seemed drawn to fights. In one particular incident that Frank recalled, two guys were picking on a third guy and getting rougher and rougher. Tommy Sr. was watching, and "he stepped up and completely whipped" both of the attackers. Another time, Tommy Sr. had stabbed a kid in class with an X-Acto knife. When that kid's friend came to his aid, Tommy Sr. had stabbed him multiple times. "His sentences always got longer because of what he did," Frank explained.

Years later in Casper, Stacy added, when Tommy Sr. came to visit, he still seemed eager to fight. A guy owed Frank twenty dollars and wouldn't pay up. "Frank was ready to forget about it, but Tommy said, 'Fuck that, let's take him on,'" said Stacy. He was not somebody who would just walk away, said Frank—for better or worse, this was what it meant to have Tommy Sr. as a friend.

When Tommy Sr. had reached out to Frank and Stacy, asking them to take Tommy for a while, they'd agreed to do so. They knew that Tommy Jr. had had a hard life. His mom, said Stacy, did meth while eight months pregnant with him and went into labor early; he was taken from her when he was born. Tommy Sr.'s mother got him back.

But it sounded as though the boy had been in and out of foster care, passed around from place to place, for years. "He's seen things no kid should see," said Stacy, not wanting to discuss particulars.

While we were having this conversation, Tommy Sr. called, and Frank put him on speakerphone. Tommy Sr. asked Frank if Tommy Jr. might have taken his grandma's checkbook with him when he left. "He loves playing with that thing," he said. Stacy left the room, checked the boy's duffel, and then said she had not found a checkbook. The call ended. When Tommy Jr. and Kanyon came back indoors, Stacy asked him if he had taken the checkbook. "No," he said, "but my grandma called the police on my dad about that." Oh, boy.

Tommy Jr. presented as reasonably okay, as confident and forthright. But a couple of days earlier, Sam, back from the Slabs in California, had seen the boy breaking beer bottles outside, near where people walked. Sam told him to stop, and Tommy replied, 'I'll break your neck.' Sam was said to have paused and then bent over so that Tommy could reach his neck. The boy didn't touch him. "He's testing us," said Stacy.

They signed him up for second grade in San Luis. Soon he got into trouble for behavior such as miming pointing a pistol at a classmate's head and saying, "I'm gonna put a cap in this." School authorities found a counselor to give him therapy. Stacy was alarmed by the boy's love of horror films and gore.

A couple of months later, Stacy told me that Tommy had started trying to touch Meadoux and Trin on the butt—weird behavior for a boy his age. The last straw was when Tommy, who was supposed to be doing his homework, dropped his pants to expose himself to Kanyon. Stacy saw and screamed at him; Frank put him over his knee and spanked him four times. Both were taken aback that the spanking didn't make Tommy cry; he seemed numb, battle-hardened. Nor did he cry when, not long after, they told him he'd be going back to live with his grandma's boyfriend. It had been four months, said Stacy. They had really tried. But that kind of behavior around girls—they had their limits.

La Puente had a new cohort of AmeriCorps workers arriving and needed some evening shifts covered at the shelter while they were

La Puente's shelter in Alamosa, Colorado

trained. Tona, the shelter's director, asked if I could work a few nights. My only hesitation was taking charge of dinner—there might be sixty people to serve, and I wasn't sure my kitchen skills were up to it. What if, Tona suggested, she asked Geneva, the longtime La Puente volunteer, to help me with that? Geneva was known for her cooking; she had even run a Mexican restaurant in Alamosa for a while. I would definitely do it with Geneva helping, I said.

Tona helped train me the first day, filling me in on the shelter's rules and the use of the logbook, and showing me the location of supplies. She walked me through intake procedures and what I suppose could be called ejection procedures if somebody broke the rules. As a case in point, she replayed recent security camera footage of a guy climbing out of the upstairs hallway window after midnight in order to smoke meth. "How do you know it was meth?" I asked her. "Because of the way he turns the pipe"—as she explained this, I could see that it was glass—"trying to make sure he gets every bit inside." The video showed a night staffer, unaware that the man was outside on the roof, closing and locking the window, and later a police officer speaking to him from the ground. Tona handed me a black plastic file-card box full of the names of guests—including him—who wouldn't be allowed back anytime soon. (I would later learn that "blackbox" had become a verb at the shelter, as in "Tona blackboxed her for doing meth.")

As we were talking, a couple arrived to check in. Tona watched me go through checking their IDs, taking their photos, getting them to fill out forms. They had been married recently in Del Norte, they said—they showed me the marriage certificate—and asked if they could share a room. I said probably, unless a family with kids arrived before dinnertime. They were white and in their thirties; the man had trouble walking and said he was a veteran with PTSD. The woman was skinny and missing bottom teeth, but what Tona noticed, she told me later, was the way her jaw periodically twitched sideways. "Almost for sure she's a meth user," said Tona. That would be something we'd need to watch. The final step in admission was helping them launder all of their clothes, which the shelter required before they could move into a room.

That first night, a Mormon church group prepared a dinner of baked potatoes with chili. The second night, Geneva whipped up a cauldron of pork green chili and served it over rice, along with tortillas and, for dessert, carrot cake donated by a different church. I was glad that she was there not only because of the tasty food but also because of her experience volunteering often at the shelter; her relaxed attitude could teach me something. Working at the shelter was taking me back to the months I spent as a corrections officer in New York. While the La Puente shelter was worlds away from a New York prison, I found that being in charge reminded me of how I'd become less nice, more inclined to say no, when I had that job. While we were cleaning up after dinner, for example, a couple appeared at the front door with their pit bull. Pets were not allowed in the shelter, but this was a service animal, the woman said, showing me paperwork to that effect. Could her partner take a shower and could the dog come in with him?

I asked her whether the dog could just wait with her outside on the porch, but she said her boyfriend really wanted the dog with him. I was about to say no when Geneva appeared and said she thought it would be okay—a decision Tona affirmed the next day. Geneva clearly had a more humane approach than I did.

She was always looking to make connections. She called an older

Hispanic man who was gracious toward her "my friend." Lots of sentences to guests ended with "dear." She was all in favor of chiding someone for ignoring the rules but then letting them proceed "this time." Her many connections to the community were clear. A thirty-something woman just out of jail turned out to be a sort of step-niece. A friend of her son, Angelo, greeted her across the counter and said he missed Angelo and also her husband. Geneva replied, to my wonderment, that the bucket lift Angelo had maneuvered too close to the power line had burned a hole in his stomach that was several inches across. "I'm getting better at talking about it now," she told me afterward. Yakking with the night guy, Rob, when he arrived, she eventually figured out that she knew his grandmother "really well."

"And how's it going for you out on the flats? How's your trailer?" she asked me. I told her things were good.

Geneva wasn't there my last day, but by then I was feeling a little more comfortable in the job. Her flexible attitude had rubbed off, I guessed—and, frankly, it was the only way you could have longevity in a job like this. During my eight hours I encountered a parade of distinctive kinds of humanity.

Here was a strange young man, dressed in military fatigues, hair dyed reddish, asking my help in calling a mental-health facility. When was his appointment, he wanted to know, and what was it for? (I later learned that about two years earlier, accused by other guests of stealing food from the shelter's guest fridge, he had set himself on fire in front of the house.)

Here was a woman, recently evicted from her apartment, who had spent the previous night in a tent. "I'm pregnant," she said. "And using drugs," said someone else.

Here was an older man from Arkansas. During intake he seemed candid about all he was fighting against: COPD, bipolar disorder, five years in prison, cancer, more. At ten p.m., he was out in front smoking a cigarette, looking completely knackered.

Another sick older guy, diabetic, had grotesquely swollen feet.

I allowed a young woman and a young man to park their bicycles in the fenced-in yard. Only after they came inside did I see that her face and arms were covered with scabs, likely the sign of a meth user.

Here were guests coming in for their meds, which they had been required to leave in our care when they checked in: Seroquel (an anti-psychotic for schizophrenia and bipolar disorder), pills for the heart, antibiotic capsules, ointments.

In my downtime, I read the logbook. That was how I learned that the cheery young guest I had had a conversation with the night before had been accused that morning of attempted rape; the police had been called, and he was arrested. I read how a woman who had been grumbling all evening about how the shelter was run by idiots had in fact been banned for three days after an altercation with staff members the day before, and yet here she was.

I had a key ring heavy with keys for a large number of doors and lockboxes. I held on to it tightly not only because, in prison, losing your keys was one of the worst things you could do, but because I remembered how, a few months before, Tona had left her office unlocked and unoccupied "for just a few minutes" only to discover, at the end of the day, that her car keys were missing and so was her SUV. She was beside herself—she had just finished paying it off, and had only liability insurance. A few hours later, to her relief, she learned from the police that the vehicle had just been "borrowed" by a guest who, as she explained on Facebook, "needed it to get back to Colorado Springs to turn himself in on a warrant for violating his parole. He was on parole for auto theft . . . 😫 😵 😩 😵‍💫."

I marveled that Tona had lasted so long as director of the shelter—now more than eleven years. At lunch one day with her and her husband, Robert, I learned that she had worked for the county mental-health service, and for a bank, and in retail, but her heart was in serving people in need. "I'm one of those people, when there's a fire, I head in that direction." Homelessness was like a fire to her. Robert, himself a former first responder (he had worked for the sheriff's office in Manassa and in Antonito), added that Tona "could have been a detective," she was so perceptive and analytical in sizing up people and their situations. Tona offered an example: a young mother had recently appeared at the shelter with her two-year-old, saying she'd been kicked out of her parents' house. She said nothing about drugs, but Tona quickly decided that was almost certainly part of the story, and she was right.

Tona seemed tough, with thick skin, but she cared a lot, which meant she second-guessed herself fairly often—something I hadn't imagined. She said she was often kept up at night wondering if she'd done the right thing. "Was I really a cunt, like the shelter guest called me?" She had asked the guest to leave, after the woman had berated an Ameri-Corps staffer and done other bad things.

The night guy, Rob, my relief, arrived a few minutes early and told me he was going to have a smoke outside before he came in. I locked the office and joined him. He was sitting in a chair with his cigarette, an extra-large Starbucks, and his cell phone, using an app called MobilePatrol. "It shows me the mug shots of everybody recently arrested by the sheriff." He said that on average, he recognized one out of every four or five prisoners. He showed me: "He was here. She was here a few nights. Oh, and this guy." He explained that he checked the app out of self-preservation, so he'd know more of what he might be dealing with. During the day he was a bus driver; the night-shift job at the shelter let him sleep some, but not as much as he needed, he said. Things were always happening—an after-hours banging at the door, some three a.m. health issue. I wished him a safe night, got into my truck, and bought coffee at a convenience store—it was a little more than an hour to my place on the flats, and sometimes late at night it wasn't easy to stay awake.

Halfway home, where I turned off the main highway, I stopped passing other cars and things got much darker. There were some street-lights in Romeo and in Manassa, but soon after I left the grid, darkness reigned. Fifteen minutes farther, where I crested a hill, the sky opened up dramatically as the highway sloped down to the Rio Grande, the starlight illuminating the flats.

And then, flashing red and blue lights from police vehicles. They were miles and miles away, and since I am a journalist and that was unusual, I decided to go by on my way home. The police were at the residence of Rhonda and Kea, the mother and daughter Robert had introduced me to on that day of my first visit to the flats. Since then I'd gotten to know them a bit better, and now I associated their place with their fierce dogs. I'd arranged for a church work group to visit them and help with some cleanup. The three dogs chained up in front had eventually stopped snarling, and that's when I'd let my guard down, stepping just inside the circle where one pit bull, the one with a dent in its head, could reach me. I'd been totally surprised when it chomped down on my foot, tearing a hole in the side of my shoe but, miraculously, barely breaking my skin.

I didn't stop that night, but I did ask around later. I learned that Kea had called the sheriff because a drunken ex-boyfriend had turned up late at night at her front door, without warning, and wouldn't go away. The drunken ex-boyfriend was the son of Terry, whose trailer now was mine. According to Paul, Terry Jr. had lived with him for a while. In fact, it was at Paul's place that he had turned up first, earlier that same evening. Paul didn't drink, and after a while he very much wanted Terry to leave. He ended up driving Terry over to Kea's. Rather than drop Terry at the front door, he had left him on the road; Terry had stumbled across a field to get to her place. I could imagine how the dogs chained up in front must have barked.

By the time I got home, the red and blue lights had stopped flashing across the flats like a strobe. Nor was there a moon. Instead the stars, those same stars that had startled Zahra when she'd arrived in Colorado, were dense and endless over the empty open, from the Sangre de Cristos to the Rio Grande and Kiowa Hill. The Milky Way was as huge and encompassing as I'd ever seen it.

While most creatures were asleep at this quiet hour, several were up and about. Largest among them were a few horses and lots of cattle. To anyone like me foolish enough to be driving in the dark, they were easy to hit, especially the black ones. You had to take it slow. Smaller were the rabbits, who would sometimes run in front of the truck for a long distance, transfixed by the headlights, and the pack rats, mice, and other tiny creatures, including insects, whose tracks you'd notice on the powdery road surface in the morning. Their presence, of course, explained the presence of birds such as great horned owls and, much more commonly, nighthawks. Nighthawks roosted on the ground, often near roadsides, and would frequently flash through my headlights as they swooped silently this way and that.

From my trailer I'd sometimes hear coyotes calling back and forth. And what I never saw but knew was sometimes there: the occasional mountain lion.

The human "prairie rats" sometimes came alive at night, cruising around while under the influence or not. Troy's son, Jason, had raised

Sam's suspicions by trolling around at night in his truck with the head-lights off. I'd come across his darkened truck, too, rolling across the prairie, and my first concern was that I might hit him inadvertently. (My second was for his mental health.) One evening when I'd been staying at the Grubers' new place and their friend Josh from Wyoming was still living at their old one, he called Frank and Stacy in distress: his beloved Great Pyrenees had disappeared. He feared it had been stolen and asked if anyone was free to help him search in the dark. Frank and Stacy didn't have enough gas to go out looking, but I did. Meadoux and Trin joined me.

After meeting Josh by the side of the road and discussing where each of us would look, the girls and I proceeded to Jack's, where they had fed the horses months before. Jack was the conservative Christian who had complained about the mural of a topless Indigenous woman in Antonito; besides being good with horses, he had a breeding pair of Great Pyrenees, and sometimes their offspring would head back to his place for a visit. It was generally ill-advised to arrive unannounced at somebody's place after dark; indeed, after I tapped my horn outside Jack's trailer, he appeared in the doorway with a pistol in his hand. But then he saw Trin and Meadoux and recognized me and beckoned us in. Jack told us he had not seen Josh's dog but would keep an eye out.

I drove around with the girls a while longer, at one point asking if they remembered the older couple we had come across the morning I drove them to meet the summer camp bus in Antonito—the man and woman from New Mexico whose vehicle had broken down in the Punche Valley. They had walked all night to get to the place where we'd found them. The girls said yes. Then they told me about how a friend of theirs from summer camp, James, had recently attempted to walk at night from Antonito to their place, a distance of almost eighteen miles, after arguing with his father. Trin said he got within a couple miles of their house before falling asleep at the side of the road. They had given him directions; I said I imagined he was also using a map app on his phone and they said no, he'd left the phone behind because his dad had "put a tracker in it." He was found the next day by his parents, who had tracked him by following his footprints on the dusty roads.

The girls went on about how weird James was. He had jumped onto a cow from the back of his father's pickup and ridden it to Mesita. He had jumped from a window into a dumpster.

"I still can't believe he walked out here barefoot," said Trin.

Now I pictured his footprints differently. And soon I remembered a lanky teenage boy crossing the railroad tracks in Antonito one winter day. "Does he also not wear a shirt even when it's cold out?"

"That's him."

Errands serendipitous and sinister, focused and random: the fugitive who had fled the police and ended up at Sundance's door had been walking around at night, as had the naked, drugged-out guy Sam and Frank had spotted near the Grubers' one morning. The prairie never looked emptier than at night, but always there were wanderers.

7

Guns, Germs, and Climate Change

> She was glad O'Malley was there instead of old Doctor Barber. She remembered Barber, sag-cheeked, shaking-handed, riddled with dope or whatever it was he took. . . . It occurred to her that everywhere she and Bo had lived there was somebody like Doctor Barber, lost and derelict and painful to see. Were they all over, she wondered, or was it just that Bo took them always to the fringes of civilization where the misfits and the drifters all congregated?
>
> —WALLACE STEGNER, *The Big Rock Candy Mountain*

> There's a starman waiting in the sky.
>
> —DAVID BOWIE, "Starman"

IT WAS TEMPTING, sometimes, to think of the San Luis Valley, lightly populated and far from cities, as existing out of time, out of the news, immune from modern stresses. But of course that was a kind of fantasy—no place in the United States was like that in the twenty-first century.

Early in 2020, when the possibility of a pandemic was more like thin clouds high in the sky than a dark storm rolling in, I met Judy McNeil-smith of La Puente for breakfast in Alamosa. Judy oversaw the Rural Outreach initiative and supervised Matt. If things got worse, she told me, La Puente had plans to limit the numbers of guests at the shelter and would stop inviting hungry members of the public to eat inside; instead they'd hand out brown-bag lunches. Outreach interviews would be conducted remotely. Lance Cheslock had already ordered a supply of N95 masks.

We hoped it wouldn't come to that, but, of course, it did. The next day, Colorado ordered restaurants like the one we were sitting in to suspend indoor dining in a bid to stop the virus. I returned to New York, where things were very bad, and resolved not to be the person who carried the virus back to remote places that hadn't yet seen it.

I was well aware that government restrictions related to the pandemic struck people as overreach in many parts of the valley, where there were still few cases. Troy called it the "baloneyvirus" and doubted it was worse than the seasonal flu. Outside the post office at Jaroso, Harold Anderson scoffed when I offered him my forearm instead of a handshake; his wife assured me that the pandemic was "something made up by the media to make money." Inside the post office, an acquaintance sounded a little less sure; he said he remembered when his grandmother had gone to Alamosa to serve as a nurse during the Great Influenza (Spanish flu) epidemic in 1918 or 1919.

In New York I read a sprawling novel of the West by Wallace Stegner that depicted one family's life over a span that included the years of that epidemic. (The family was widely believed to be based on his own.) The father, Bo Mason, is an energetic, self-reliant, bull-headed man who hates being told what to do and can't stand the concept of quarantine, which has been imposed on the region where they live. It's wintertime, and Bo finds himself "disgusted, vaguely grouchy, irrationally sore at the farmers who sat around" and couldn't think of anything to do but tell stories about the flu. The suckers' quarantine will be his opportunity, he resolves, and he drives south from Canada in a blizzard to buy some bootleg liquor in Montana and bring it back for resale in Saskatchewan, which is dry. Bo navigates snowdrifts and desolate farmsteads on his way to a town where he hopes to convince a barkeep to sell him some hooch. But "the whole bunch from the Last Chance is in the hospital," he's told. As Bo presses on, ignoring rules and coming into contact with people who are clearly sick, I simultaneously wondered whether he would make it home with the goods and dreaded finding out what would happen if he did. As one critic wrote in 2020, "Bo, a rambunctious avatar of the unconfined, can-do spirit of the West, is a mortal danger to everyone around him."

Eventually the coronavirus made its way around the San Luis Valley. It started in towns, especially Alamosa, and enclosed agricultural facilities such as potato warehouses. La Puente implemented the measures Judy had shared with me over breakfast. But the group's managers hadn't anticipated that the run on canned goods and other groceries that accompanied the start of the pandemic nationwide would affect its network of food banks. "The stores that we depend on for their surplus food suddenly didn't have any," Lance told me later. "We couldn't even find food to buy" from commercial distributors.

They pivoted quickly. The food bank's director, working the phones, got in touch with a California-based wholesaler who had supplies but required a minimum order of one trailerful, which would cost around $30,000. Lance told me that the group got to work painting a sign on plywood to place near the street, asking for donations, and also put the word out on Facebook. Almost before the paint had dried, he said, they had raised $30,000, and the money kept pouring in. "By the time we were done, we had enough for two trailersful." That tided them over during the early days of the pandemic.

The monthly all-staff meetings transitioned from a church's community room to Zoom. While this meant that I could attend from New York, it did feel as though some of the life had been sucked out of the meetings. People looked pretty sleepy at eight a.m., except for Matt Little.

Using the weak signal from his cell phone, Matt would join from his home out on the flats. Often the video was jerky and there would be gaps in the sound, but that didn't matter, because Matt brought the prairie to the Zoom. I recognized where he sat on his couch as being just about a foot away from a plastic bin full of chicks I had seen on my last visit; I imagined I could hear their peeps. Typically, Matt being Matt, he didn't sit still for the whole meeting but would carry his phone outside, where he could make progress on his chores. I'd catch glimpses of his goats, his turkeys, his horses, Willow's daughter, the hay in the back of his pickup truck. The sun would flare into the picture and you'd know he was on the move, impatient, restless. Everyone else's Zoom image was static, but Matt's was a live-action video. I sat in my home office in New York and wished I were there.

With the police killing of George Floyd in Minneapolis later that spring, things around the country got worse. New York was among the many cities rocked by protests starting at the end of May. My students joined some of the marches, as did journalist friends who got roughed up by police. A colleague watched as a peaceful march from Brooklyn "devolved into pandemonium" in lower Manhattan when looters swooped in. On June 1, he cataloged all fifty-eight high-end storefronts in SoHo that had been damaged by looters the night before. My students marched; my daughter, too. My wife and I attended a gathering in a Bronx park that remained peaceful.

On May 30, the Alamosa *Valley Courier* published a long letter to the editor by Calvin Brown, a La Puente volunteer. Under the headline "Justice for Floyd," the letter was a cri de coeur about America's race problems. It concluded, "The time for inaction has passed, and if we ever want to get past the 'false peace' we need true understanding. Or there will be more riots. Signed, The only Black man in Alamosa, Calvin Brown."

Of course, Calvin Brown was not the only Black man in Alamosa—the mayor was a Black man; Zahra had Black sons—but you could understand how there were times when he might have felt that way.

I was not surprised to learn that a Black Lives Matter protest was planned for Alamosa three days later—such demonstrations were happening everywhere. It was to be in the town's main intersection, where some less-organized sign waving about Floyd's murder had already taken place. People who attended the protest told me what happened, and I was also informed by two long articles published in the *Valley Courier* by Susan Greene, a seasoned Denver-based journalist who lent her expertise to small-town newspapers when important stories came up.

This larger protest began in the early evening, right outside Milagros Coffee House. A dozen or so people took part, most of them young, white, and female. Several happened to work for La Puente. Also participating were a husband and wife—he a twenty-seven-year-old lawyer named James Marshall who championed criminal justice causes and, on Facebook, had posted negative things about the police. He'd also advised his Facebook friends about "how not to die while protesting. 1. Be white. 2. Carry a freedom stick" (slang for a firearm). Marshall, who called his practice Marshall Law, had attended law school at the University of Colorado and gotten his undergraduate degree from

Ohio State University, where he had been president of the rifle club. (His wife, a child-welfare caseworker for the county, had worn a pistol to a previous protest.) One protestor would later remark to Susan Greene that Marshall was the loudest in the crowd that evening—"but, like, not in a good way."

The demonstrators carried signs—Marshall's said, "MURDER IS MURDER NO MATTER BLUE DID IT"—and chanted slogans. To get drivers' attention, they filed into the crosswalk when traffic was stopped by a red light and then walked out of it when the light turned green.

Waiting at a red light around six p.m. was a black pickup truck driven by a forty-nine-year-old veteran and transplant from Texas named Danny Pruitt. Pruitt, after living for a while at the Blanca RV Park, had bought seven acres in an off-grid subdivision east of Fort Garland and was preparing to build a house there. It was later said that he was driving into town for a hamburger. (The land had been bought and subdivided by Malcolm Forbes in the early 1970s, around the same time that Tony Perry was investing farther south on the flats. It was more costly than Perry's Rio Grande Ranches, as it had trees and was closer to the mountains.) Susan Greene's article reported that the subdivision "has drawn many Texans and Oklahomans, off-roaders and gun people, and at least two residents who recently were using Confederate flags as window coverings." Greene wrote that on Facebook, a week earlier, Pruitt had

> posted an article about a soldier credited with saving lives in Kansas by ramming a shooting suspect with his pickup truck. He previously had posted a picture of his own Dodge Ram 4x4, writing, "How does it go if you can't Dodge it ram it if you can't see it well hit it."
>
> [Three days before he drove into town,] he shared five Facebook posts related to the protests. One was a meme picturing Black looters that read, "I don't know about you, but this doesn't look like they're grieving to me." . . . One sought prayers for President Donald Trump: "He's fighting an evil we can't even imagine." One showed a T-shirt printed with an American flag

and the words "You don't have to love it, but you don't have to live here either." And one was a photo of Clint Eastwood as Dirty Harry with his gun drawn, and a reference to the line, "Go ahead, make my day."

Video feeds from nearby stores showed Pruitt's truck moving into the crosswalk while people were still in it, including Marshall's wife, and protestors jumping out of the way. The videos don't reveal whether the light had changed to green before he did. They do show James Marshall, who had been in front of Pruitt's truck, pulling a pistol from his waistband as the truck moved by and turning to fire at him through the truck's rear window.

Pruitt, shot in the back of the head, came to a stop in the intersection. Then he continued driving twelve more blocks before he passed out. Marshall would later tell Alamosa police officers that the truck had hit his wife, a claim that did not appear to be supported by the video. Pruitt was transported to hospitals in Colorado Springs and Denver, where he spent weeks in a coma. Later, with the bullet still in his skull, he returned to the valley to recuperate with his sister. A GoFundMe account set up for him raised more than $150,000. James Marshall was arrested and charged with attempted murder. He pleaded guilty to a third-degree felony and was sentenced to eleven years in prison.

To me, Marshall's actions fell wide of the usual narrative—the criminal defense attorneys I knew were not pistol packers. Then again, only a week before, two Brooklyn attorneys of color had been charged with throwing a Molotov cocktail into an unoccupied police cruiser. Local sentiment leaned heavily against Marshall, particularly out on the flats. This was so even though nobody I spoke to had been anywhere near the protest; nor had they read Greene's articles. Rather, they had seen aggrieved posts from Pruitt's family and supporters. It was as though the pandemic had ushered in a new, expanded role for virtual communities: not only did the fight that brought Marshall and Pruitt together have roots on Facebook, it was now the scene of the aftermath.

Ever since George Floyd had been killed and Black Lives Matter protests had begun, I had noticed on social media that the blocking of roads by protestors, the impeding of travel, hit a particular sore spot among conservatives.* Chants like "Whose streets? Our streets!" upset them. At Troy's annual Fourth of July potluck, I played devil's advocate a little bit, broaching the idea that Pruitt's aggressive driving might have contributed to his fate, but this was always rejected. For the second year in a row, one of my neighbors wore a belt holster with a sizable pistol in it. The year before, he had told me that he planned to sell his AK-47 and use the proceeds for a rifle, but recent events had changed his mind. Instead, he said, "I'm buying a second AK! And keeping it in the truck, in case of protestors." The father of a family visiting from Mississippi said they had packed three firearms for the journey—"it's just common sense."

The strong feelings around the necessity of firearms coincided with strong feelings about the tyranny of mask-wearing rules. "You people and your masks!" Troy had said to me, exasperated, when, earlier in the week, I'd picked up a couple of his propane tanks to refill in town. I'd pointed out, with some pleasure, that he now had a disposable one hanging from his rearview mirror. "It's just in case I have to go into a store!" he explained. The black fabric and elastic straps of my masks reminded him of "half a bra—maybe a B cup."

Nobody at Troy's potluck wore a mask except for me. After a while I took it off so as not to stand out as the weirdo city person (and also, perhaps, to stop thinking about the widening gulf in the United States concerning everything from vaccines to racism). A lot of what my neighbors had to say about the pandemic echoed what was being said on Fox News at the time (e.g., "not much different from the common flu, which is also a coronavirus"). As one had written on Facebook, "I am NOT afraid of this stupid virus. I have NOT missed the fact that more people died in america in 2009 from swine flu than have died worldwide from coronavirus—so we can quit with the whole 'deadly' nonsense. I DO roll my eyes every time another anything in any state is shut down for this—nothing shut down in 2009 and they still managed to get it under control." The writer had some chronic health issues, and I hoped she wouldn't get the virus; one on one, she was a kind and

---

* In fact, a year later, Republican-controlled legislatures in Oklahoma and Iowa granted immunity to drivers whose vehicles strike and injure demonstrators in public streets.

funny person. Also, this was early in the pandemic, before the death toll approached one million in the United States and six million globally, as it did in March 2022—and denial was a little bit easier.

From Troy's I drove over to the potluck at Paul's. Here the scene was a bit different: Paul wore a mask, as did one of the other guests, a retired nurse from Texas. I kept mine on. But the fact that we all wore masks didn't mean we thought about the virus the same way. The week before, Paul, to my amazement, had asked me, "So, do you think it could all be a hoax?"

"What—the pandemic?"

"Yeah, I don't really know who to believe." He was wearing a mask just to cover his bets.

"Believe *me*—I live in New York. The hospital where my neighbor works has freezer trucks outside for bodies. Another neighbor has died. It's not a hoax."

Paul had applied stripes of masking tape six feet apart on his deck for social-distancing purposes. But he was tolerant of those who ignored them—which was most of his guests, including the young man and woman who commanded everyone's attention in the middle of the deck. Both were slender and attractive and appeared to be around thirty years old. Both looked as though they had done some hard living. The man had silver rings and studs and tattoos and wore layers of denim and leather; the woman also had many tattoos, and her short jean cutoffs showed off a lot of them on her sunburned legs. One of the man's earrings was in the process of becoming her nose ring, but it wasn't going smoothly.

"Owwwww!" she said from a chair, stamping a cowboy boot. He bent over her head, trying to ease the stud through the cartilage in her nostril. It was hard to gauge his progress because there was some blood. The retired nurse from Texas, whom I'd met before, filled me in on what had happened fifteen minutes before: the woman in the chair had admired the many rings in the man's ear and asked if she could have one of them. For her nose.

"Are you okay, honey? Anything I can do?" asked the nurse.

"It used to be pierced there—maybe that's why this is happening." She then revealed to the older woman that she had once been a nurse herself. She seemed smart, and nice, and it made me wonder what she was doing out here. She'd had a bit to drink, and maybe those things were connected.

Paul had a diverse group of prairie friends. Inside were a politically conservative Mormon couple, another neighbor who seemed conservative but swore to me he wasn't ("I just believe in the Constitution"), and a longtime pizza parlor employee who lived with his son and was talking about having just lost his job—the place had closed due to the pandemic.

An hour and a half later, the retired nurse's husband and I followed the much-pierced man—I'll call him Harry—out to his car. Gunsmithing was a hobby of his—I'd met several men on the prairie who shared this interest—and he had offered to show us his work.

He was driving a small sedan without license plates and explained that he'd just bought it, adding that it had a "clean title." He popped the hood and reached inside the engine compartment to where he had hidden the first gun—a pistol with a silencer. We oohed and aahed— the silencer was, of course, illegal. "I could get a few years for that, so I hide it," he explained. He also took out an AK pistol (an AK-47 rifle modified into pistol form) and a Colt revolver. The nurse's husband joked that around here you need a gun that can fire a lot of rounds in case you run into "a whole herd of mule deer."

"Or a whole herd of protestors," said Harry.

He talked about going back to Oklahoma in a few days to resume work on the machinery used in fracking—"valves, other stuff." He liked the idea of living in Oklahoma or Missouri because "they're both open carry," with no permits required, "and I've carried a gun since I was fifteen. The people I've gotten to know, I've had to." One night at two a.m., he said, guys he recognized from high school in San Luis broke into his grandpa's general store in Mesita with the intention to rob it. "But my gun had bullets in it and theirs didn't." His shirt was unbuttoned enough to reveal his chest tattoo: two Derringer pistols, crossed like short swords.

Somehow the Grubers came up, and that's when I realized I'd already heard a story about Harry: he had stopped by one night when Stacy and the girls were visiting relatives in Wyoming and had gotten drunk with Nick, the lost boy who was sleeping on the Grubers' couch. Harry had wanted to wrestle Nick, who was rather puny. Frank was there and told me that in the course of defending himself, Nick had pulled on Harry's thumb until it dislocated, causing considerable pain. According to Frank, Nick's response to this triumph of David over Goliath (and Harry's howls of anguish) was to apologize effusively. "I told him later he should have owned it. He did it purely in self-defense." Stacy told me that Harry was "like a baby version of Sam"—a wild man enamored of weaponry, getting high, and going a little bit crazy. I also thought of Angelo Duarte and of Troy's son, two more dashing hell-raisers who had done time in jail.

It was feeling late, and I got in my truck to go. But the men, and others milling about, were effectively blocking the driveway—like protestors, Harry joked. I revved my engine, getting in the spirit of things. Harry mimed brandishing a pistol at me, then blasting away as I rolled by.

Even if few people had been infected yet by Covid-19 in my part of the flats, much of the turmoil of the outside world filtered in via television and social media. I stopped by a neighbor's place; he told me, "If you have any money in the bank, get it out." But why? "Last night it took one trillion dollars to cover the daily bank rate"—I wasn't sure what this was—"as opposed to the two hundred million dollars in the last banking crisis." The core problem, he added, wasn't the pandemic but that the media overdramatized the Covid situation. I allowed that this might be true in certain situations, but I told him I believed there were solid reasons for alarm. I noted that only eight people so far had died of Covid in the valley but pointed out that the figure was bound to go higher. My neighbor told me that he doubted that eight had died. I scrolled through my emails until I found the SLV Public Health Daily Update of June 29, 2020, forwarded to me from La Puente. In addition to the deaths, it said there were 420 known infections in the six counties of the valley, 98 of which had resulted in people seeking medical care. I handed the phone to him, and he read it. "Okay, well, I believe you about this," he said.

But there was so much disbelief. A friend of the Grubers' had shared a post on Facebook that purported to demonstrate that the George Floyd video was faked. There was broad support for Trump's threats to send troops to cities such as Portland, Oregon, and Seattle, which had "lost control." Matt Little, to my surprise, told me that the pandemic was intentional. Did he mean that China had released the virus on purpose? No, he meant that unnamed global elites had released it expressly to "start a race war" so they could impose further lockdown restrictions "and martial law," leading to gun confiscation. The evidence was always just something people had read on Facebook.

There were some surprises, though. Whereas I had expected people who opposed the Black Lives Matter protests to be pro-police, many were not—including, in their Facebook posts, Frank Gruber and Luke Kunkel. Both, I knew, had spent time locked up, and neither thought police power was the answer. All the same, Luke objected to the message of "Black lives matter." "Don't all lives matter?" he asked me. I was reflexively about to tell him that of course all lives mattered, but the protests were about anti-Black racism, not about saying white lives don't matter, when Luke added some nuance: Black people, in his view, "aren't just looking for equality, they're looking for superiority." And then I saw that Luke, who had nothing, was saying that he was against being *disadvantaged* compared to Black people. He lived in a universe of poor people where he was competing for a small share of the available resources. Equality, he said, would be fine with him.

In any case, the turmoil in the outside world had reenergized Matt and Luke's interest in prepping. The worse things got, in terms of civil unrest, the more they believed they'd soon be forced to rely on their own devices. (Both would eventually see the electoral loss of Donald Trump in November 2020 as a fraud and further evidence that people like themselves needed to prepare for total anarchy.)

Fewer cows were finding their way to my place that summer, which was good, as I was still working on the fence. But the reason there were fewer cows was bad. The land was really dry, and the dark green kochia weed, which had grown a foot tall a couple of summers before, was either barely an inch tall or missing entirely. Drought was to blame: most of the San Luis Valley, and much of the West, was experiencing "abnormally dry to exceptional drought" conditions—the worst designation given by the National Oceanic and Atmospheric Administra-

Abandoned trailer home

tion. In fact, rainfall had been below normal for several years. Beyond my place, the prairie was browner. I could see it when I drove over the one-lane Lobatos Bridge on my way into Antonito, too: the Rio Grande was more like a *rio pequeño*.

The drought was also apparent in the sky, as July turned to August and forest fires sprang up around the region. When the fires were nearby, as with the Spring Creek fire, started by a Danish immigrant in 2018, we could see columns of white and gray smoke rising from the mountaintops, up into the clouds. When they were farther away, as with the 186 Fire near Durango in 2019, we would see (and sometimes smell) diffuse smoke coming in from the west, making the view less clear (and, occasionally, the sunsets more brilliant). The year 2020 would be an extreme fire season that saw major fires in twelve western states, and the three largest fires on record in Colorado, including the giant Pine Gulch fire near Grand Junction.

Drought on the ground, smoke in the sky. And then in September, something else that suggested a climate in crisis.

The valley is a great place to see migrating birds. The premier attraction is the arrival of sandhill cranes every spring and fall, particularly in the wetland wildlife refuges around the town of Monte Vista.

"Monty," as it is known, hosts an annual crane festival. Tourists sign up for bus tours, but anyone can drive the "tour loop" and see thousands of cranes. Usually they are standing, in flocks numbering from scores to hundreds, often in water, but occasionally they go airborne, an enthralling sight. The birds also make an otherworldly, gentle clacking sound as they chatter among themselves, which I've found easiest to hear toward the end of the day, when the wind is right and the people have gone back to town.

Lance Cheslock gave me my introduction to valley bird life. As much as helping the poor is his life's work, watching birds is his weekend pleasure: year-round he will relax by driving, often with his wife, to good birding sites, be they near the sand dunes, along the Rio Grande, or hours away in Utah or New Mexico. In addition to cranes, Lance had shown me ground-nesting owls, falcons, eagles, and other birds of prey. One summer day near Los Sauces, we even saw a pelican—like many of the birds, it was just passing through. When I wondered about the family of birds hanging around my mobile home, I texted Lance a poor cell-phone photo. He shot back, "Does it perch in high places? Eat flying insects?" Yes and yes. Another text: "Say's phoebes."

It wasn't only serious birders who followed avian life in the valley. The Gruber girls, as I have mentioned, had named the ravens who visited them Coo and Caw—and, under a collapsed shack nearby, had discovered a disused raven nest. (Stacy and Frank's youngest child, born in the valley, was named Raven.) The McDonald kids had named a particular raven with a green feather Bob, and a hummingbird Fred. Paul posted photos on Facebook of many of the birds that stopped by his place, including a great horned owl. A member of the Conejos Writers Circle, which I visited one month, told me about seeing a flock of maybe forty eagles one weekend the year before—feasting on tilapia, she guessed, dumped by a commercial fish farm.

In September 2020, though, something awful happened that took everyone by surprise. On September 7 and 8, which is still considered summertime in the valley, temperatures dropped from 87 to 27 degrees. Fifteen inches of snow fell in Alamosa and six to eight inches elsewhere. Winds gusted up to seventy miles per hour. People took to social media to post photos of dead birds on their driveways, sidewalks, and lawns. They weren't just any birds; they were colorful gems: little bursts of yellow and red, many of them warblers. As days went by, it became clear that a huge number had died over a wide area of the Southwest. Paul posted a photo of three yellow birds from his yard on social media and asked if anyone knew what they were. (His friends agreed they were Wilson's warblers.) My neighbor Woody told me he had "tons" of dead birds at his house and believed it was caused by the cold. "Red, yellow, green ones" were both dead and alive; "the dogs ate a couple." Oddly, they now had a bird *never* normally found in the area, living in a short tree on their land: a woodpecker.

The Monte Vista Journal published a report from a local expert that lent some context:

> The timing of the storm was especially unfortunate for migrating songbirds. Migrating birds expend tremendous energy during migration and rely on the autumn abundance of seeds, flowers and insects to restore energy. However, the 14 plus inches of snow the Valley received effectively cut off the food supply for these birds and left them wet, weakened, hungry and cold. Many birds died in the process or were seen to be near death. They were easily approached in their diminished conditions.

He reported that a science teacher at the local high school had her students do a mortality survey of birds around a nearby historic building. They found "24 juvenile Violet-green swallows, 5 adult Violet-green swallows, 1 MacGillivray's Warbler, 1 Wilson's Warbler, 1 Pine Siskin and 1 juvenile Barn Swallow. That count is conservative as the janitors are reported to have removed a few more." He had done his own carcass count along a four-mile stretch of valley highway nicknamed the Gunbarrel: "3 American Robins, 3 Vesper Sparrows, 3 Hermit Thrushes, 2 Green-tailed Towhees, 3 Mountain Bluebirds, 1 Western Bluebird, 2 Starlings and 1 Wilson's Warbler. If this is extrapolated to other county and state roads in our Valley, the mortality would have amounted to thousands of birds from highways alone."

My neighbor with the most vivid report, perhaps not coincidentally, lived not in a house or a mobile home but in a camper trailer about the size of mine. Camaro Jim, you might say, was closer to the weather than most. He had gone inside as it started getting cold on the first day of the storm but ventured back out after hearing two thunderclaps in the late afternoon. Jim, who is not prone to hyperbole, said he found himself amid "thousands and thousands and thousands" of birds flying three to four feet above the ground, heading south. The wave of birds lasted twenty or thirty minutes, he said, and reminded him of the old black-and-white Hitchcock film *The Birds.* Only this was in color—mostly yellow but also red and green. When it was over, he said, the ground around his trailer was covered with birds. They weren't dead but seemed stunned. "You could just pick 'em up," he said, and he did, gathering up an armload. He placed some underneath his trailer and brought others inside, "just hoping they'd warm up and get better." But they all wanted to go back outside. In the morning, the blanket of snow "was just covered with them," to the point that he didn't want to drive because he didn't want to squash them, though most were already dead.

I returned to the valley about a week after all this. My property was dotted with wisps of yellow feathers and down, as though kids dressed up for Halloween had marched through and lost details from their costumes. The semi-sheltered path between Troy's house and his shop had five little mounds of red and yellow feathers—and here you could still see that some had once been birds, because their little bodies were out of the wind. But dead birds fall apart fast, and I guessed they wouldn't be visible for long.

In a webinar sponsored by a conservation group, a scientist named Arvind Panjabi showed the main routes taken by birds migrating south. Up to 2.7 billion birds do this every year, he said, most of them traveling at night. The birds that died in September—hundreds of thousands of them, if not millions—had flown into a perfect storm. The backdrop was an even bigger disaster: a decline of almost 30 percent in the number of birds in western forests of North America over the past fifty years, described by Panjabi and others in the journal *Science.* The root cause of both appeared to be, in general terms, climate change. The scientist concluded by sharing some steps ordinary people could take to help birds, such as keeping cats indoors, marking windows so birds won't crash into them, reducing the size of lawns and growing native plants, and "watching birds and sharing what you see."

But these steps seemed unlikely to counterbalance the powerful forces driving climate change. At least my neighbors, with their modest carbon footprints, absence of lawns and picture windows, and attention to what was happening outside, seemed to be doing right by the birds, intentionally or not.

A woman I chatted with in line at Hometown Food Market in Antonito agreed that it had been cold when all the birds died but said the real cause was God: the calamity was a harbinger of the biblical "end of days"—a sign that the end of the world was near. It struck me that in this one instance, those who believed in science and those who believed in the supernatural were in agreement about the meaning of the disaster.

But you can't write about the San Luis Valley without saying a bit more about the supernatural. Judging by their ubiquity, the best-selling books about the San Luis Valley in recent years are the ones written about the supernatural by Christopher O'Brien. The best known, *Secrets of the Mysterious Valley* (2007), declares on its cover, "No other region in North America features the variety and intensity of unusual phenomena found in the world's largest alpine valley, the San Luis Valley of Colorado and New Mexico." The book talks about reports of "UFOs, ghosts, crypto-creatures, cattle mutilations, skinwalkers and sorcerers, along with portal areas, secret underground bases and covert military activity." And, indeed, the valley is known for supernatural weirdness. The book has been updated at least once; I would not be surprised to find the massive bird die-off of 2020 in a future edition.

That said, while the books are short on evidence, that doesn't mean that some of what they describe isn't true. Early in my acquaintance with Matt Little, we stopped by his first residence on the flats to pick something up. As we turned off the main road, I noticed the carcass of a dead animal, and he said, "Oh yeah, that's a mutilated cow." *What?* He stopped so that I could view the tawny body. Just as I had read in multiple accounts of such deaths, the animal's anus appeared to have been removed with a square cut—it was plain as day. But there was no sign of blood in the soil. Matt said that until the rancher came to take a look, there were no tire tracks at all near the animal; nor did he see footprints. Nor had animals like coyotes stopped by to feed. It had been a week or more since the animal's death; now it looked desiccated, and though in this case there was no telling, many accounts suggested that the mutilated animals had internal organs removed, presumably via the butthole.

But how and by whom? Cattle mutilations weren't unique to the San Luis Valley, but it had seen a lot of them. Christopher O'Brien had a whole book on the subject (*Stalking the Herd: Unraveling the Cattle Mutilation Mystery*). Soon after Matt showed me that cow, the *Costilla County Free Press* published an article about other mutilations—ranchers Manuel Sanchez and Erminio Martinez had both reported them in the past month. Martinez was quoted as saying, "I found one of my cows with her tongue, udder, and sex organs removed. It appears that some type of surgical knife was used. But there was no sign of blood [and] the cuts were so precise. In my opinion, if it were a predator, they would tear at the hide and pull at it until they reached the cavity." That wasn't what this looked like.

On the goofy side, one valley tourist attraction is the UFO Watchtower on State Highway 17, also known as the Cosmic Highway. It's a raised platform (and private campground) from which one can get a second-story view of the valley; a sign there declares that psychics have identified "two large Vortexes" on the eastern side of the platform. ("A Vortex is described as an opening to a Parallel Universe which is full of energy. One of the Vortexes spins clockwise and the other spins counter clockwise.")

The United States military admitted in 2017, after a media report, that it had a previously secret office that collected information on UFOs, much of it provided by its pilots. After the release of a Pentagon report to the U.S. Senate Intelligence Committee in the summer of 2021, the former head of the secret office told *60 Minutes*,

> Imagine a technology that can do 6-to-700 g-forces, that can fly at 13,000 miles an hour, that can evade radar and that can fly through air and water and possibly space. And oh, by the way, has no obvious signs of propulsion, no wings, no control surfaces and yet still can defy the natural effects of Earth's gravity. That's precisely what we're seeing.

In their own ways, it seemed that the military and the UFO people were talking about the same thing.

I was struck by the way many educated, sober-minded people in the valley had supernatural-type stories to tell. The same day that historian Loretta Mitson had led our group to an ancient circle of volcanic stones of unknown provenance, she had pointed to a mountain to the south of us, Cerro de la Olla, which was just north of Taos. The previous fall, two bowhunters looking for elk had stumbled upon two strange sights. First were two beings basically human-shaped except for their extremely large heads, which may have been hoods; the second, which they saw a couple of days later on the same mountain, was a large white structure that looked a bit like a circus tent with a long extension. Seconds after the men laid eyes on these objects, they disappeared. The two men were quoted in the weekly *Taos News:* "We're a couple of guys that don't believe in much, but we believe now."

Then practically everyone else in our group shared a story about some encounter with the supernatural. One man had seen mutilated cattle. So had Reyes Garcia, the retired philosophy professor whose family raised cattle. Reyes also recalled being surrounded one night by bright light; Loretta had a sober-minded accountant friend with a similar story. Lance Cheslock knew a pharmacist from La Jara who woke up to two crop circles on his property; a photo appeared on the front page of the *Valley Courier.* Ronald Rael, the professor of architecture at Berkeley, described what sounded like ghosts in the historic property he had bought and was preserving in the crumbling settlement of Conejos, concentrated in the spaces where slaves had once lived.

So far as I know, I have never seen a ghost or a UFO. But I think I would be foolish to disbelieve something just because I cannot explain it. For his book *Lonely Planets: The Natural Philosophy of Alien Life,* the astrobiologist David Grinspoon drove to the valley from his home in Denver to talk to believers in UFOs. He spent some days in Crestone, which he called "a spiritually restless town . . . that attracts aliens, hippies, and New Age entrepreneurs." He watched the sky at night while immersed at a nearby hot springs and saw

two spinning galaxies, one from the inside and one from the outside. I saw eager clusters of bright young stars just leaving their nebular nest and entering galactic life, and tired, old red giant stars taking one last lap around the galaxy. . . . I saw enormous clouds of dark, obscuring dust drifting down the Milky Way. I saw stars that we now know have planets circling them, and many more that surely must have planets. Closer to home, I saw Jupiter and Mars promenading through the starscape. . . . I saw many satellites speeding along and winking out when they fell into Earth's shadow, and occasional high-flying aircraft, each flashing its own distinctive rhythmic stripe across the sky, the silent songs of mechanical birds. . . .

It was all there, except no UFOs.

Grinspoon asked his fellow springs bathers for advice on seeing UFOs. "One woman who had experienced many sightings told me that the most important thing is that *you have to invite them.* They will not show up for just anyone, in just any state of mind. I asked if she could tell me anything more specific about how you invite them. She said that you go to a very dark place and focus on inviting them, on receiving them, on wishing them to be with you, and you try to communicate to them that it is safe to come." And sometimes, then, they show up.

As a scientist, Grinspoon thinks that evidence should precede belief. He says that if asked, Do you believe that the universe is full of extraterrestrial intelligent beings and do you think it possible that some of them are now on Earth or have been in the past?, he'd say yes. But if asked, Do you believe that reported UFO sightings are alien spacecraft and that aliens walk among us?, he'd say no. He sees no reason to link cattle mutilations to extraterrestrial life, as many do, but I'm pretty sure he doesn't think it's impossible. "There are some mysteries," he writes in *Lonely Planets.* "Are we being unpatriotic to the flag of science if we admit there are some mysteries?"

By summer the surge in demand at La Puente's Alamosa food bank was past. But the pandemic meant that clients could no longer come in and browse the shelves; rather, they lined up outside and then, one at a time, waited to be served. The food bank put out a call for some extra hands. I signed up for a slot. Others did, too, including La Puente's director of outreach, Callie Adams.

Before the doors opened, I helped unload a van that brought donated produce from Walmart and other local businesses, including boxes of melons, lettuce, and rotisserie chickens (cooked but now frozen). Then I started packaging bags of potatoes and onions and placing carts of them near the table set up at the front door. Callie staffed the table at the door, signing people in and then sharing their orders with me and other volunteers, who filled them.

Most of the clients had been there before—they could come once a week. But early in the afternoon a first-timer, a young man wearing a big backpack, said he had just arrived in town and was looking for "snacks." We had a few things that qualified—packets of cookies, day-old pastries, yogurts. A friendly female volunteer asked if he knew his way around. He replied aggressively, saying that he'd already heard about camping by the river but didn't plan on it because "I hate homeless people." Next Callie took over, explaining that she needed to sign him in.

"Can't I just take those snacks?" he asked, gesturing at some.

"As soon as we get you into the system," she said. "It'll just take a minute."

He began digging in his heels, said he didn't want to answer questions. A lot of activity on our side of the table kind of stopped as we waited to see how much of a problem he was going to be. Callie stayed perfectly even in her manner. *First name, last name?* He was Benjamin Franklin, he said. He was born on today's date about two hundred years ago. His first language was Russian, and his ethnicity was purple.

I felt myself getting annoyed at the way he appeared to be trying to provoke Callie, and at his disrespect for the simple process. He was, after all, about to get food for free. I was wondering whether Callie might tell him to leave, whether there might be a scene and if volunteers like me might need to back her up. But we took our cues from her, and she was unshakable, not challenging anything he said. After he finally received his "snacks" and went on his way, I asked Callie about it.

"How did you stay so calm?" I asked, truly curious. "I might have lost my temper."

"I just don't react to snarky answers," she said. "I taught high school for too many years. He obviously has mental-health issues." She explained how she trained her AmeriCorps volunteers to deal with this kind of situation. "It's hard for them because often they want to engage—they have a lot of ideals. But this is not the right person to engage with. They're not assholes, they're just in crisis—you have to repeat that to yourself."

She went on: "When they're personally attacking you, demanding service from you in a violent way, that's yelling *at* you. Otherwise they're yelling *to* you because they're frustrated and in crisis. There are a lot of people who come in very angry—not at us, but at the situation they're in."

I thought about that for some time. Not reacting felt unsatisfying to me, like tamping down a natural response. But then I pictured Callie in a classroom and thought of the ways student misbehavior could be unrelated to a particular teacher. In that kind of institutional setting, it wasn't always personal—some students were just going to act up. And I could see that the humble storefront of the food bank was an institutional setting, of a sort. We had what he wanted, and that gave us power over him—that seemed to be what he was reacting to. Callie's experience had given her wisdom. And it was of a piece with an ideology that underlay much of what La Puente did, which was, in my own paraphrasing, *You can't really know their pain, so don't judge.*

But what about judging? Wasn't forming opinions part of what made us human? I grappled with this problem on the flats, where I was surveying my neighbors about whether they'd gotten a Covid-19 stimulus payment from the federal government and what they'd decided to do with it. This was a happy subject for most of them, since life tended to bring few of these windfalls.

I started with the Grubers. Like many Americans, they had received federal stimulus payments totaling $3,200 in the twelve months starting in April 2020. Most of the mini-windfall went to paying off debt, especially to Sam and Cindy, whom they still owed for their property, but also to their neighbor "Car Wash" Kevin, who had sold them an old Toyota sedan on credit. They then bought a new generator and wood for an addition to the house Frank was building. Finally, they bought computer equipment, including a special printer and supplies,

and a laptop. Stacy described this to me in terms of making money—
the equipment would allow her to sell custom vinyl stickers to friends
or to strangers at crafts fairs. But, from the custom Broncos T-shirt she
had made for Frank, I could see that some of its value was in pleasure,
in things they made for themselves.

Another neighbor showed me the shiny used ATV he had bought. I
knew that his household had some debt and no savings.

Another neighbor had spent stimulus money on car repair and
bought a new television and a new tablet computer.

I brought the subject up with Matt Little when we met for coffee
in the spring of 2021. Immediately he saw why I was interested. "It's
about toys versus what you need, right?" He himself had spent $500
on an assay fee to learn about how much precious metal was in an ore
sample, as well as $3,500 on a "shaker table" ("it's like a big sluice box")
to help in extracting ore from rocks. By contrast, Luke had bought a
$500 welding rig ("which he don't need") and a dredge—a floating
machine that sucks up silt from the bottom of a creek, while the opera-
tor stands nearby in the water. But none of their claims had a real creek
where they could use it. And it was hard to picture Luke in the water.

Yes, there is a lot to be said about spending for pleasure, and people
on the flats had precious few opportunities for it. That was not to say
they didn't judge one another, however. According to one neighbor,
the McDonalds, who had lived in the windowless wooden box house
until the dad was arrested for sexually abusing his kids, had been notably improvident: "Costilla County would give families gas money to
get back and forth to the school bus stop. Zane would use the gas
on his generator to power the TV that was always on"—or when the
generator wasn't working, he'd just turn on the car and power the TV
from that. And they'd quickly spend all of their welfare money at the
start of every month on shopping trips to Alamosa, and inevitably be
broke by month's end.

That spring, Stacy and Frank had met a family that had arrived in
the past year from the East Coast and lived in a trailer about a mile
away. The family had become briefly famous when their oldest child,
a son, fifteen, disappeared one afternoon during the winter. He was a
handsome boy; when the sheriff's office posted a notice announcing
that he was missing, someone commented that he looked like Kurt

Cobain of Nirvana. There was speculation that he might have met someone online who had driven in and picked him up. The notice said he'd last been seen on his bicycle near Road G: "He was supposed to go down to the river, but he never arrived and his bike was later found near an abandoned trailer on Road G."

The sheriff's office and many neighbors joined in the search for the boy. At first they focused on the canyon along the river. When that was unsuccessful, the high school principal loaned the sheriff's office a drone. Together they used it to buzz around various prairie dwellings, abandoned and otherwise, in the area. The sound of the drone prompted the boy to open the door of the trailer where he'd been squatting, to see what was going on. The drone's camera spotted him; deputies arrived soon after.

The boy had since gone back East to live with his grandmother—apparently he'd had differences with his stepmom in the trailer on the flats. But Stacy and Frank, in the course of joining the search, had become friendly with the family. So one day when I was visiting, Stacy asked me if I, as a volunteer for La Puente, would consider driving the dad into Alamosa? His truck was out of commission, but he'd received his $1,400 stimulus payment and there were things he wanted to buy.

I went there directly to talk with him about it. The family's trailer was improbably small—hardly larger than my camper trailer—and I could barely believe that five people (now four) lived there. In place of a lawn it was surrounded by a sea of discarded clothes. I tapped my horn and the dad came outside.

He wanted to buy a new go-cart and motorbike from Tractor Supply in Alamosa, he said. They were holding the items for him, and he was eager to go ASAP. And he didn't trust his truck to get him into town and back. I thought, *A go-cart?* I told him I needed to check my schedule but would let him know the next morning.

I returned home to think about it. This did not seem to be an errand that would rise to the level of free help from La Puente. It would require a commitment of probably half a day. And all for a couple of things that, by most people's standards, were not necessary purchases and possibly not even wise ones, given the family's modest resources. I made myself dinner, drank a beer, and decided not to do it.

But later, as I lay in bed, I changed my mind. It was actually something Zahra had said that made me. After moving from the prairie into town, she had told somebody she had avoided things like vodka because "I got six kids. I can't afford to have that. I got to pay for water and take care of them, that's why. Whereas others, they spend their money on the wrong things because that's what make them feel better."

Go-carts and minibikes weren't the same as vodka. But they did seem to fall into the same category of possibly unwise purchases that would make a person feel better. In the morning I texted Stacy to tell the guy I could pick him up around lunchtime. (He didn't have a working phone and she had said she'd be going by that morning.)

She texted me back an hour later to say, "he got a ride just a few mins ago" and didn't need me anymore. I shouldn't have been surprised—if he had $1,400, he also had the cash to pay somebody for gas, if not their time. But I was disappointed. It would have been a chance to get to know him.

I drove by his place the next day to check in and see if he'd gone through with it. Nobody was home at the trailer, but down the hill I heard engines and saw lots of action—a minibike and a go-cart racing around, kicking up clouds of dust. A blond girl, maybe eight, ran up the hill to me, unafraid. I told her I was there to see if her dad needed another ride anywhere. She said no, he got the minibike and was on it with her mom, and the truck worked now, too! She looked thrilled, and I got the feeling that the whole family was happy today.*

My fence grew in fits and starts. It was harder work than I'd expected, even as I gained expertise. The hardest on my body was setting new fence posts: YouTube showed guys pounding them in with the heavy post drivers that slide over the top of a T-post. You'd lift it up and drop it down, again and again, until the T-post sank into the earth. All of them seemed to be doing it in the rich soil of the Midwest, not in the hard sand of the desert. Here the sand was loose for the first couple of inches, and it was easy to start the hole, but then the soil could become

---

* Sociologist Matthew Desmond, in his book *Evicted*, describes how a woman, Larraine, blows all of her food stamps on a lobster dinner for herself—and he also quotes her explaining the logic of it, given her certainty that she'll always be poor.

Troy and Grace
Courtesy of Grace Nielsen

dense and unyielding. A couple of hours of pounding and my arms and shoulders and neck would be aching.

I asked Troy for advice on digging the holes. Years ago he had used an auger attached to the back of his tractor to dig post holes, he said. His tractor now had a flat tire, but he thought I might be able to rent an auger I could tow behind my truck. He said it could be especially useful in setting the thick wooden posts I'd need to attach gates to my fence. Handheld post-hole drivers weren't so helpful for those big posts—"you really just have to dig a hole" with a shovel, and it helps to have a hose nearby to loosen the ground as you go. But even with that, said Troy, sand will probably keep sliding into the hole, so that by the time you have a hole that's two or three feet deep, you also have a hole that's two or three feet across. That's when you set the big wooden pole in, and keep it balanced upright as you fill the dirt back in.

With three sides of my fence essentially finished, I prepared for the final stretch: the side between my property and Troy's. It had not been fenced before and, awkwardly, it was not entirely clear where the property line should be drawn. There was another reason I had saved it for last: fencing Troy out of my property was, in truth, the *worst* aspect of building a fence. During the years nobody lived there, the place had remained untouched due to his oversight. My land had once belonged to him, and he had briefly lived on it. People knew that, still associated Troy with the land years later, and I believe that's one reason nobody had messed with it during its years of quiet abandonment. I wanted Troy to keep feeling proprietary. But also I wanted to fence out the cows.

When Troy came over, he would often skip the road and drive on a dirt trail from his property. I told him I was getting ready to finally finish the fence and suggested substituting a cattle guard for the gate on our property line, so that he could continue to drive over without having to get out of his truck and open a gate. But Troy discouraged me. He explained that cattle guards were expensive, hard to install without a crew, and required concrete to support them.

Finally, I had to discuss the property line. Troy had once showed me a T-post set in the sand by the previous owner, who, he said, had measured it with string and told him, "I think this might be it." But I suspected that it was off. The county has a Web-based property map with software that lets you drop pins and measure distances. I used it to get fairly exact GPS readings of where the property line was between me and Troy, and then I pounded little wooden stakes at the lot's corners, after locating them with my phone. I tied a long string between the two corners and pounded in a line of more wooden stakes where my fence posts would go. I thought it important to show the line to Troy before I built the actual fence. But I was a little nervous about it—I knew that property lines can become an issue between neighbors. I liked Troy and didn't want there to be any problems between us.

We had just finished having morning coffee at his kitchen table when I brought it up. Troy allowed that he had half an hour or so free, and I offered to drive us over. We got out of my truck, and Troy looked at my line of stakes. His eyes then went back to the T-post set in the sand by the previous owner. It was closer to my house. "Are you sure that's not it?" he asked. I tried to explain why I was, without getting technical: Troy was not big on computers, GPS, or technology in general, and I didn't want to bully him with tech. If he wanted, I said, I would go buy us a long length of string and we could start from scratch and measure with that. No pressure. Troy looked one way for quite a while and then turned his head 180 degrees and looked the other. I held my tongue and thought, *If it's only a difference of a few yards, I will compromise.*

Then Troy said, "I guess this feels like the middle." We shook hands.

I brought up my fence the next day when I was talking with my neighbor Robert. Robert had close-cropped hair and a big bushy beard. He had come to the flats from Denver, where he had worked in the state police auxiliary and in a weed store. Originally he was from Tennessee. He had done a stint in the army and was a thirty-second-degree Mason. A $25,000 settlement from a motorist who had struck him on his motorcycle was the seed money that had allowed him to buy land and build a simple house near me. He liked firearms, and we'd shot at cans with his AK-47. He'd picked up a used one-man gasoline-powered auger when he was building a pallet fence for his marijuana grow, he said. It was basically a big screw, three feet tall and six inches in diameter, with handles and a little engine on top. How had I never heard of such a tool? He offered to loan it to me.

Then he took a call on his cell: Robert was growing a bail bonds business, and the phone was his lifeline. When the call ended, he looked worried.

"A methhead I wrote a bond for skipped his court appearance. If we can't find him, I could be out five thousand dollars," he said. He paused. "Would you go up to Blanca with me tomorrow? He lives off-grid near his mom. If he's home and I can arrest him, it would help to have somebody else there." In exchange, if we caught him, Robert would pay me one hundred dollars. "How about we skip the money," I suggested, "and you help me drill holes for my last line of fence posts, whether we catch him or not?" Robert agreed.

I was fine with the arrangements until the next morning, when Robert called and asked, "Do you have a ballistic vest?" Um, no. Did most people? Robert said that was okay, and that he'd be over soon. But as we motored up to Blanca in his rickety GMC pickup, the question prompted us to have an important and, from my end, heartfelt conver-

Robert holsters his Taser.

sation about how prepared I was to take on the role of bounty hunter. Robert revealed that he would be approaching the house of the fugitive with the aforementioned vest, an official BAIL ENFORCEMENT AGENT badge, a pistol, a Taser, and handcuffs. I, on the other hand, had a pair of sunglasses.

"So I've been thinking about that," said Robert. "This guy has done state time, he's a felon. I'd feel more comfortable with a deputy there, so I'm going to call them once we're in town." I seconded the idea.

In the event, Costilla County had only two deputies on duty, and neither was available to help; they said they had pressing matters to attend to. We listened to their calls using Robert's police scanner app and learned that these included helping locate a lost dog and escorting a funeral procession. Robert also tried the state patrol, but those officers, too, were tied up. Eventually he said, "I'm just going to go there myself. You can stand by the truck, keep an eye out, call 911 if anything bad happens."

I said that was okay. Then I tried to picture what this might look like: Robert getting blown away by the fugitive firing through his window, me discovering that my phone had no signal and running down the road, trying to hide in the brush from the felon on my tail.

The reality was somewhat different. Robert parked his truck at the front gate of the property, which was on the slopes of Blanca Peak. A pit bull and a large German shepherd ran up barking but stayed with me as a woman came out of the main house and Robert walked past the gate to speak with her. She, I would later learn, was the fugitive's mother. She had put up money for the bond, which now, Robert told her, she could lose. But she said she didn't know where he'd gone. Her other son was also in prison. The dogs stopped growling, and at the risk of looking less intimidating, I petted the German shepherd. Meanwhile, seeing that we'd left the doors open, the pit bull jumped into the truck. I wondered how this might complicate our exit.

Long story short, we left empty-handed. Robert would return soon to drive away a pickup truck and a Nissan Maxima that had been signed over to him to cover the bond. He would mock up a WANTED poster with the guy's picture and post it to different Facebook groups. He would appear at my place the next day with his gasoline auger, and we would drill eighteen post holes in less than an hour.

With my fence nearing completion, I went to see Ronald Rael, the architecture professor I had met on the history tour with Loretta Mitson. Ron was still in the valley, teaching remotely and waiting out the pandemic with his wife and son. He was celebrated for an installation of seesaws at the border wall with Mexico. Each seesaw fit through the border fence, using the fence itself as a fulcrum; if a Mexican kid sat on one side and an American on the other, they could play. I wanted a chance to talk to somebody who had given so much thought to walls and fences, and Ron agreed to see me.

His family's ranch, which had been theirs for five generations, was situated between me and the town of Antonito in an area called

La Florida ("The Flowery Place"). This kind of land, with its cotton-wood trees and fields irrigated not with pumps and pivots but with ditches from rivers, was lush and lovely in a way the prairie was not. It sat on the south branch of the San Antonio River on what was presumed to be the route of the famous Diego de Vargas expedition from Santa Fe to the San Luis Valley in 1694. In fact, said Ron, the scribe who had recorded the daily dispatches from the Spanish settler was "my sixth great-grandfather on my father's side." A neighbor had found a horseman's spur nearby, and an authority at Adams State University had judged it to be from the seventeenth century.

Ron had been using his time productively. Graduate students from Berkeley had been helping him build experimental adobe structures using 3-D printing technology. He showed me into the latest one. It was cool, naturally lit, and quiet, the perfect place for a talk.

I reminded Ron that on the day we'd met, he'd been preoccupied with something more mundane than experimental architecture, which was fixing a fence. He had leased a field to a guy with cows; as part of the deal, the man agreed to maintain the fences. Instead, said Ron, the man's cows, numerous and underfed, had pushed through a fence in search of grass and invaded his neighbors' property. The neighbors were unhappy, and now Ron, who had other demands on his time, had to fix it himself. He'd been wearing work boots and driving his dad's ancient pickup truck, which wouldn't start at lunchtime until he adjusted something under the hood and we gave it a push. The truck had a shovel and fence tools in the back, and I'd felt a kinship to him.

I told Ron how, for my book *Coyotes,* I had snuck into Arizona from the Mexican state of Sonora with undocumented Mexicans. It was nighttime. We climbed over a total of four barbed-wire fences; the last of these, strong and taut, was still not hard to scale. Most of my companions were headed to work in Idaho, where they knew (because they had worked there for years) that they were needed and expected. That they had to endure this gauntlet didn't seem entirely fair. I had my doubts about fences and wondered whether Ron felt the same.

First off, he said, "there's a difference between a fence and a wall." Out here fences were for animals, and "I have no problem building or fixing a fence because there's just a complex set of issues related to where a cow should eat and where a cow shouldn't eat." The barriers I had crossed north of Sonoita had since been "upgraded" by the government into walls, though to Ron that was too simple a descriptor. "A steel structure that's filled with concrete for hundreds of miles has the violence embedded in it associated with a militarized wall, as a medieval kind of structure." Such a barrier "blocks wind and animal migrations, causes ecological damage, and causes border crossers, whether people or animals, to put themselves into extreme and dangerous situations."

It also creates "long-lasting psychological and cultural walls" that promote a feeling on the builder's side that what's being kept out is dangerous. Reports in recent months of "caravans" of would-be migrants arriving from the south were of a piece with this. "Caravan," said Ron, was the wrong word. "To me that word sounds threatening. I remember that that first 'caravan' was arriving around Thanksgiving. And I asked, Why don't we call these people pilgrims? Instead of a caravan, [we might say] that pilgrims are arriving who are seeking a better life, who are seeking freedom from persecution." Even if the numbers were large, they could be seen as "people who are in danger, who could be welcomed."

We talked about the historical meanings of the land around us. I had just read an account of the de Vargas expedition and knew that in his day, grants of frontier land were made to colonists who could "settle" them—establish towns, help expand Spanish dominion. The Utes that de Vargas ran into at San Antonio Mountain, just south of here, did not attack until the Spaniards started killing (and eating) their buffalo: Utes cared about the food more than about any concept of owning land. The historian William Cronon has written of how Europeans in New England "bounded" the land, turned it into a place of "fields and fences." This was a completely different view from that of the Indigenous tribes they displaced, who for hundreds of years had moved across the land according to the seasons and the food and resources available at different times of year. By measuring land and dividing it into parcels, Europeans also transformed it into units that could be bought and sold, and *owned* by individuals for their exclusive use—another idea foreign to the Indigenous. Ron opened Google

Maps on his phone and showed me how early Hispanic communities had divided land in yet another way. East of my property and south of San Luis were lots that, he explained, had been created in "enormous strips" so as to traverse different habitats. Each landowner, according to the values of the time, could thus have access to water, to fields, and sometimes to high ground as well.

I asked whether Ron was familiar with the Robert Frost poem that considered the nature of fences. He said he knew it well. Frost's "Mending Wall" describes the poet working with his New England neighbor to repair the stone wall that divides their properties. The neighbor feels it is important to keep the wall in good repair because "Good fences make good neighbors." But Ron noted that while people think that this was Frost's message, too, "in fact he's lamenting the entire time the making of a fence, and he says that it should not be necessary at all." The architect appeared to endorse the famous contrary lines of the poem: "Something there is that doesn't love a wall, / That wants it down."

Ron's graduate students needed him, so I headed back to the prairie. Our conversation had made me feel it was okay to fence the cows out of my property. Frost had suggested that you don't need a fence where you don't have cows. But I could say to the poet, altering his line, *Here there are cows,* and they trample my sagebrush and leave their massive cowpies and scare me at night when they bellow and rub against my trailer. (It is one of life's ironies that one of the indispensable tools of barbed-wire fence building, leather gloves to keep hands from being cut by the barbs, are made from the hides of cows. It reminds me that the first walls of Sing Sing prison, where I worked, had been built by prisoners themselves.)

But poets, it seemed clear, did not like fences or walls. And unfenced land was part of the valley's great beauty. It was also part of the idea of the West. Public lands kept that idea alive, but they also seemed to impose a kind of suspended animation; they felt a bit like a museum. Unfenced private land such as I was on seemed all the more precious because you knew that someday, somebody might throw up a fence to declare, *This is mine. Keep out!* I was not immune to the thought that fences were a vexation to the wandering spirit, to the vagabond, to the tribal Indigenous hunter, and to the landless itinerant cowboy. Cole Porter tried to channel that spirit with the classic song "Don't Fence Me In," repeating that phrase nine times and conjuring up the sky, the breeze, and the cottonwood trees.

I loved the spirit of that song. But I wanted to have my fence.

EPILOGUE

Sanctuary and Exile

America's margins have often been the best vantage point from which to survey [our] weaknesses.

—JELANI COBB

Same hurt in every heart / Same trailer, different park.

—KACEY MUSGRAVES, "Merry Go 'Round"

WHEN TONA RUYBAL of La Puente had first driven me onto the flats, I hadn't understood everything I was seeing. There were the tiny homesteads scattered sparsely across the land. And there was the land itself. Human habitation (and private property) started at the one-lane Lobatos Bridge, which we crossed slowly, the thick boards of the deck creaking under the tires. I vaguely knew that was the Rio Grande River flowing underneath, a little ribbon of green across the brown prairie. But I hadn't understood that the rocky crevice it flowed through was the start of the Rio Grande rift, a fissure in the lithosphere that begins in the San Luis Valley and deepens as it heads south, becoming a gorge eight hundred feet deep around Taos and extending into Mexico. A friend's photograph, taken from atop a small mountain nearby, made this vivid.

The Rio Grande Gorge at its beginnings
near the Lobatos Bridge, just north of New Mexico
Photo copyright 2020 by Michelle L. LeBlanc

More than three hundred years before, in July 1694, Spanish explorer Diego de Vargas crossed the same river, going in the other direction. De Vargas had been on a six-week mission to "reconquer" Indigenous people north of Santa Fe, as well as to trade for or confiscate corn, and was on his way home. But the country was largely unknown to him; the river ran high and presented a barrier to the Spanish soldiers and the mules and horses with them. At the de Vargas crossing, two miles north of the little bridge I was on, and also about two miles from the place I would buy, the land flattened out, the river widened, and, helped by an Indigenous guide, de Vargas found a way across that would lead him back to Santa Fe.

The de Vargas crossing has no historical marker, but it still has petroglyphs that likely predate the Spanish: a rock outcrop there is decorated with human-shaped figures, a sunburst, something that resembles a question mark, and something that might be a snake. It also once featured sheep—destroyed, says the out-of-print *San Luis Valley Rock Art,* by someone who was attempting to chisel off a section of rock and steal it. The area exudes a sense of antiquity, both geological and human. What must have seemed like invasion and apocalypse to the Indigenous people, of course, came to be celebrated as a beginning by the Spanish, Mexicans, and then Americans who saw the area as empty, a wilderness frontier that settlers might tame with farms and ranches. What one sees today is a stunning natural space that is also real estate— raw land available for purchase, at a very low price, a landscape upon which even a person of very modest means can imagine leaving a mark.

And even if you're not a nineteenth-century-style homesteader, the wide-open spaces of the valley evoke a sort of ongoing frontier, virtuous because unsettled, pure because off-grid. However, these days the grid is not far away. Convenient sources of manufactured energy, such as gasoline and propane, change everything, as do the big-box stores in Alamosa, military flyovers, and cell phones.

Another change in our lifetime is a reassessment of humankind's relationship with nature. Ideas of dominating the natural world, of taming and subjecting it to the human will, are in retreat as Americans, with some foot-dragging, join other countries in responding to climate change, a crisis that our country, in producing so much carbon dioxide, has had such a big hand in creating. Younger people are attracted to the valley as a place to try out living lightly on the land, independent of the grid. In certain ways they seem reminiscent of the hippies who embraced the "back to nature" movement in the 1960s, alienated from conservative social mores, but in other ways they're responding to today's ecological emergency.

The Costilla Land Company and the San Luis Southern railroad pitched the valley to farmers as seemingly random as German immigrants in Iowa (who turned them down), Seventh Day Adventists (who came and founded Jaroso), and Japanese immigrants from California (who settled near Blanca and successfully raised garden vegetables, which they shipped out on the railroad). The Denver & Rio Grande Railroad did similar pro-farming promotions. But these blandishments gave way to a very different sort of pitch when Tony Perry and similar land promoters arrived on the scene. The genius of these 1970s subdividers was to subtract from the land the idea of agriculture. They sold a dream of simple land ownership in a pristine mountain setting—of life not on a ranch, if you will, but on a ranchette.*

And fifty years later? I came expecting certain sorts of people and found, in fact, many more sorts of people. Among the qualities they shared was a desire to be away from things, to actively not be in a city like Denver, much less New York or Los Angeles. Sometimes I've wondered if we can see in them an answer to the question, Who is America for, and who is it not? Generally speaking, the flats residents I met were not the young and idealistic (though there were exceptions). Rather, they were the restless and the fugitive; the idle and the addicted; and the generally disaffected, the done-with-what-we-were-supposed-to-do crowd. People who, feeling chewed up and spit out, had turned away from and sometimes against institutions they'd been involved with all of their lives, whether companies or schools or the church. The prairie was their sanctuary and their place of exile. Lance Cheslock had used the metaphor of figurative painting: just as the object is defined by its borders (the artist draws an outline of the person before filling it in), so is society defined by the people out on the edge. Their "outsiderness" helps define the mainstream.

Another metaphor occurred to me on a summer day at Mountain Home Reservoir. A friend who had been asked to leave La Puente because of drug use had invited me to meet him there, with friends of his who had kayaks. Just as Coloradoans who try skiing in the Midwest or the East are often disappointed, I think it's fair to say that easterners who come to a Colorado reservoir may be crestfallen—you call this a lake? The shores are basically dirt, the fish are stocked (i.e., dropped from airplanes), and there are few trees and no docks or picturesque cabins around the edge, only a concrete boat ramp. In the afternoon, as the wind picked up, my friend and I paddled out gamely just the same. We pulled our boats up onto the far shore and walked around, examining, among other things, the dam that had created the reservoir. It

---

* A tract of half-sized lots near me were in fact sold as "ranchettes."

wasn't much to see, but the spillway next to it was epic: this was a wide concrete channel meant to save the dam itself if the water rose too fast. Rather than washing out the dam, the excess water would pour down the spillway, which faced the flats. In the meantime, it looked like a honey trap for skateboarders (except for the problem of how you'd stop at the bottom). Afterward I thought that the valley itself was kind of a spillway for the dam of contemporary society. Those who could not be contained in the mainstream reservoir could be swept over the edge, and come to rest somewhere out on the prairie.

The pull of the land endured over time, in part because of disappointment elsewhere and the imagined promise of a new start. A hundred years ago, homesteaders came in search of opportunity. That promise is faded; as Wallace Stegner wrote in 1943, "There were no places on earth any more where opportunity lay new and shining and untouched. The old days when people used to rush to Dakota or California or Alaska in search of easy wealth were gone forever." (Harold Anderson in Jaroso was fond of saying—and it seemed to be true— "Nobody ever got rich in the valley.")

The attractive power of valley life endured even so. Matt Little wasn't after easy money. Rather, pushed from his West Virginia home by the death of his wife and the fire that destroyed their house, he Googled "cheap land colorado" and found a new beginning. A food service job at Adams State University sustained him at the start. Briefly homeless when that job ended (though he refused to call it that), he found stability and new purpose when he got hired by La Puente. As I finished this book, the grant that had funded Matt's Rural Outreach work had ended, and in its place, La Puente put him in charge of a program of small grants to flats dwellers for home-improvement projects. He no longer delivered much free firewood—in fact, for the first time ever, he was driving an SUV instead of a pickup truck—but he said that was fine, that the mission to connect prairie people to resources was now largely self-sustaining. He had made it official with Willow—they married late in 2020. The broken femur and a bout of testicular cancer had set him back, though. Now he seemed to be moving at a less frantic pace, putting fewer miles on his vehicle and devoting more time to family and his menagerie of horses, wolf-dogs, ducks, and chickens. His son Joshua, after a long wait, had moved into supportive housing in Alamosa that Matt thought would bring stability to his life.

Matt's dream of mining with Luke had receded a bit, due to his own poor health and Luke's. When Luke stopped by to check on my power shed, it seemed he had to catch his breath after walking only fifty feet. Ditto when I ran into him at the Walmart in Alamosa. He told me that he had been diagnosed with a hole in his heart and was scheduled for open-heart surgery in Denver. A few weeks later, he told me he didn't have the money to get to Denver and had rescheduled it for a month later. When I checked in after that, he told me he'd canceled the surgery altogether, and not just because of money but after deciding he would live out his life "with the cards I was dealt with."

Tona left La Puente after almost thirteen years as the shelter's director. The job had required her to be on call twenty-four/seven, and she said she was tired. A new job helping valley high schools connect their students to mental-health care would be a welcome change. Her friend Geneva, around the same time, had found new love with a retired electrician from Texas and was dividing her time between Texas and the valley.

My neighbor Paul had a long stretch of happiness characterized by lots of cooking (he posted pictures of his creations on Facebook) and hosting friends for meals. He set up a chicken coop that regularly produced eggs. He finally got his remaining teeth extracted and, with help from La Puente, acquired a set of gleaming dentures that made him look like a prairie movie star. He adopted a new dog, which was promptly bitten by a rattlesnake; its face swelled up, but it survived. Worse were his familiar mental tortures—namely, the gusty winds of spring, the houseflies of late summer, and the presence of new neighbors down the road. I almost thought his mental state could be charted on a graph; it trended gradually up and down, and seemed headed down as I was writing this, due to new concerns about high blood pressure.

Zahra had some big news: she'd earned a commercial driver's license and gotten a job driving trucks out of Denver. Her kids and husband, now living outside Alamosa in a trailer on the property of her husband's family ranch, missed her but benefited from the extra income, she said—50 percent more than what she had been making booking medical appointments on the phone. In fall of 2021, just before I stopped by, Zahra had rendezvoused with Paul in Antonito to show him her rig. He said she looked great—maybe a little more "rednecked out" than previously with her cowboy hat and leather jacket.

Lance of La Puente had found his gregarious nature challenged by the pandemic; spending workdays at home was difficult for him. A new hobby seemed to help: a friend of a friend had sent him a high-end telescope, and on dark nights he would head out to photograph the heavens from different spots in the valley. One night he asked to set up at my place, and I got to peer with him at deep sky objects (such as the Hercules Cluster and Andromeda Galaxy) that were light-years away. At the same time, over cups of tea, he told me he'd recently recovered from a breakthrough case of Covid; the apparent source was an anti-vaxxer relative who had stayed with him and his wife for a few days. That was the first time I'd heard of anyone getting a breakthrough case, but many more soon followed, including more than a score of La Puente staff, all of them vaccinated.

My neighbor Troy Zinn had cataracts removed from both eyes, belatedly. Like many others, he resisted doctor appointments but then reached a point where daylight caused him agony, even with two pairs of sunglasses on. A long wait ensued for laser surgery appointments in Colorado Springs, one trip for each eye. But afterward, he was effusive in his excitement: "It's all incredibly vivid, it's awesome, everything is so beautiful."

But then, just as the calendar changed to 2022, Covid finally visited the neighborhood. Its first victim was "Car Wash" Kevin, the first person I met in my prairie cold calls for La Puente, the one just back from opiates rehab whose T-shirt said "SINGLE AND READY TO JINGLE." (He was also the friend who sold the Grubers the Toyota on credit.) Kevin's prairie nickname derived from a period in his life when he detailed cars in Aspen and Las Vegas. He had also worked as a dealer in casinos and was known for his cultivation of weed and support of Donald Trump. A friend of the Grubers, Kevin had recently baked Trin a birthday cake that contained inside it coins, a credit card, a pocket knife, and bullets. Tie Rod Tony hadn't seen Kevin for a while, so he stopped by after Christmas and found him lying on the floor, blue in the face but alive. After he gave him mouth-to-mouth resuscitation and kindled the wood stove, Kevin rallied. Tie Rod got Troy to spell him overnight. They speculated that Kevin might be suffering from Covid. Troy called an ambulance when he began to fade again, but Kevin angrily refused to get in. A day later he was dead.

A few days later, Tie Rod Tony went to the hospital and received a positive Covid test himself. He returned home to the prairie and told Troy he thought he was going to be all right. Then two days later, his nephew opened the door to the bathroom to find Tony naked and dead, on the toilet. "Just like Elvis," commented one of his friends, trying to find light amid a lot of dark news.

Several days of fever and nausea then ensued for Troy himself. He slept in his truck for three days until Grace left to visit family in Denver; then he moved indoors to the couch and spent the rest of the week there, barely able to get up. He was never tested but felt "pretty sure" he had Covid, too.

Stacy Gruber had gotten vaccinated following surgery on her back—one of a relatively small cohort of prairie people who had received the vaccine. The surgery had treated an arachnoid cyst along her spine that had caused her months of pain. Some follow-up procedures might prove necessary, and she felt the doctors would be more attentive if she were vaccinated. When I saw the family afterwards, late in the summer of 2021, Frank was excited about a robust marijuana harvest at his home garden but distracted by pain in his leg; an ER doctor had told him it was likely a torn ligament or pulled hamstring. But six weeks and three ER visits later, a different doctor determined that Frank had a blood clot and, fearing he'd have a stroke, had him flown by helicopter to Denver for immediate surgery. He'd required two stents to replace damaged arteries, but the doctors said the prognosis was reasonably good—if he could stop smoking. As of this writing, Frank, a smoker for thirty-two years, had not had a single cigarette.

The girls were growing up: Trin, the oldest at seventeen, and Meadoux, now fifteen, had moved into their own small trailers on the property. Trin was taking online courses in ranch management and preparing for a GED exam in the spring. She told me and others that she thought she might be gay. Stacy said to me, "That's fine—we are proud of her for being true to herself. All I want is for my girls to be the best people they can be and for them to be happy with themselves and have a life they want to live." Coming from a happy family, they had a big advantage. With limited skills and experience, would they be able to keep safe and thrive in the world beyond the prairie?

Tommy Jr., the eight-year-old boy the Grubers had taken in for a time, was settled in a foster home in Denver that seemed to be working out. I hadn't thought of him in a while when, late in 2021, Frank posted on social media that Tommy Sr. had been shot and killed by police. I felt bad for the boy and bad for Frank, but I'd never met Tommy Sr. myself—I didn't think. Then I looked more carefully at the photos Frank posted: I had met Tommy Sr. It was just the month before, when I took my wife to visit the Grubers at home for the first time. Along with Frank and Stacy and all the girls, several of the dogs, and a baby goat was a couple who looked to be in their forties who greeted us without offering their names and then gave up their chairs; the man had called me "sir." After a few minutes they had quietly left. When Frank posted the shocking news, I texted him: had I met Tommy Sr. without knowing it?

He confessed that I had—and Tommy's new wife, as well. They hadn't introduced themselves because Tommy was on the lam. He faced new assault charges and, if convicted, risked being locked up for years as a habitual offender. Frank said his friend was understandably depressed about this. On Facebook, Tommy had even posted, "I will die on my feet before I'll live on my knees! I will not beg for a life that will be spent in a prison cell!" He had not died on his feet but rather in a stolen car, in which police had discovered him asleep at night in the mountain town of Gunnison. According to police, an officer attempting to arrest him ended up getting dragged when Tommy gunned the engine and tried to escape; after that police opened fire.

Frank told me that as a young man, he had left Denver for Wyoming, and later for the flats, in order to escape the social world he grew up in. And, after meeting Stacy, he had largely succeeded in that—the prairie was his refuge, a place for living a healthier life. But it seems worth mentioning that the prairie was also, if briefly, a refuge to his fugitive friend, a place where the things you didn't want to find you usually didn't.

These sad endings were the foil to my romantic love of the land, the sky, and the weather: the prairie had aspects of a rural ghetto. There were folks with outstanding warrants, there was relationship abuse, there was addiction. (My wife quipped that I could title this book *Little House on the Prairie, with Meth.*) People were "doing without" in so many ways, from job opportunities to quality education and access to medical care. And yet a big difference from real ghettos was that it was seldom a generational poverty; most of the prairie people had arrived recently, usually the result of conscious choice. My neighbors, like the early settlers, had chosen to be out there, no matter the hardships. That added something hopeful to the whole equation.

So did the setting itself, and not just for me. Neighbors posted to social media photos of the same dramatic clouds, the same rainbow. The sky made a difference to them and to me, as well: I was enthralled by the spaces. I just loved being in the middle of so much of it; to me it was (and is) one of the most beautiful places in the world, an antidote to civilization. Often as I approached, having driven through the relatively populated Front Range towns of Denver, Colorado Springs, and Pueblo, I'd be listening to music and swept up in an elation brought on by the space—the land opened up and so did I. It could happen while driving around the valley, as well, noticing the clouds or the golden glow in the grass when the sun got low: euphoria struck.

Early in my valley days I drove south from Alamosa, turned east at Romeo, and proceeded through Manassa and then into the empty country. Off the highway I saw the skeleton of a wooden shed, intricate and tipping over but not quite fallen; anywhere else, kids would have given it a little push and hastened its demise. But this ruin, quite beautifully, hung on. The land was wonderfully devoid of human traces, except for the occasional barbed-wire fence and Bureau of Land Management sign. But a few miles on, the road crossed the Rio Grande and there was dissonance: the empty, ransacked mobile homes in the middle of nothing, the desecrations that appeared to have escaped the notice of federal officials. This was before I had taken the measure of the whole space—before I realized that, in crossing the river, I had entered a different county, where the land was privately owned. Where there are few or no people, it is easier to imagine things.

Months later, my sister pointed me to an article in a map lovers' journal about a giant lake that had shown up in the northern valley, according to mapmakers, in 1863, and then disappeared in the 1880s. As drawn, the body of water, labeled San Luis Lake or Sahwatch Lake, was twenty-one miles long by six miles wide and shaped like a pickle. (By contrast Colorado's largest natural lake, Grand Lake, measures only a mile wide.) Despite not actually existing, this "monster lake appeared on no less an authority than the official government map of Colorado." Indeed, Colorado's first territorial governor, William Gilpin, had described it in detail in an 1869 book promoting the area just southeast of the mythical lake (even as he'd failed to disclose his own vast land holdings—options on five-sixths of the Sangre de Cristo land grant). "Perhaps we have Governor Gilpin to thank for a fascinating mythical lake that lingered on maps years after government surveyors had removed it from official reports," concludes author Wesley Brown, who cofounded the Rocky Mountain Map Society in 1991, in his article "A Mystery Lake in Southern Colorado."

I wanted to stick around long enough that I could feel fairly certain I had no delusions. I wanted the view from the ground—close-up, first-person, continuous, ongoing. Bruce Chatwin's classic *In Patagonia*, about his travels through the southern part of South America, hardly ever mentions that he was writing about parts of a country called Argentina. He wanted the magical side of things. I did, too, but not at the expense of real people in actual situations. At a time when more and more people seem to believe that almost anything can be true, I wanted a book that could be fact-checked, populated by people who are indisputably real.

And so I came, saw, and left, came, saw, and left, over and over again. I built a fence because it felt right, and because I plan to stay a while longer.

Acknowledgments

The following people helped make this book possible. I'd like to thank:

My sister Beth Conover, for pointing me to La Puente, and also her husband, Ken Snyder. My sister Margo Conover, for help and company in Santa Fe and Española. My father, Jerry Conover, for hometown hospitality (and a humidifier), and my sister Pam Conover, and Jon Adams, for assistance above and beyond.

My readers Eliza Griswold, Margot Guralnick, and Jay Leibold.

James Marcus for assigning me the story at *Harper's Magazine* and publisher John R. MacArthur for supporting my work. And before that, Chris Outcalt at *5280* for assigning me to write about South Park and Geoff Van Dyke for seeing the story to publication.

Jonathan Segal, my editor at Knopf, and Kathy Robbins, my agent. I could not ask for better. Also Sarah Perrin at Knopf and Janet Oshiro at The Robbins Office.

Everyone at La Puente, especially Lance Cheslock but also Matt Little, Teotenantzin Ruybal and Rob Lockwood Jr., Judy McNeilsmith, Callie Adams, and Amanda Pearson; and Shanae Diaz (for beer, coffee, and *Bless Me, Ultima*).

Also in Colorado, Geneva Duarte, Loretta Mitson, Rachael Cheslock, Ryan Barnes, Amy Scavezze, Mary Van Pelt, Mark Dudrow and Michelle LeBlanc, Reyes Garcia, Paul Andersen, Richard de Olivas y Córdova, Calvin Moreau, and Jody Guralnick and Michael Lipkin.

Kelsey Kudak and Katherine Boss for research. Scott Lankford, Andrew Meyers, and Robert Boynton for reading suggestions. Arlene Stein, for help with words. Elizabeth Beim, for years of being there for me.

Jess Bruder for brainstorming and the e-bike, and Bryn Adams and Abby Perrino for conspiracy theories.

And Margot, for everything.

Notes

EPIGRAPH

vii *This is the country I love the most*: From the preface to Andrew Moore's *Dirt Meridian* (Bologna, Italy: Damiani, 2015), 12.

PROLOGUE

7 *"Wait—does this place belong to"*: To avoid confusion with a similarly named person, "Tie Rod Tony" is a pseudonym.

CHAPTER 1: CHEAP LAND COLORADO

9 *The San Juan Mountains*: *Colorado Encyclopedia*, "Colorado Geology."

11 *Blanca, named for the snow*: To the Diné, or Navajo, people, the mountain is called Sisnaajini. For more on its meaning to them, see Harold Carey Jr., "Mount Blanca (Sisnaajini) Navajo Sacred Mountain," *Navajo People* (blog), January 7, 2013.

31 *"I want you to see that gravestone"*: Oddly, this gravestone appears to be a duplicate of one in Texas. Notes at findagrave.com suggest it was previously photographed elsewhere in the region, "next to Highway 160 . . . below a shrine."

CHAPTER 2: MY PRAIRIE LIFE, PART I

57 *Illegal drugs, however*: Bill Whitaker, "Whistleblowers: DEA Attorneys Went Easy on McKesson, the Country's Largest Drug Distributor," CBS News, December 17, 2017.

57 *60 Minutes ran a report*: The CBS News investigation was conducted jointly with *The Washington Post*.

62 *"Fighting was the entertainment"*: Beryle Vance and Elma Pagett, "Jack Dempsey—'The Manassa Mauler,'" *The San Luis Valley Historian*, 1995, Vol. XXVII, No. 2.

70 *Off-grid life seems to be growing*: Some recent attempts to count off-gridders have correlated social media posts tagged #offgridliving with location data. That approach would miss many off-gridders on the flats, who only occasionally use that tag, if in fact they post at all.

CHAPTER 3: SO MANY DIFFERENT KINDS OF PEOPLE, OR MY PRAIRIE LIFE, PART II

97 *Frank Gruber, using his one bar*: The scan is here: James Rose Harvey, "El Cerrito De Los Kiowas," *Colorado Magazine,* November, 1942, www .historycolorado.org. Loretta Mitson, citing other sources, believes the battle took place in the 1850s.

   Frank said that his interest in Native American history stemmed in part from Stacy's Native ancestry—two grandparents were part Lakota Sioux. Sam also claimed Lakota ancestry. Matt Little's great-grandmother was Cherokee.

100 *Loretta remembered that some young people*: See also, "Searchers Locate Manassa Woman's Body," *Pueblo Chieftain,* March 10, 1996; and "Colorado Woman Dies of Exposure," *Albuquerque Journal,* March 11, 1996 (though this article incorrectly states the number of people in the car).

CHAPTER 4: RAW LAND

110 *Calvin Trillin wrote about the conflict*: Calvin Trillin, "A Cloud on the Title," *The New Yorker,* April 18, 1976, 122.

110 *dialect of Spanish unique to the area*: Sam Tabachnik, "The Quest to Save a Dying Spanish Dialect in Colorado's San Luis Valley," *The Denver Post,* November 22, 2020.

113 *only 6 percent of the land grants*: *Colorado Encyclopedia,* "Mexican Land Grants in Colorado."

113 *"It's difficult to overestimate the level"*: Robert Sanchez, "The Long-Forgotten Vigilante Murders of the San Luis Valley," *5280,* December 2019.

114 *Gilpin asked Congress to confirm the legitimacy of the arrangement*: "U.S. Statutes at Large, Vol. 16 (1869–1871), 41st Congress," Library of Congress. Also see Thomas L. Karnes, *William Gilpin, Western Nationalist* (Austin and London: University of Texas Press, 1969).

116 *The owners of what became known as Costilla Estates*: P. R. Griswold, *Colorado's Loneliest Railroad: The San Luis Southern* (Boulder: Pruett, 1980), 3, 23.

117 *"The earliest American explorers"*: Clarence A. Lyman, *The Fertile Lands of Colorado and Northern New Mexico,* 12th ed. ([Denver?]: Denver & Rio Grande Railroad, 1912), 42, 47, 53.

119 *Shortages of water*: Griswold, *Colorado's Loneliest Railroad,* 115.

119 *Farms that survived*: Harold Anderson said he made a living from cattle, selling hay from fields irrigated with well water, and driving his semitruck—

but it didn't sound like a big living. He quipped that a definition of child abuse was "giving your kid the farm."

119 *Betting on that strategy*: John D. MacArthur, the corporate titan, was the father of John R. (Rick) MacArthur, the publisher of *Harper's Magazine,* who assigned me to write about the San Luis Valley in 2017. At the time, neither Rick nor I knew about the connection between the land I would become interested in and his father's investments.

119 *Water from wells*: Until the 1970s, well water in the valley made its way to fields mainly via ditches. Then center-pivot irrigation arrived, allowing water to be sprinkled around vast areas in circles. Chet Choman recalled going to see what he believes was the first center-pivot system in the valley, south of Blanca, around 1971: "We went out there to look at this thing, because we were convinced it was going to get stuck in the sand and flip over itself and be one big disaster. We sat there for five minutes but nothing happened." The technology, which was invented in Colorado, was a success and has been widely adopted across the United States and much of the world. It's responsible for the giant green circles visible from the air over farm country. In some places, agriculture made possible by wells paired with center-pivot irrigation is thought to have depleted aquifers.

122 *Subdividing could generate*: Hubert B. Stroud and William M. Spikowski, "Planning in the Wake of Florida Land Scams," *Journal of Planning Education and Research,* September, 1999, Vol. 19, Issue 1, 27–39.

124 *In all, he thought*: For context, the Costilla County manager told me the county has approximately 45,000 subdivision parcels out of 104,000 parcels total; the county's population is only about 3,700.

128 *The U.S. Senate Special Committee*: "Frauds and Deceptions Affecting the Elderly: A Report of the Subcommittee on Frauds and Misrepresentations Affecting the Elderly," United States Senate, Special Committee on Aging, January 31, 1965.

128 *A star witness*: Bob Caro, "Misery Acres," *Newsday,* January 7–10, 1963. Also see www.robertcaro.com.

129 *The FTC claimed that*: See "Land-Sale Victims May Get $14 Million in FTC Agreement," *The Washington Post,* May 9, 1979; "Buyers to Get Refunds on Worthless Land in Colorado," *The New York Times,* May 10, 1979; and Federal Register, Vol. 44, No. 96, May 16, 1979, 28671 Federal Trade Commission, Proposed Rules, Consent Orders: Bankers Life and Casualty Co., et al.

CHAPTER 5: OWNERSHIP

151 *"an average life expectancy of forty-eight years old"*: One study published in 2018 determined the life expectancy of individuals with Autism Spectrum Disorder (ASD) to be thirty-six years and found that they are forty times more likely to die of accidents than other people. Another study found

that the leading causes of death for those with ASD were heart disease, suicide, and epilepsy; the suicide rate among those with ASD was said to be nine times higher than in the general population. See Michael A. Ellis, "Early Death in Those with Autism Spectrum Disorder," *Psychology Today*, October 7, 2018.

169 *The county sheriff's office*: Facebook page for Costilla County Sheriff's Office, May 3, 2019. https://www.facebook.com/profile/100064414343613/search/?q=boswell.

169 *Just over a year later*: Facebook page for Costilla County Sheriff's Office, June 17, 2020. https://www.facebook.com/profile/100064414343613/search/?q=puppies.

169 *Oregon had an open case*: "Klamath County Man Faces 32 Animal Neglect Charges," KOBI5.com, October 2, 2017.

170 *In Florida he had been charged*: Debbie Salamone, "Suspect in Puppy Scam Fights Extradition to California," *Orlando Sentinel*, September 12, 1989.

170 *Six years earlier*: Stephen Floyd, "Animal Neglect: Beatty Man Charged After Animal Seizure," *Herald and News* [Klamath Falls, Oregon], October 3, 2017.

170 *Costilla County charged Ken*: "Charges Filed in Costilla County Animal Cruelty Case," Denver Dumb Friends League, October 14, 2020, www.ddfl.org.

170 *A majority of the dogs*: Becky Talley, "Denver Dumb Friends League Seeks Donations After Aiding in Rescue of More than 100 Dogs," *Our Community Now*, July 14, 2020, ourcommunitynow.com.

CHAPTER 6: LOVE AND MURDER

177 *She called Leroy, a member of the African nationalist group*: Leroy is a pseudonym.

178 *People she knew*: Kemetic Orthodoxy, as described at the House of Netjer's Kemetic Orthodoxy website (www.kemet.org), was founded in Illinois in the late 1980s and has points of convergence with Zahra's beliefs—but she said it is different from her spiritual practice.

188 *Mojaves were especially venomous*: Alexandra Hicks, "Mojave Rattlesnake (Crotalus scutulatus)—One of the World's Most Venomous Snakes," Wild Snakes: Education and Discussion, November 18, 2020, www.wsed.org.

190 *"Mexicans of Costilla and Conejos counties"*: Charles F. Price, *Season of Terror: The Espinosas in Central Colorado, March–October 1863*, 123 (Boulder: University Press of Colorado, 2013). Price offers a thorough history of the rampage.

191 *Alamosa woman who killed and ate her boyfriend*: According to Lance Cheslock, the two had first met over a meal at La Puente's shelter.

193 *Specifically, he thought*: Merle Baranczyk, "Mike Rust Family Finds 'Huge Relief' His Remains Discovered," *The Mountain Mail*, May 2, 2016.

193 *Sheriff's deputies dug up*: Arlene Shovald, "Affidavit Reveals How Police Found Suspect in Rust Case," *The Mountain Mail*, June 23, 2016.

194 *Wahhaj and one of his wives*: Janon Fisher, "New Mexico Compound Leader Believed She Could Reincarnate Jesus Christ Through the Body of Dead Disabled Boy," New York *Daily News*, August 31, 2018.

194 *They believed that once the demons*: Madison Park, "Timeline of What Has Happened in the New Mexico Compound Case," CNN.com, August 24, 2018.

194 *Reuters would later report*: Andrew Hay, "Defendants in New Mexico Compound Case Hit with New Charges," Reuters, March 14, 2019.

195 *Though the child-abuse charges were dismissed*: Richard Gonzales, "Feds Indict 5 New Mexico Compound Residents on Terrorism and Gun Charges," National Public Radio, March 14, 2019.

198 *Late in 2020*: Michael Levenson, "Fugitive Arrested After Remains of 3 People Are Found in Colorado," *The New York Times*, November 19, 2020.

198 *From the local paper*: "A Look Back at 2017 in the Valley," *Valley Courier*, December 30, 2017.

198 *Regular updates followed*: Elise Schmelzer, "Adre 'Psycho' Baroz Arrested in Connection with 3 Bodies Found in Rural Southern Colorado," *The Denver Post*, November 19, 2020.

199 *On November 25, 2020, police executed a search warrant*: Daniela Leon and Lauren Scharf, "Court Documents Reveal Gruesome Killings in Connection to Human Remains Found in San Luis Valley," Fox 21 News, January 22, 2021.

199 *The story of Psycho*: Sylvia Lobato, "Suspect in Five Killings Speeds Through Antonito and Chama," *The Conejos County Citizen*, June 21, 2017.

199 *he was found frozen under a bridge*: "Identity Released in Weekend Death," *Valley Courier*, January 29, 2019.

207 *This was Tommy, said Stacy*: Tommy is a pseudonym.

CHAPTER 7: GUNS, GERMS, AND CLIMATE CHANGE

218 *"disgusted, vaguely grouchy, irrationally sore"*: Wallace Stegner, *The Big Rock Candy Mountain* (New York: Penguin Books, 1991), 247.

218 *"the whole bunch from the Last Chance"*: Wallace Stegner, *The Big Rock Candy Mountain*, 260.

218 *As one critic wrote*: A. O. Scott, "Wallace Stegner and the Conflicted Soul of the West," *The New York Times*, June 1, 2020.

220 *A colleague watched as a peaceful march*: "Looting and Shooting in Manhattan After Peaceful Protest in Brooklyn," *Bedford + Bowery* (blog), June 1, 2020.

220 *On June 1, he cataloged*: Daniel Maurer, "Over 50 Storefronts Smashed During Night of Mayhem in Soho," *Bedford + Bowery*, June 6, 2020.

221 *"posted an article about a soldier"*: Susan Greene and Keith Cerney, "Triggered: How One of Colorado's Smallest Protests Became Its Most Violent, COLab, June 27, 2020.

223 *In fact, a year later*: Reid J. Epstein and Patricia Mazzei, "G.O.P. Bills Target Protesters (and Absolve Motorists Who Hit Them)," *The New York Times,* April 21, 2021.

226 *I noted that only eight*: As of January 6, 2022, the toll was 167, per San Luis Valley Public Health Partnership.

229 *temperatures dropped from 87 to 27*: "September 8–10, 2020, Early Season Winter Storm," National Weather Service.

230 *"The timing of the storm"*: John Rawinski, "Summer Snowstorm Devastating to Migratory Songbirds," *The Monte Vista Journal,* September 22, 2020.

231 *In a webinar sponsored by a conservation group*: "Unraveling a Migration Mystery," https://youtu.be/tqq-jwDzUbM.

231 *The backdrop was an even bigger disaster*: Rosenberg et al., "Decline of the North American avifauna," *Science,* October 4, 2019, Vol. 366, Issue 6461, 120–24.

233 *Soon after Matt showed me that cow*: *Costilla County Free Press,* June 8, 2017.

233 *On the goofy side*: "UFO Watchtower," tripadvisor.com.

233 *The United States military*: Helene Cooper, Ralph Blumenthal, and Leslie Kean, "Glowing Auras and 'Black Money': The Pentagon's Mysterious U.F.O. Program," *The New York Times,* December 16, 2017; and Gideon Lewis-Kraus, "How the Pentagon Started Taking U.F.O.s Seriously," *The New Yorker,* April 30, 2021.

233 *"Imagine a technology"*: Bill Whitaker, "UFOs Regularly Spotted in Restricted U.S. Airspace, Report on the Phenomena Due Next Month," CBS News, May 16, 2021.

234 *"We're a couple of guys"*: Stacy Matlock, "A Taos Close Encounter of the Hunters and Aliens Kind," *Taos News,* September 5, 2019.

234 *"two spinning galaxies"*: David Grinspoon, *Lonely Planets: The Natural Philosophy of Alien Life* (New York: Ecco, 2004), 345–46.

235 *"There are some mysteries"*: Grinspoon, *Lonely Planets,* 351.

247 *I had just read an account*: *La Vereda: A Trail Through Time,* by Ruth Marie Colville (Alamosa, CO: San Luis Valley Historical Society, 1996).

247 *The historian William Cronon*: *Changes in the Land: Indians, Colonists, and the Ecology of New England,* by William Cronon (New York: Hill and Wang, 1983).

249 *Cole Porter tried to channel that spirit*: While Porter wrote the music, the lyrics were partly written by cowboy poet Robert (Bob) Fletcher. See Philip George Furia and Michael L. Lasser, *America's Songs: The Stories Behind the Songs of Broadway, Hollywood, and Tin Pan Alley* (New York: Routledge, 2006), 192–93.

EPILOGUE: SANCTUARY AND EXILE

250 *"America's margins have often"*: Jelani Cobb, "What Black History Should Already Have Taught Us About the Fragility of American Democracy," *Daily Comment* (online newsletter), *The New Yorker,* November 5, 2020.

251 *It also once featured sheep*: Ron Kessler, *San Luis Valley Rock Art* (Monte Vista, CO: Adobe Village Press, 2000), 158.

254 *"There were no places on earth"*: Wallace Stegner, *The Big Rock Candy Mountain* (New York: Penguin Books, 1991), 330.

260 *"Perhaps we have Governor Gilpin"*: Wesley A. Brown, "A Mystery Lake in Southern Colorado," *Portolan* no. 100 (Winter 2017): 56. A more recent governor of Colorado is presently involved in another enterprise regarding water in the valley. Former governor Bill Owens is a principal in a company that hopes to spend millions of dollars on a pipeline that would send water from San Luis Valley aquifers to sprawling cities of the Front Range. See Bruce Finley, "Developers Seeking Water for Booming Front Range Look to the San Luis Valley, Where Farmers Already Face Well Shut-Offs," *The Denver Post,* September 16, 2019.

Index

Page numbers in *italics* refer to illustrations.

mountain lions, 11, 27, 60–61, 64, 202, 214
Mount Blanca Valley Ranches, 127
Musgraves, Kacey, 250
Muslims, 178, 194–95
Muumuu Ranch, 26
"Mystery Lake in Southern Colorado, A"
    (Brown), 260

National Oceanic and Atmospheric
    Administration (NOAA), 227–28
Navajo (Diné) people, 11, 263n
Nebraska, 94
Nederland, Colorado, 86
Nevada, 112, 123
New Black Panther Party, 182
New Buffalo commune, 92
New Hampshire, 117
New Jersey, 90
New Mexico, *10*, 11, 14–15, 44, 70, 74, 76,
    96, 99, 109, 112, 114, 121, 163, 199
New Mexico Territory, 113, 190
Newsday, 128
New York City, 187, 219–20, 224
New Yorker, 110
New York State, 70
New York Times, 12, 89, 198
New York University, 153
Nicholson, Jack, 94
Nick (Grubers' friend), 80, 82–83, 102–4,
    158–59, 207, 225–26
Nielsen, Grace (Troy's wife), 46–47, 152,
    162, 164, 168–69, *241*, 257
nighthawks, 214
non-Hodgkin's lymphoma, 79
Noriega, Manuel, 49
Norris, Chuck, 63

Obama, Barack, 91, 98, 168
O'Brien, Christopher, 232, 233
Ohio State University, 221
Oklahoma, 150, 223n, 225
186 Fire, 228
opioids, 5, 38, 49, 57–59, 73

Oregon, 29, 70, 73, 91, 166–67, 169–70
Orlando, Florida, 124
Otero, Shirley Romero, 110
Owens, Bill, 269n
owl, great horned, 201, 214, 229

Pacheco, Salina, 62–64
Packer, Alferd E. (Alfred), 191
pack rat nests, 170, 214
Pan-Africanism, 177, 182–83
Panjabi, Arvind, 231
Paul (Armando's neighbor), 18–19, *19*, 135,
    159–63, 166, 169, 176–81, 214, 224–25,
    229–30, 255–56
Penitentiary of New Mexico riot, 199
permaculture, 184, 252
Perry, Al, 123–24, 127, 130
Perry, Tony, 123–27, 129–30, 221, 253
petroglyphs, 97
Phillips, M. Penn, 123
phoebes, Say's, 229
Pine Gulch fire, 228
Pittsburgh, Pennsylvania, 49
Planned Parenthood, 12, 94
police and sheriffs, 39, 47, 58, 85–86, 88,
    164–66, 194–95, 212–14, 222, 227,
    243–45
Polish immigrants, 88, 90
Polk, James, 113
Pollan, Michael, 38
polygamists, 180
Poncha Pass, *10*, 109
Porter, Cole, 249, 268n
Portland, Oregon, 227
potato cellars, 119, 121, 142
potato gun, 84
potsherds, 97
poverty, 13–14, 17, 23, 25, 29–30, 56, 70,
    130, 138
prairie dogs, 142
prairie rats (human), 206–7, 214–15
preppers, 70, 146, 148, 200, 227
prisons, 199, 210–11

Ted Conover is the author of several books, including *Newjack: Guarding Sing Sing* (winner of the National Book Critics Circle Award and a finalist for the Pulitzer Prize) and *Rolling Nowhere: Riding the Rails with America's Hoboes.* His writing has appeared in *The New York Times Magazine, The New Yorker, Harper's Magazine,* and many other publications. He is a professor and past director at the Arthur L. Carter Journalism Institute of New York University.

A NOTE ON THE TYPE

This book was set in Minion, a typeface produced by the Adobe Corporation specifically for the Macintosh personal computer, and released in 1990. Designed by Robert Slimbach, Minion combines the classic characteristics of old-style faces with the full complement of weights required for modern typesetting.

Composed by North Market Street Graphics, Lancaster, Pennsylvania
Printed and bound by Berryville Graphics, Berryville, Virginia
Designed by Maggie Hinders